Data Modeling with Microsoft Excel

Model and analyze data using Power Pivot,
DAX, and Cube functions

Bernard Obeng Boateng

BIRMINGHAM—MUMBAI

Data Modeling with Microsoft Excel

Copyright © 2023 Packt Publishing

Group Product Manager: Kaustubh Manglurkar
Publishing Product Manager: Apeksha Shetty
Book Project Manager: Farheen Fathima
Senior Editor: Sushma Reddy
Technical Editor: Devanshi Ayare
Copy Editor: Safis Editing
Proofreader: Safis Editing
Indexer: Manju Arasan
Production Designer: Prafulla Nikalje
DevRel Marketing Coordinator: Nivedita Singh

First published: November 2023

Production reference: 1221123

Published by Packt Publishing Ltd.
Grosvenor House
11 St Paul's Square
Birmingham
B3 1RB, UK.

ISBN 978-1-80324-028-2
www.packtpub.com

I dedicate this book to the Almighty God, who is the light of all knowledge, for guiding me to this milestone. To my wife, Georgina Konadu Boateng, and children, Kristodea, Kristoadom, and Owuraku, for their sacrifices and support. To the Finex Skills Hub team in Ghana for their immense support throughout this journey.

Foreword

This *Data Modeling with Microsoft Excel* you have in your hands or are reading via a digital device is going to change you for good. *Bernard Obeng Boateng* has taught dashboard creation and data modeling to thousands of people at conferences and classrooms over the last decade. I have seen him deliver data modeling sessions at Global Excel Summit London, Excel Virtually Global, Australia, Excel Office Hours Nigeria, and at other conferences around the world. For all the eight years I have known Bernard, he has been building reports that involve a deep level of data modeling for companies.

This book is structured to be engaging and practical, with a focus on making you instantly ready for the real-world application of the knowledge. Bernard uses a conversational style and lots of illustrations to ensure you don't have to read any sentence twice. You will find this book both enjoyable to read and exciting to practice the data modeling concepts it presents.

Bernard starts by helping you understand what data modeling is and why it is very important in your analytical work within Excel. He then takes you on an exciting journey through the paradise that is hidden within Excel and called Power Query. After getting you well-grounded in the use of Power Query, he walks you through how to serve up interactive computations through Power Pivot and Cube functions. Finally, he teaches you how to build beautiful, interactive, and robust dashboards that will be a joy for managers and decision-makers to use.

I congratulate you on taking the first step on this exciting journey to becoming a very proficient, creative, and value-delivering Excel reports builder. You will find the knowledge gained useful across all analytical tools and change your way of thinking in relation to data wrangling. Bernard has poured his more than a decade of experience and his refined teaching style into this book.

I would advise that you don't just turn the pages but that you simultaneously practice what you learn so that the teaching becomes ingrained in you.

Michael Olafusi
Microsoft Excel MVP & Founder of MHS Analytics Inc.

Contributors

About the author

Bernard Obeng Boateng is a 3x Microsoft Excel MVP, Microsoft Certified Trainer and Excel Expert with over 10 years working experience in Banking, Insurance, and Business Development. He has a first degree in BSc. Admin from the University of Ghana Business School and is certified in Business Analytics from the World's leading Business School, Wharton. He also holds the Advanced Financial Modeler (AFM) certification from the Financial Modeling Institute, Canada and the Financial Modeling and Valuation Analyst (FMVA) certification from the Corporate Finance Institute, Canada.

He is lead trainer at Finex Skills Hub, `www.finexskillshub.com`, a digital skills training hub dedicated to delivering workshop-styled training in Power BI, Financial Modeling and Microsoft Office Suite in Ghana. He is co-founder of Business Evolution Systems & Training Ltd `www.best-gh.com`, a business development and training consultancy firm in Ghana. Bernard has an active online audience of over 19,000 followers on LinkedIn and has provided training to several corporate firms and individuals in Ghana.

Sample of Bernard's work portfolio can be found here: `www.obboat.com`

YouTube: `https://www.youtube.com/@FinexSkillsHub`

I want to thank the people who have been close to me and supported me, especially my wife Georgina Konadu Boateng and children Kristodea, Kristoadom and Owuraku. I am grateful to the Finex Team: Osbert, Ferdinand, Ernest, Dii-Winga, Priscilla, Daniel and Naa for always providing the support needed.

About the reviewers

Jennifer Viola is a passionate and innovative Data Analytics and Business Intelligence professional with 20+ years of experience working with data across many industries.

She has a Bachelor's of Business Administration (2006) and a Masters of Investigations (2022). Her experience combined with her education successfully niches between Business and IT and makes her a well versatile addition to any company looking to improve their bottom line using data to achieve their goals and overall success.

She is published author for TDWI's Journal of Business Intelligence (2016), and she has mentored and been an educator in the industry since 2016. She enjoys helping and seeing others have successful careers in Data Analytics, too.

Tejanshu Salaria has completed his undergrad degree in Electronics and Communication engineering and master's in information system with major in finance. Business Development, Finance and analytics are the fields which excite him to innovate something and to build a career where he can help people to grow and make an impact on an organization. He has experience in leadership and has served fortune 500 companies for 7+ years now. He has Significant Experience in: Business Intelligence and Strategy, Data Analysis, Data Engineering, Project Management and Financial Modeling.

Victor Momoh is a Petroleum Engineer during the day and an Excel Enthusiast at night. He is passionate about data and numeracy, so his love for Microsoft Excel does not come as a surprise. Victor is a certified Microsoft Excel Expert (2010,2019/365). An international speaker at various global events and one who is passionate about sharing knowledge through LinkedIn, his YouTube channel, ExcelMoments, and a telegram group, Nigerian Excel Users (NEU) which he runs alongside some Excel MVPs.

Victor's contributions to the Excel community got him the award of Microsoft Excel MVP back in 2022 and in 2023.

I would like to appreciate Bernard for putting out such quality material and for the privilege to be a technical reviewer for this book.

Table of Contents

Section 2: Creating Insightful Calculations from your Data Model using DAX and Cube Functions

5

6

Section 3: Putting it all together with a Dashboard

7

8

9

Choosing the Right Design Themes: Less Is More with Colors   227

10

Publication and Deployment: Sharing with Report Users   259

Preface

Data Modeling with Microsoft Excel is an essential resource for anyone looking to harness the full potential of Microsoft Excel in data analysis.

This book delves deep into the advanced features of Excel, specifically focusing on Power Pivot, Data Analysis Expressions (DAX), and Cube Functions. These tools are pivotal for anyone working with large datasets and seeking to perform complex data modeling and analysis efficiently.

This book is not just about learning the functionalities; it's about understanding how to apply these tools in real-world scenarios to derive meaningful insights from your data. Whether you are a business analyst, a data scientist, or someone who regularly works with data in Excel, this book will equip you with the skills to transform the way you interpret and present data, enhancing your analytical capabilities and decision-making processes.

Who this book is for

This book is for Excel users looking for hands-on and effective methods to manage and analyze large volumes of data within Microsoft Excel using Power Pivot. If you are new or already conversant with Excel's Data Analytics tools, this book will give you insight into practical ways to apply Excel's Power Pivot, Power Query, DAX and Cube functions to save you time on routine data management tasks.

What this book covers

Chapter 1, Getting Started with Data Modeling, introduces the concept of data modeling, explaining its significance in today's data-driven world. Readers will learn the basics of data modeling in Excel and understand why it is a crucial skill for effective data analysis.

Chapter 2, Data Structuring for Data Models, focuses on organizing data to optimize its use in Power Pivot. The chapter provides strategies and best practices for structuring data tables to facilitate efficient data analysis and modeling.

Chapter 3, Preparing Your Data for the Data Model, guides readers through the process of cleaning and transforming raw data into a more usable format using Power Query, setting the stage for effective data modeling.

Chapter 4, Data Modeling with Power Pivot, will show you how to use Power Pivot for advanced data modeling, including techniques for connecting tables using relationships.

Chapter 5, Creating DAX Calculations from Your Data Model, introduces DAX (Data Analysis Expressions), teaching you how to create powerful calculations and measures directly within your data models.

Chapter 6, Creating Cube Functions from Your Data Model, explores Cube Functions as an alternative to DAX, offering flexibility in extracting and manipulating data from the data model.

Chapter 7, Communicating Insights from Your Data Model Using Dashboards, emphasizes the importance of dashboards in communicating data insights. It covers how to create effective dashboards that convey the story behind the data clearly and compellingly.

Chapter 8, Visualization Elements for Your Dashboard, will show you various visualization tools such as slicers, pivot charts, conditional formatting, and shapes, and how to use them to enhance the effectiveness of your dashboards.

Chapter 9, Choosing the Right Design Themes, delves into the principles of design in the context of data presentation, focusing on the strategic use of colors and themes to create visually appealing and informative dashboards.

Chapter 10, Publication and Deployment, guides you through the process of publishing and deploying your Excel models and dashboards, ensuring that the insights are accessible and understandable to end-users, online and offline.

To get the most out of this book

An understanding of Excel's features like Tables, Pivot Tables and some basic aggregating functions will be useful but not a requirement to come along.

Software/hardware covered in the book	Operating system requirements
Excel	Windows, macOS, or Linux
Power BI	

Conventions used

There are a number of text conventions used throughout this book.

`Code in text`: Indicates code words in text, database table names, folder names, filenames, file extensions, pathnames, dummy URLs, user input, and Twitter handles. Here is an example: "We can connect these two normalized tables using the common column `Course ID`."

Bold: Indicates a new term, an important word, or words that you see onscreen. For instance, words in menus or dialog boxes appear in **bold**. Here is an example: "we can have separate lookup tables that will give us the details for each **Customer ID**, **City**, and **Product ID**."

> Tips or important notes
> Appear like this.

Get in touch

Feedback from our readers is always welcome.

General feedback: If you have questions about any aspect of this book, email us at `customercare@packtpub.com` and mention the book title in the subject of your message.

Errata: Although we have taken every care to ensure the accuracy of our content, mistakes do happen. If you have found a mistake in this book, we would be grateful if you would report this to us. Please visit `www.packtpub.com/support/errata` and fill in the form.

Piracy: If you come across any illegal copies of our works in any form on the internet, we would be grateful if you would provide us with the location address or website name. Please contact us at `copyright@packt.com` with a link to the material.

If you are interested in becoming an author: If there is a topic that you have expertise in and you are interested in either writing or contributing to a book, please visit `authors.packtpub.com`.

Packt is searching for authors like you

If you're interested in becoming an author for Packt, please visit `authors.packtpub.com` and apply today. We have worked with thousands of developers and tech professionals, just like you, to help them share their insight with the global tech community. You can make a general application, apply for a specific hot topic that we are recruiting an author for, or submit your own idea.

Share Your Thoughts

Once you've read *Data Modeling with Microsoft Excel,* we'd love to hear your thoughts! Scan the QR code below to go straight to the Amazon review page for this book and share your feedback.

https://packt.link/r/1-803-24028-8

Your review is important to us and the tech community and will help us make sure we're delivering excellent quality content.

Download a free PDF copy of this book

Thanks for purchasing this book!

Do you like to read on the go but are unable to carry your print books everywhere?
Is your eBook purchase not compatible with the device of your choice?

Don't worry, now with every Packt book you get a DRM-free PDF version of that book at no cost.

Read anywhere, any place, on any device. Search, copy, and paste code from your favorite technical books directly into your application.

The perks don't stop there, you can get exclusive access to discounts, newsletters, and great free content in your inbox daily

Follow these simple steps to get the benefits:

1. Scan the QR code or visit the link below

https://packt.link/free-ebook/9781803240282

2. Submit your proof of purchase

3. That's it! We'll send your free PDF and other benefits to your email directly

Part 1: Overview and Introduction to Data Modeling in Microsoft Excel

This part is structured to guide both beginners and intermediate users through the foundational concepts and advanced applications of data modeling in Excel. Here, we delve into what data modeling is, why it is essential in today's data-driven environment, and how Excel can be a powerful tool in this realm. You'll also learn how to clean and transform your data using Power Query, ensuring it is in the best possible shape for modeling.

This section has the following chapters:

- *Chapter 1, Getting Started with Data Modeling*
- *Chapter 2, Data Structuring for Power Pivot*
- *Chapter 3, Preparing your Data for the Data Model*
- *Chapter 4, Data Modeling with Power Pivot*

1

Getting Started with Data Modeling – Overview and Importance

Think of how a business plan lays out the written roadmap for companies to understand and make sense of all the moving parts of their business: the drivers, resources, and processes required to achieve success. This plan often serves as the manual companies consult to understand how all the pieces of the business puzzle fit together.

In the same way, large and complex datasets require a structure or a blueprint that allows data analysts to visualize how different data points can be structured and connected to deliver insights for action or decision making.

This underscores the significance of data modeling in the field of data analytics, and it is precisely where data modeling in Microsoft Excel proves invaluable.

In this first chapter of the book, we will break down the concept of data modeling within and beyond Microsoft Excel. The chapter will cover the advantages of using a data model to manage multiple sources of data. You will go on to understand some practical use cases on how to use the data model to look up and reference related tables and understand the architecture and features of Power Pivot, the engine for data modeling in Microsoft Excel. Throughout the journey, best practices will be highlighted and covered.

At the end of the chapter, you will be in a good position to understand how data modeling can help you connect and manage datasets from multiple resources to deliver insights quickly and efficiently in your data analytics project.

The following topics will be covered in this chapter:

- Understanding the concept of data modeling
- The importance of a data model in Microsoft Excel
- Practical use cases for a data model
- Introduction to Power Pivot in Excel
- Best practices with Power Pivot

Understanding the concept of data modeling

Data modeling is the process of structuring and organizing data in a way that it can be easily analyzed and reported. Think of it like arranging books in a library. If you just threw all the books into a room, it would be hard to find what you need. But if you categorize them by genre, author, or publication date, it becomes much easier to locate a specific book.

Similarly, data modeling helps in organizing data so that you can easily derive insights from it.

Just as a business plan serves as a blueprint for a company, a data model acts as a blueprint for creating and visualizing the relationships between different datasets. This activity is known as data modeling.

It serves as the backbone for your visuals and calculations, allowing for more complex data analysis. A data model gives you a visual or conceptual view of how the datasets you are working with connect to produce the results or insights you need. Getting it right can be the difference between well-optimized data analytics and analytics filled with redundant data that offers little insight.

Microsoft offers the following definitions for a data model in Excel and Power BI:

- A data model allows you to integrate data from multiple tables, effectively building a relational data source inside an Excel workbook.
- Data modeling is the process of analyzing and defining all the different data types your business collects and produces, as well as the relationships between those bits of data. By using text, symbols, and diagrams, data modeling concepts create visual representations of data as it's captured, stored, and used in your business. As your business determines how data is used and when the data modeling process becomes an exercise in understanding and clarifying your data requirements.

In Excel, a data model can help you connect to one or many tables and summarize the data with PivotTables.

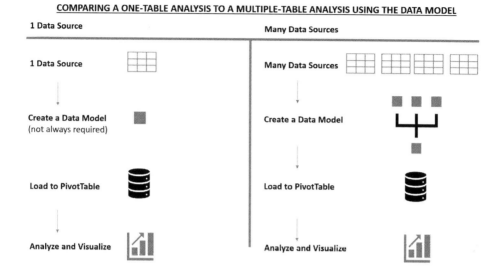

Figure 1.1 – Comparing a one-table analysis to multiple-table analysis

Besides Excel, the concept also applies to other database management systems, such as Power BI, Access, Oracle, and so on.

With a data model, analyzing your data becomes easier because you can clearly define each dataset, the role it plays, and how it connects to other datasets to give you the results you need.

Comparing a one-table analysis to multiple-table analysis in Microsoft Excel

Often, we store our data in a range of cells in Microsoft Excel. Converting data stored in a range of cells into a table makes it easier for you to reference the dataset for calculations and further analysis using a PivotTable. This is called **Structured Referencing**. Standing in the range of cells, you can insert a table in Excel by going to **Insert > Table** in the ribbon or simply pressing *Ctrl + T*.

When data is stored in a table, simple aggregations such as SUM, AVERAGE, and COUNT can be performed using the table name and the column. For instance, summing sales from a table named Table1 can be simply done using =SUM(Table1[Sales]).

Data in the table can also be used in a PivotTable. This way, when the source data changes with the addition of more rows or columns, the PivotTables automatically update with the new data in the table when it is refreshed. This avoids the need to update the source reference of cells in the PivotTable.

Most Excel users tend to store all their data in one table for their analysis. This can be referred to as **One-Table Analysis**. There is nothing wrong with this approach. However, if the data you are working with grows and you have a situation where you need to add other tables to your analysis, it can become complex with just one table and a PivotTable.

Creating a data model in Power Pivot in Excel allows you to have access to multiple tables for your analysis without the need for complex lookup formulas. It improves performance and gives you a clear overview of how the tables relate.

Let's now explore some of the key advantages of using a data model in Power Pivot.

Here are some reasons to use a data model:

- It gives you a broad overview of your datasets or tables. This ensures that all the tables and datasets you require in your model are accurately captured. Take a look at the following example data model for a sales report.

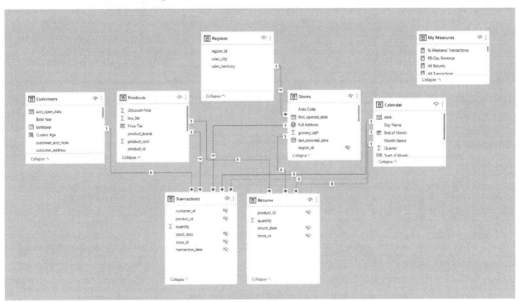

Figure 1.2 – A Diagram view of an example sales report data model

You'll realize that even though there are several tables used in the creation of the final dashboard, the data model gives a good overview of how each table connects and contributes to delivering the final results.

- It is an abstract representation of the real-world situation you are analyzing. With the data model, you are in a good position to generate accurate measures and calculations for the KPIs in your report.

- The data model helps reduce the occurrence of redundant data. That is, the repetition of the same data at different points in your dataset. This helps improve performance when your data increases.

- The data model can also be a good blueprint for developing web or frontend applications for your dataset. For example, **PowerApps**, **AppSheet**, **Caspio**, and **Squirrel** are some of the applications that can benefit from a well-designed data model.

Most of these are low-code tools that use data models as a blueprint to create interactive apps for users. The data model then becomes an indirect way for developers to document the data that will be required to build these apps.

So far, we have covered what a data model is and the reasons you should consider using data models to structure datasets that are broken up into relational components and that need to be connected and properly visualized in order to effect the maximum efficiency and insight that is possible.

In the following section, we will look at some practical use cases of a data model. We will look at the case of an accountant and a salesperson and see how data models can help reduce the efforts and processes required in analyzing data.

Practical use cases for a data model

This section explores practical use cases of data models in various workplace scenarios.

The accountant

Mr. Owusu Yeboah is a chartered accountant. He enters his accounting records in the **Journal** tab, a table he has created in Microsoft Excel to record the **Date**, **Description**, **Amount**, **Debit Account**, and **Credit Account** of all transactions.

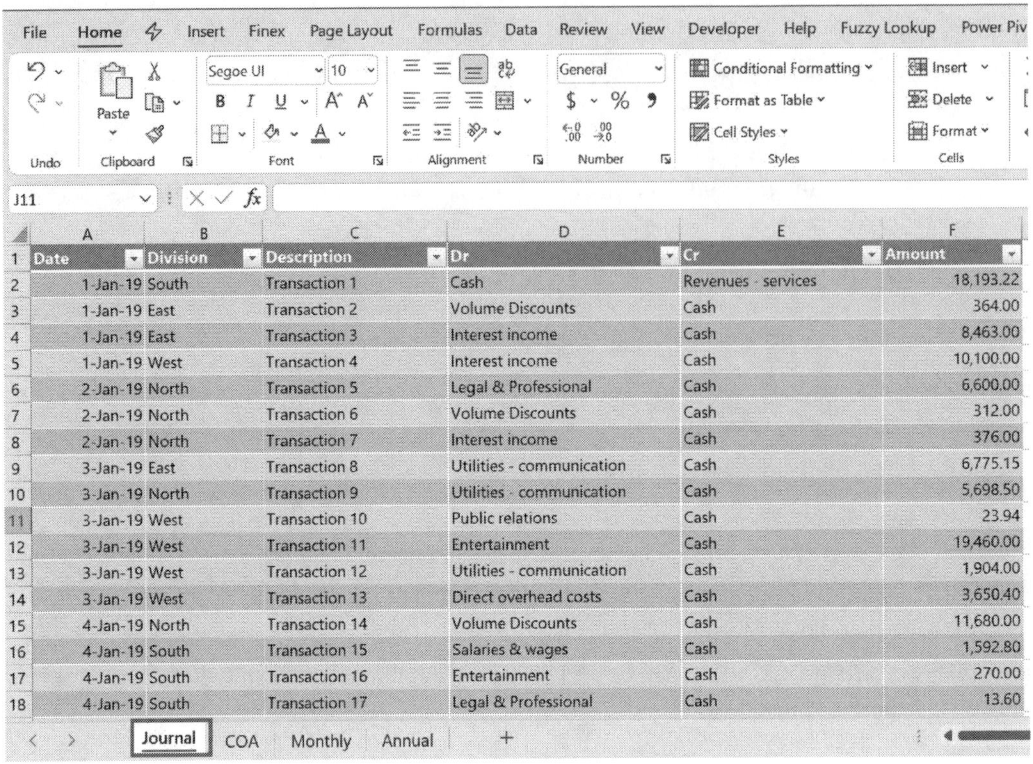

Date	Division	Description	Dr	Cr	Amount
1-Jan-19	South	Transaction 1	Cash	Revenues - services	18,193.22
1-Jan-19	East	Transaction 2	Volume Discounts	Cash	364.00
1-Jan-19	East	Transaction 3	Interest income	Cash	8,463.00
1-Jan-19	West	Transaction 4	Interest income	Cash	10,100.00
2-Jan-19	North	Transaction 5	Legal & Professional	Cash	6,600.00
2-Jan-19	North	Transaction 6	Volume Discounts	Cash	312.00
2-Jan-19	North	Transaction 7	Interest income	Cash	376.00
3-Jan-19	East	Transaction 8	Utilities - communication	Cash	6,775.15
3-Jan-19	North	Transaction 9	Utilities - communication	Cash	5,698.50
3-Jan-19	West	Transaction 10	Public relations	Cash	23.94
3-Jan-19	West	Transaction 11	Entertainment	Cash	19,460.00
3-Jan-19	West	Transaction 12	Utilities - communication	Cash	1,904.00
3-Jan-19	West	Transaction 13	Direct overhead costs	Cash	3,650.40
4-Jan-19	North	Transaction 14	Volume Discounts	Cash	11,680.00
4-Jan-19	South	Transaction 15	Salaries & wages	Cash	1,592.80
4-Jan-19	South	Transaction 16	Entertainment	Cash	270.00
4-Jan-19	South	Transaction 17	Legal & Professional	Cash	13.60

Figure 1.3 – Journal showing accounting entries

In another worksheet named **COA**, he has a table containing his chart of accounts with account codes, sorted to classify the various accounts into assets, liabilities, equity, revenue, and expenses. The other columns in his chart of accounts describe how each account has to be treated to produce a monthly and an annual financial statement.

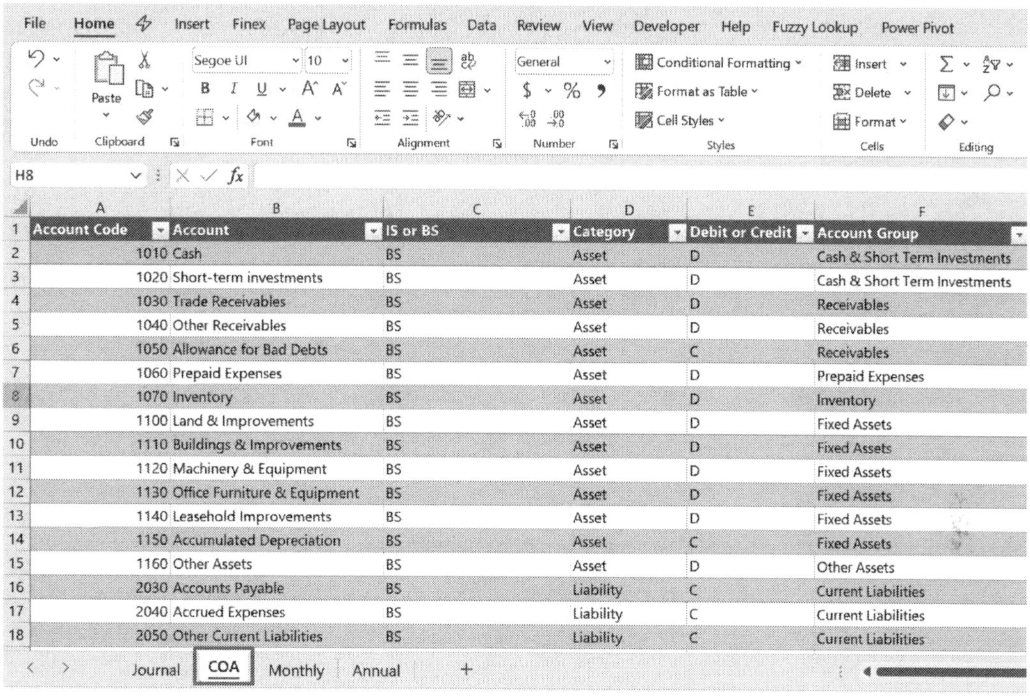

Account Code	Account	IS or BS	Category	Debit or Credit	Account Group
1010	Cash	BS	Asset	D	Cash & Short Term Investments
1020	Short-term investments	BS	Asset	D	Cash & Short Term Investments
1030	Trade Receivables	BS	Asset	D	Receivables
1040	Other Receivables	BS	Asset	D	Receivables
1050	Allowance for Bad Debts	BS	Asset	C	Receivables
1060	Prepaid Expenses	BS	Asset	D	Prepaid Expenses
1070	Inventory	BS	Asset	D	Inventory
1100	Land & Improvements	BS	Asset	D	Fixed Assets
1110	Buildings & Improvements	BS	Asset	D	Fixed Assets
1120	Machinery & Equipment	BS	Asset	D	Fixed Assets
1130	Office Furniture & Equipment	BS	Asset	D	Fixed Assets
1140	Leasehold Improvements	BS	Asset	D	Fixed Assets
1150	Accumulated Depreciation	BS	Asset	C	Fixed Assets
1160	Other Assets	BS	Asset	D	Other Assets
2030	Accounts Payable	BS	Liability	C	Current Liabilities
2040	Accrued Expenses	BS	Liability	C	Current Liabilities
2050	Other Current Liabilities	BS	Liability	C	Current Liabilities

Figure 1.4 – Sample chart of accounts

For Mr. Owusu Yeboah to determine the ins and outs of each account or create a trial balance, he would need to use a lot of lookup formulas to connect the two tables. Aside from this, when new data is added to the tables, he must manually update all his workings to capture the new entries. Using Excel tables to store data is one way to avoid manually updating calculations when your data changes.

How does a data model help in this situation?

Using a data model, Mr. Owusu can upload and connect the two tables using common columns. These common columns are used to establish a relationship between the tables and make it possible to create a data model. He can then create an extra calendar table to help him create a month-on-month or annual financial statement.

A calendar table in Excel is a special table with a series of sequential dates that helps you keep track of dates and times in your data. It's great for looking at things such as sales or expenses by day, month, or year. If your data is missing information for certain dates, a calendar table makes it easy to spot those gaps so you can fill them in. This ensures you're not missing out on important details when making decisions.

In addition to helping Mr. Owusu Yeboah sort and analyze his data over time, a calendar table makes sure that all the date information in his various tables lines up correctly. This helps him avoid mistakes and makes it easier to combine different sets of data. It also lets Excel perform more advanced calculations for him, such as figuring out his total sales for each month or calculating averages over specific time periods.

His data model will look something like the following screenshot:

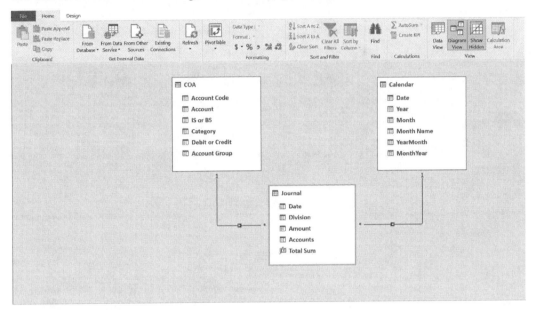

Figure 1.5 – A screenshot of a data model with accounting data

This will help him easily capture new information in the journal and chart of accounts and create a dynamic financial statement for his users.

The salesperson

Ferdinand Attobra is a sales executive with Finex online electronics shop. Daily, he is required to create a report that captures top-performing products, branches, and customers to his supervisors.

Order Date	Customer ID	Store ID	Product ID	Quantity	Revenue	Cost
1/6/2018	CustID- 401		10001 ProdID-28000011	11	2332	1650
1/6/2018	CustID- 525		10002 ProdID-28000021	5	10525	8770
1/6/2018	CustID- 214		10001 ProdID-28000031	8	2744	2320
1/6/2018	CustID- 030		10003 ProdID-28000041	6	10476	8508
1/6/2018	CustID- 204		10004 ProdID-28000051	10	3720	2890
1/6/2018	CustID- 494		10005 ProdID-28000061	13	4056	2990
1/6/2018	CustID- 096		10006 ProdID-28000071	7	18998	13566
1/6/2018	CustID- 496		10007 ProdID-28000081	3	393	270
1/10/2018	CustID- 290		10008 ProdID-28000091	11	5544	4400
1/10/2018	CustID- 496		10007 ProdID-28000101	12	4476	3120
1/13/2018	CustID- 334		10009 ProdID-28000111	15	8625	6900
1/13/2018	CustID- 210		10010 ProdID-28000121	4	6324	4716
1/13/2018	CustID- 590		10011 ProdID-28000131	5	3340	2400
1/13/2018	CustID- 424		10012 ProdID-28000141	2	3514	2358
1/13/2018	CustID- 175		10013 ProdID-28000151	7	12453	10549
1/13/2018	CustID- 541		10009 ProdID-28000161	13	3718	3120
1/15/2018	CustID- 494		10005 ProdID-28000171	12	7008	5220
1/20/2018	CustID- 453		10001 ProdID-28000181	6	14994	10482
1/20/2018	CustID- 210		10010 ProdID-28000191	15	6090	4500
1/20/2018	CustID- 572		10014 ProdID-28000201	7	14014	11676
1/20/2018	CustID- 254		10004 ProdID-28000211	15	5340	4320
1/20/2018	CustID- 334		10009 ProdID-28000221	4	1324	904
1/20/2018	CustID- 096		10006 ProdID-28000231	9	3483	2610
1/20/2018	CustID- 290		10008 ProdID-28000241	8	2048	1600
1/21/2018	CustID- 245		10015 ProdID-28000251	2	4600	3456
1/26/2018	CustID- 397		10016 ProdID-28000261	13	4303	3302

| < | > | | Transactions | Lookup | + | |

Figure 1.6 – Sales transactions

To create his report, he downloads four datasets from his sales software:

- **Transactions**: This captures all the revenue as well as the cost of sales per transaction. The table also has fields that identify the customer, product, and store information related to each transaction. This is represented by **Customer ID**, **Product ID**, and **Store ID**.

  Apart from the **Transactions** table, there are three other tables he uses to look up the details of each customer, product, or store that appeared in the **Transactions** table.

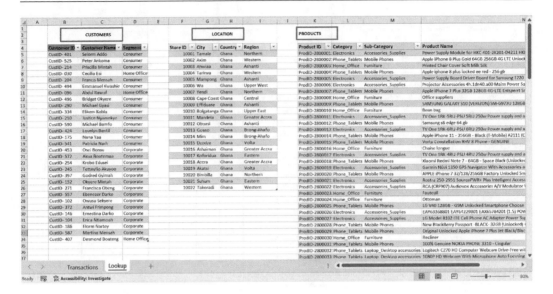

Figure 1.7 – Sample lookup tables

- **Customers**: This table has the unique details of all the shop's customers' IDs, their names, and their customer segments.

- **Products**: This table contains the unique details of the product IDs, their categories, sub-categories, and their names.

- **Location**: This table contains the details of each store ID, the city, region, and country.

The challenge Ferdinand faces in creating his report is how he can use the various IDs stored in the **Transactions** table to look up the customer, product, and store involved in each transaction.

How does a data model help in this situation?

Using a data model, Ferdi can upload and connect the **Customers**, **Products**, and **Locations** tables to the **Transactions** tables using the **Customer ID**, **Product ID**, and **City** columns respectively. This is where a calendar table, created as supplemental data but very useful, would get connected as well. He will then use this model to generate his daily reports to analyze sales by **Product**, **Geography**, **Customer**, and **Date**.

The model will look like the following screenshot:

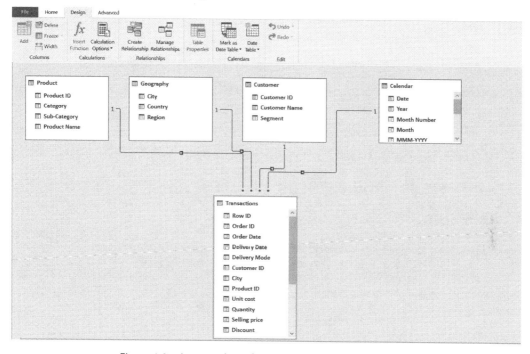

Figure 1.8 – A screenshot of a data model showing sales data

From the two case studies, we can appreciate that using Excel's data model can help us overcome some of the typical challenges in our routine office work.

Excel's data model allows you to integrate data from multiple sources in an efficient manner. This is what is called an **Entity Relationship Diagram (ERD)**.

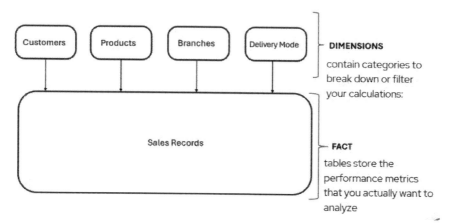

Figure 1.9 – Sample ERD for a sales report in Excel

Apart from this key advantage, the data model can also do the following:

- Store and analyze data beyond Microsoft Excel's 1-million-row capacity. This brings a whole new capability to regular Excel.

- Create more powerful formulas to help you analyze your data more efficiently.

- Work together with tools such as Power Query to transform, shape your data, and maintain a dynamic connection to your data sources.

In the next topic, we will dive into the main tool for data modeling and explore some best practices to help you get more insights from your datasets.

Introduction to Power Pivot, Excel versions, and installation

Power Pivot is the main authoring tool for data models in Microsoft Excel.

Power Pivot allows you to load large volumes of data from various sources, perform more powerful calculations, and create insights easily from your datasets.

Power Pivot works as a downloadable add-in for the Excel 2010 and 2013 versions. Excel 2016 and more recent versions have the add-in already available in-app.

Power Pivot was inspired by **Microsoft SQL Server Analysis Services** (**SSAS**) to ultimately make self-service business intelligence possible for regular Excel users. This means a novice Excel user can still crunch key insights from datasets directly in Excel.

The key features of Power Pivot include the following:

- An in-memory engine that can compress large datasets into smaller units making it easier to load data beyond Excel's typical capability

- A diagram view that makes it easy to manage relationships and create hierarchies in your data model

- A dynamic date table feature that allows you to create automatic date dimensions for your dataset

- A powerful calculation engine for calculations using **Data Analysis Expressions** (**DAX**), the native calculation language for Power Pivot

Now that we have a good idea about Power Pivot, we will look at where we can find and install this tool in earlier and older versions of Microsoft Excel in the next section.

How do I install Power Pivot?

To install or enable Power Pivot in Excel, please go through the following steps:

1. Open a new Excel workbook and go to the **Data** tab:

Figure 1.10 – Enabling the Data tab in Microsoft Excel

2. In the **Data Tools** group, go to the **Power Pivot** window:

Figure 1.11 – Enabling the Power Pivot tab in Microsoft Excel

3. If this is the first time you are using Power Pivot, you will see the following pop-up message:

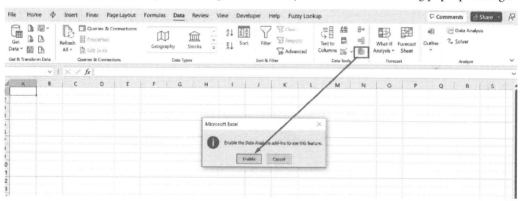

Figure 1.12 – Pop-up message while enabling Power Pivot

4. Click on **Enable**. After a few seconds, the Power Pivot window will open to confirm that the installation was successful.

Figure 1.13 – Enabling the Power Pivot Tab in Microsoft Excel

5. You will find a new Power Pivot **Command** tab on your ribbon when the process is completed.

Figure 1.14 – Process is complete

You should find the **Tab** present anytime you open a new workbook.

There are situations where the Power Pivot tab is not available when you open a new workbook. This could be because of low disk space or memory issues with the computer. A quick way to resolve this will be to restart your computer or create some disk space and follow the following steps:

1. Go to File | Options | Add-ins, select COM Add-ins, and click on Go.

    This will display the following screen:

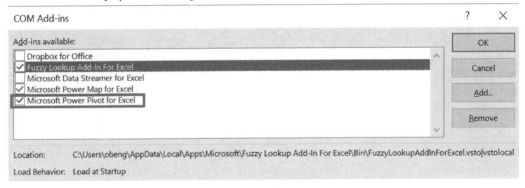

Figure 1.15 – Resetting the Power Pivot tab in Microsoft Excel

2. Unchecking and checking the box will reset the tab and you should find it available in the **Command** tabs area again.

We have now installed Power Pivot. In the next section, we will take a tour to understand how we can take full advantage of some of the features of the tool for our data modeling.

Exploring the features of Power Pivot

In this section, we are going to explore some of the key features of Power Pivot. It's important you begin learning about these features to help you use and apply them when we start working with data.

Figure 1.16 – Components of Excel's Power Pivot

Some of the useful features of Power Pivot are described here:

- **Command** tabs: Here, you will find the **Home** and **Design** tabs. The **Home** tab contains a group of icons for the following:

  - Formatting

  - Calculations

  - Sorting and filtering

  - Views (data and diagram view)

  - Connecting to data sources (get external data)

- The **Design** tab contains icons for managing the following:

  - Columns

  - Calculations

  - Relationships

  - Creating calendars

- **Formula** bar: This displays the formulas for your calculated column and measures when you select them. You can also use the field to create formulas from scratch.

- **Views**: The **View** group under the **Home** tab is useful for switching between a tabular view of your datasets or a diagram view. You can also use this menu to turn off some aspects of Power Pivot.

- **Calculated Column**: This area helps you to calculate and add new columns to your original datasets.

- **Calculation Area**: You can create your measures and store them in this section of Power Pivot. You can turn this section off using the option in the **View** group.

- The view in Power Pivot is similar to the worksheet view in Microsoft Excel. However, in Power Pivot, you can't edit cells or create calculations by referencing cells. Calculations are done using the columnar view in the data using a formula language called DAX.

What is DAX?

Think of DAX as a more powerful version of the regular Excel formulas you might already know, such as SUM or AVERAGE. DAX allows you to do more complex things with your data, such as summing up sales for a specific time period or calculating year-over-year growth, all while working within your data model.

So, if you're using a data model in Excel to help make sense of your business data, DAX is the tool that helps you ask specific questions and get precise answers from that model. It's like having a super-smart calculator that can quickly crunch the numbers in different ways, helping you make better business decisions. We will go into this in detail in subsequent chapters. These calculations can result in a new dimensional column or a new measure.

Beyond understanding the features of Power Pivot, it is important to adopt some best practices when working with this tool. In the next section, we will cover some of these best practices.

Best practices with Power Pivot

To get the best out of your Power Pivot and data model, there are some best practices you need to adopt to ensure optimum performance. We discuss some of these best practices here:

- Ideally, all datasets that are added to the data model should be named tables. This makes it easy to identify the tables when creating your DAX formulas.

- Update your source data to limit the number of columns and rows you import into Power Pivot. This will improve performance and give you a better response for your calculations. You can achieve this by normalizing your data. We will discuss this in the next chapter.

- Avoid creating calculations that shape and transform your data in Power Pivot. You can do all the data transformation and shaping in Power Query and then after, load it to Power Pivot. We will discuss Power Query in detail later in the book.

- Use the **Diagram** view in **View** to get an overview of your datasets and how they connect to each other and the **Data** view to audit or explore the content of each dataset.

- Ensure that the data type in each column is consistently formatted. For example, a column that contains dates should not have text input.

Sticking to these rules will greatly improve the performance of Power Pivot.

Summary

The objective of this chapter was to help you understand the concept of data modeling. We have covered the key advantages of using a data model in analyzing large and complex datasets. The chapter introduced you to tables, PivotTables, and Power Pivot and how the data model you create in Power Pivot helps you analyze data from multiple table sources. To help you put this in context, we looked at two practical use cases of a data model for an accountant and a salesperson. This should help bring the concept home and help you apply it to any dataset you analyze at work.

After reading this chapter, you are now also able to identify the key components of Power Pivot, the main authoring tool for data modeling in Microsoft Excel and Power BI. In this chapter, we also covered some best practices with a data model to help you improve the performance of Power Pivot.

In the next chapter, we will see best practices for laying out data. The chapter will help you further improve the performance of your Power Pivot calculations for large datasets.

Questions for discussion

1. Name five features of Power Pivot and the role they play in data modeling.

2. What is DAX?

3. List the key advantages of a data model in analyzing your work.

2

Data Structuring for Data Models – What's the best way to layout your data?

How do you structure your data for the data model? Getting your data in the right shape and form is important in the data modeling process. In this chapter, we will learn about the three golden rules for data structuring. These rules make it easier to model your data and create your calculations and analysis in Microsoft Excel. You will understand the concept of data normalization and the advantages it has over flat tables for analysis. The chapter will round off with an introduction to **Power Query**, Microsoft Excel's data transformation tool. When you encounter data layouts that do not conform to the best practices described in the chapter, Power Query plays a critical role in shaping and transforming the data.

The following topics will be covered in this chapter:

- Data structuring – understanding the three golden rules
- Denormalized and normalized data
- Understanding the role of primary keys and foreign keys

Data structuring – understanding the three golden rules

To get the best out of **Power Pivot**, we need to lay out our dataset in a way that will improve performance and help us get the right insights from our datasets. The following figure summarizes the ideal layout for a single dataset or table:

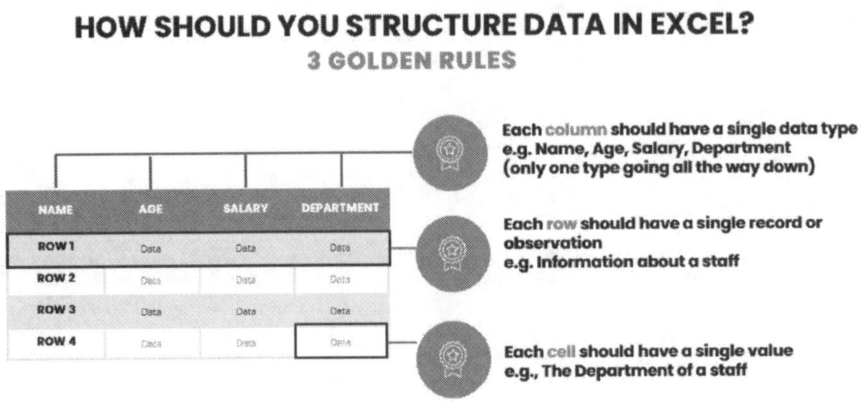

HOW SHOULD YOU STRUCTURE DATA IN EXCEL?
3 GOLDEN RULES

Each column should have a single data type e.g. Name, Age, Salary, Department (only one type going all the way down)

Each row should have a single record or observation e.g. Information about a staff

Each cell should have a single value e.g., The Department of a staff

Figure 2.1 – The three golden rules for laying out your data in a single dataset

Let's look at each of these rules in detail:

- **Rule 1**: Each column should have a single data type. As we learned in *Chapter 1, Getting Started with Data Modeling*, Power Pivot manages data using a columnar structure. It is therefore important to commit one data type to each column of your dataset.

  For example, if you have data for a payroll containing the names of staff members, one column should be dedicated to the names of staff with the same format and no other data type. Apart from this, there shouldn't be any column in your dataset that contains similar names of staff members. This way, your dataset is more likely to be longer and not wider.

- **Rule 2**: Each row in your dataset should represent a single record of your observation or data units.

  Using the same payroll example, the rows in your dataset should represent information on one staff member with no duplication in any other row in your dataset. What this means is that you should find the information you need on a particular staff member – age, salary, department, and so on – in the same row that contains their name. This represents one record of staff entry in the database.

- **Rule 3**: Each cell in your table should have a single value. If a cell contains text, it should not be combined with a number or any other data type.

  For example, if you are entering the addresses of your staff into your payroll, cities and zip codes should be placed in different cells. This way, you should have separate columns to analyze your dataset by city or zip code.

The preceding rules are standard and are also applied to datasets in Access, SQL, and other relational database management systems. Abiding by these rules makes it easy to calculate in Power Pivot using **DAX** and later generate summary reports using pivot tables.

However, sticking to these rules may not be sufficient for good performance and calculations in a large dataset that has many columns. Many columns in a dataset can lead to **data redundancy** in a table. Data redundancy is defined as the repetition of the same data at different points in your table.

In the next section, we will look at some examples of this and discuss how to prevent it in our analysis.

Understanding data redundancy

Data redundancy is a situation that occurs when the same data is stored in multiple places within a database. This means that the same information is repeated in different fields, tables, or records. It is often unintentional and can cause problems within a database. For example, suppose you have a customer database that includes customer details such as name, address, and phone number. If you store this information in multiple tables, such as one for orders and another for customer information, it creates data redundancy. This means that if a customer's information changes, you will have to update it in multiple places, which can be time-consuming and can lead to inconsistencies.

Similarly, if you have a product database that stores the product name, price, and description and you create another table that stores the same information, you end up with redundant data.

As discussed in the earlier section, storing your dataset in one table in Excel can be convenient. It makes it easy to analyze your data using pivot tables. However, for large datasets, this often leads to data redundancy.

To help us understand the challenges of data redundancy, let's take the example data in the following figure, showing orders received from and delivered to customers of an e-commerce shop in Ghana:

Row ID	Order ID	Order Date	Delivery Date	Delivery Mode	Customer ID	Customer Name	Customer Segment	City	Country	Region
1	OrdID-2018-0000011	1/6/2018	1/13/2018	5-7 Day	CustID- 401	Selorm Addo	Consumer	Tamale	Ghana	Northern
2	OrdID-2018-0000021	1/6/2018	1/8/2018	2-3 Day	CustID- 525	Peter Ankoma	Consumer	Axim	Ghana	Western
3	OrdID-2018-0000031	1/6/2018	1/8/2018	2-3 Day	CustID- 214	Priscilla Mintah	Consumer	Tamale	Ghana	Northern
4	OrdID-2018-0000041	1/6/2018	1/9/2018	2-3 Day	CustID- 030	Cecilia Esi	Home Office	Ahwiaa	Ghana	Ashanti
5	OrdID-2018-0000051	1/6/2018	1/8/2018	2-3 Day	CustID- 204	Francis Mensah	Consumer	Tarkwa	Ghana	Western
6	OrdID-2018-0000061	1/6/2018	1/6/2018	Pick up	CustID- 494	Emmanuel Kwashie	Consumer	Mampong	Ghana	Ashanti
7	OrdID-2018-0000071	1/6/2018	1/9/2018	2-3 Day	CustID- 096	Abdul Rawuf	Home Office	Wa	Ghana	Upper West
8	OrdID-2018-0000081	1/6/2018	1/8/2018	Pick up	CustID- 496	Bridget Okyere	Consumer	Yendi	Ghana	Northern
9	OrdID-2018-0000091	1/10/2018	1/10/2018	Pick up	CustID- 290	Michael Gyasi	Consumer	Cape Coast	Ghana	Central
10	OrdID-2018-0000101	1/10/2018	1/10/2018	Pick up	CustID- 496	Bridget Okyere	Consumer	Yendi	Ghana	Northern
11	OrdID-2018-0000111	1/13/2018	1/14/2018	Pick up	CustID- 334	Elikem Kobla	Consumer	Effiduase	Ghana	Ashanti
12	OrdID-2018-0000121	1/13/2018	1/18/2018	5-7 Day	CustID- 210	Justice Nyamekye	Consumer	Bolgatanga	Ghana	Upper East
13	OrdID-2018-0000131	1/13/2018	1/14/2018	Express 1 Day	CustID- 590	Michael Bamfo	Consumer	Mandela	Ghana	Greater Accra
14	OrdID-2018-0000141	1/13/2018	1/14/2018	Pick up	CustID- 424	Lovelyn Bentil	Consumer	Obuasi	Ghana	Ashanti
15	OrdID-2018-0000151	1/13/2018	1/13/2018	Pick up	CustID- 175	Nana Yaa	Consumer	Goaso	Ghana	Brong-Ahafo
16	OrdID-2018-0000161	1/13/2018	1/18/2018	5-7 Day	CustID- 541	Patricia Narh	Consumer	Effiduase	Ghana	Ashanti
17	OrdID-2018-0000171	1/15/2018	1/20/2018	5-7 Day	CustID- 494	Emmanuel Kwashie	Consumer	Mampong	Ghana	Ashanti
18	OrdID-2018-0000181	1/20/2018	1/25/2018	5-7 Day	CustID- 453	Osei Bonsu	Corporate	Tamale	Ghana	Northern
19	OrdID-2018-0000191	1/20/2018	1/23/2018	2-3 Day	CustID- 210	Justice Nyamekye	Consumer	Bolgatanga	Ghana	Upper East
20	OrdID-2018-0000201	1/20/2018	1/22/2018	2-3 Day	CustID- 572	Akua Boatemaa	Corporate	Mim	Ghana	Brong-Ahafo
21	OrdID-2018-0000211	1/20/2018	1/23/2018	2-3 Day	CustID- 254	Krobo Edusei	Corporate	Tarkwa	Ghana	Western

Figure 2.2 – Sample sales data showing data redundancy

You would observe that the columns in the highlighted section, from **G** to **K**, contain information that is linked to other columns in the same table. For example, Customer Name is linked to Customer ID and the Country column to the City column.

This means that every time a particular customer orders from the shop, we can choose to enter the transaction with just the `Customer ID` and avoid creating another column in the same table that repeats the customer's name several times alongside the `Customer ID`.

This is the same situation with entries related to the customer's location, that is, **Region** and **Country**, which are linked to their city. The country the customer bought from is repeated multiple times in another column unnecessarily. This repetition of data is what is termed data redundancy.

Problems caused by data redundancy

Beyond increasing the size of your database, data redundancy can lead to the following problems in large datasets:

- **Insertion anomaly**: An insertion anomaly is a problem that occurs when it is not possible to insert a new record into a database without also adding additional data that may not be relevant or necessary. This can happen when a database is not organized efficiently.

  Take the example of a customer order database where customer details such as name, address, and phone number are stored in the same table as order details such as order number, product name, and quantity. If a new customer places an order, all their details will have to be entered again even though they have already been entered before. This leads to redundancy and is inefficient. We could enter the order with just the customer's ID and the quantity the customer has ordered. The extra details on the customer can be stored in a separate customer table where we can look up these details. An insertion anomaly occurs when a new record cannot be inserted into a database without also adding additional data that may not be necessary. This can be prevented by properly organizing the database to store the unique details of the customer once in a customer table. If this customer makes an order, we can then record that order with just a customer ID. This is possible because we can always know who that customer is when we go to the customer table.

- **Deletion anomaly**: A deletion anomaly is a problem that occurs when deleting a record from a database results in the unintentional loss of other related data that should be retained. Again, this can happen when your database is not organized efficiently. For example, suppose you have a database table that stores information about customers and their orders. The table has two columns, one for the customer's name and another for the order number. If a customer places an order, their name and order number are added to the table. If a customer cancels their order, the row that contains the order number and the customer's name is deleted from the table. However, if the customer has no other orders, their name is also deleted from the table, even though they are still a valid customer. This is an example of a deletion anomaly because deleting an order results in the unintentional loss of customer data.

  If we had a separate table in our database that stores only the details of customers, customer details would still be maintained even when there is no order from them in our orders table.

Another example of a deletion anomaly could be a database that stores information about students and their courses. If a student drops a course, the row that contains the student's name and the course number is deleted from the table. However, if the course is the only one that the student is taking, their name is also deleted from the table, even though they are still a valid student. This can cause problems with data consistency and can make it difficult to retrieve accurate information from the database.

This can be prevented by properly organizing the database. We will go into the proper ways to organize data later in this book.

- **Modification anomaly**: Another type of problem that is caused by data redundancy is a modification anomaly. This is similar to a deletion anomaly but it has to do with changes in the records we have in our database. If the orders we recorded have the same data type repeated in several places, then any change or modification of the data must be changed in exactly the same way in all locations. Take a correction of a product name in our sales data. To modify the name of the product, we have to go back and change all the records containing the product name. If we miss any name or there is an alternative spelling of the product name somewhere, it could lead to inconsistencies in our analysis. This type of change is easier to implement if that product name was stored once in a product register and not in the sales records. In the sales record, the product name will only be represented by the product ID.

Another example of a modification anomaly could be a database that stores information about products and their suppliers. If a supplier's name changes, it must be updated in the database to ensure that the correct supplier is associated with each product. However, if the supplier's name is misspelled or updated inconsistently across multiple records, it can cause problems with data consistency and make it difficult to retrieve accurate information from the database.

These problems can be prevented if we normalize our data. Let's now discuss the concept of data normalization and go through some differences between denormalized and normalized data.

What is data normalization?

Data normalization is the process of organizing data in a database in a way that reduces redundancy and improves data integrity. The goal of data normalization is to eliminate some of the problems with data redundancy such as insertion, deletion, and modification anomalies, which can occur when a database is not properly organized.

To illustrate the process of data normalization, let's consider the following example.

Suppose we have a database table that stores information about students, including their ID, name, address, course ID, course name, and course instructor. The table looks like this:

Student ID	Student Name	Student Address	Course ID	Course Name	Course Instructor
10001	Bernard	11 Sanshie, East Legon	101	Excel for Work	Mr. Boateng
10001	Bernard	11 Sanshie, East Legon	102	Data Analytics	Mrs. Konadu
10002	Ferdinand	1 Oxford, Osu	101	Excel for Work	Mr. Boateng
10003	Naa	14 Kay Road, Adenta	102	Data Analytics	Mrs. Konadu

Figure 2.3 – Database with student information

As you can see, this table has redundant data that can lead to data anomalies. For example, if we need to update the address of a student, we would have to update it in multiple rows, which can be time-consuming and error-prone.

To normalize this table, we can follow a series of steps:

1. Identify the primary key: The primary key is a unique identifier for each record in the table. In this example, the primary key is the student ID.

2. Eliminate redundant data: To eliminate redundant data, we can separate the course information into a separate table, with a foreign key relationship to the student table:

Course ID	Course Name	Course Instructor
101	Excel for Work	Mr. Boateng
102	Data Analytics	Mrs. Konadu

Figure 2.4 – Course information

3. Create a new table for the course registration information: To further normalize the data, we can create a new table for the course registration information, with a foreign key relationship to both the student table and the course table.

Student ID	Course ID
10001	101
10001	102
10002	101
10003	102

Figure 2.5 – Course registration information

We can connect these two normalized tables using the common column `Course ID`. This creates a relationship between the two tables.

Normalized datasets are more efficient than denormalized datasets. Let's look at some key differences between the two in the next section.

Denormalized and normalized data

Denormalized data combines redundant data into one table while normalized data stores related data in separate tables. Each type has its pros and cons when analyzing data. However, for data modeling, normalized data is ideal. We will go into the process of converting denormalized data into normalized data in the next section.

The following table lists the important differences between normalization and denormalization:

Criteria	Normalized Data	Denormalized Data
Definition	Data is organized in such a way that each piece or dimension of the data is stored in only one place in separate tables.	Data is organized in such a way that multiple pieces of information are stored together in one place.
Duplication	There is minimal duplication of data.	There is high duplication of data.
Data Redundancy	No data redundancy exists.	Data redundancy may exist.
Storage	More tables are needed to store the data.	Fewer tables are needed to store the data.
Data Integrity	Data is maintained with high integrity.	Data integrity may be compromised due to data redundancy.
Maintenance	Maintenance is easier, but querying may be more complex.	Maintenance may be more difficult, but querying is generally simpler.
Scalability	Normalized data is more scalable in handling large amounts of data.	Denormalized data is less scalable in handling large amounts of data.
Performance	Normalized data may require more joins, slowing down performance.	Denormalized data may have better performance due to fewer joins.
Flexibility	Normalized data allows more flexibility in making changes to the data structure.	Denormalized data is less flexible, and changes may require more effort.
Use Case	Normalized data is best for transactional systems.	Denormalized data is best for analytical systems.

Figure 2.6 – Differences between normalization and denormalization of data

Understanding the key differences between normalized and denormalized data can help you structure your data properly. A well-structured dataset can help you write simpler DAX calculations and optimize the performance of your entire dataset.

Now, we will take a second example and learn the steps to convert denormalized data into normalized data in Microsoft Excel.

We will start off by downloading the sample workbook containing the sales data. As explained, the data is in a denormalized form. We are going to go through the steps to transform the data into a normalized form.

You will observe that there are 19 columns in the dataset. Taking a glance through all the columns, you will realize that some of the columns are related. For example, we can generate or look up values for region and country by using data in the city column as a lookup value.

Expanding on this example, if I have a **Customer ID** number, I can use this to look up the **Customer Name** and **Customer Segment**.

This also applies to **Product ID | Product Category | Product Sub-Category | Product Name**.

These groups of columns have been segmented to help you spot the linkages, as shown in *Figure 2.3*:

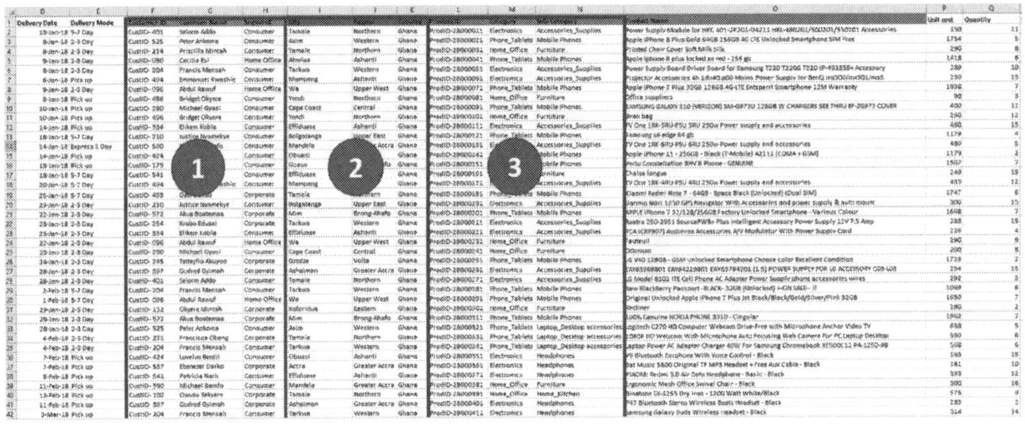

Figure 2.3 – Segmented headers that show related columns

Instead of repeating the entries in these lookup columns in our main tables several times, we can have separate lookup tables that will give us the details for each **Customer ID**, **City**, and **Product ID**.

To illustrate this concept of creating lookup tables for each ID, let's copy the headers of the columns and transpose them into the following list. The steps to do so are as follows:

1. Highlight the column headers.

2. Copy (*Ctrl + C*).

3. Go to cell V2 on your worksheet.

4. Press *Ctrl + Alt + V* for the **Paste Special** dialogue box and then select **Transpose** in the menu.

After the preceding steps, we should see the **Paste Special** dialogue box shown in *Figure 2.4*:

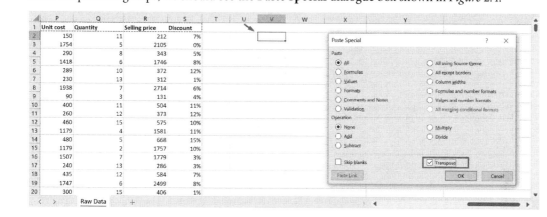

Figure 2.4 – Transposing copied list of headers

This should give you the list of headers in a vertical list, as shown in *Figure 2.5*:

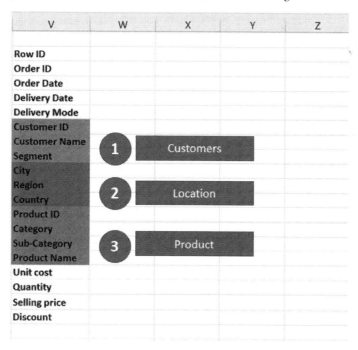

Figure 2.5 – Segmented blocks of related columns

At this point, we can use the numbered segment blocks to create distinct lookup tables that will provide the details for each **Customer ID**, **City**, and **Product ID**.

We can now cut each block or group of headers and mock up how these tables will look, as in *Figure 2.6*:

	V	W	X	Y	Z	AA	AB	AC
1								
2	Row ID		Customer ID		City		Product ID	
3	Order ID		Customer Name		Region		Category	
4	Order Date		Segment		Country		Sub-Category	
5	Delivery Date						Product Name	
6	Delivery Mode							
7								
8								
9								
10								
11								
12								
13								
14								
15								
16								
17	Unit cost							
18	Quantity							
19	Selling price							
20	Discount							

Figure 2.6 – Creating lookup tables from the original sales table

To maintain a relationship between our original table and these three lookup tables, we need to define a key field from each table to be present in our original table. We will duplicate these headers into our original table to help us keep them connected. To make it easier, we will move our original table below our lookup tables.

Our updated view or schema will now look like this:

Customer ID	City	Product ID
Customer Name	Region	Category
Segment	Country	Sub-Category
		Product Name

	Row ID
	Order ID
	Order Date
	Delivery Date
	Delivery Mode
	Customer ID
	City
	Product ID
	Unit cost
	Quantity
	Selling price
	Discount

Figure 2.7 – Mockup of our relational database

As indicated earlier, the preceding three tables represent our lookup tables, giving us details on each **Customer ID**, **City**, and **Product ID**. They connect to our original table using the same duplicated headers below them.

This way, we can enter every sales transaction using just the **Customer ID**, **City**, and **Product ID** without repeating the extra details that cause redundancy.

Data modeling will now help us connect these tables using common relationships between the tables.

Understanding table relationships

In a data model, relationships refer to the connections between different entities or tables within a database. There are three types of relationships in a data model: one-to-many, many-to-many, and one-to-one. Let's discuss each type in detail along with some examples.

One-to-many relationship

In a one-to-many relationship, one record in a table is associated with multiple records in another table. This is the most common type of relationship in a database.

For example, a customer may place many orders, but each order is associated with only one customer. In this case, the customer table is on the one side of the relationship, and the order table is on many sides. The relationship is established by creating a foreign key in the **order** table that refers to the primary key in the customer table.

Another example is the relationship between a department table and an **employee** table. A department may have many employees, but each employee is associated with only one department.

Many-to-many relationship

In a many-to-many relationship, one record in a table can be associated with multiple records in another table, and vice versa. This type of relationship requires a third table, called a junction table or bridge table, to connect the first two tables.

For example, consider a music streaming service that has a **user** table and a **song** table. A user can listen to many songs, and a song can be played by many users. To represent this relationship, we need a third table called a **playlist** table that contains foreign keys to both the **user** and **song** tables. Each record in the **playlist** table represents a user's specific playlist, which may contain many songs.

One-to-one relationship

In a one-to-one relationship, each record in one table is associated with only one record in another table.

For example, in a hospital database, each patient may have only one medical record, and each medical record is associated with only one patient. In this case, the **patient** table is on the one side of the relationship, and the **medical record** table is on the other side. The relationship is established by creating a foreign key in the **medical record** table that refers to the primary key in the **patient** table.

Another example is the relationship between an **employee** table and a **payroll** table. Each employee has only one payroll record, and each payroll record is associated with only one employee.

Understanding dimension and fact tables

In a relational database, a **fact table** is a table that stores quantitative information or facts about a business process or activity, such as sales, inventory, or customer transactions. A fact table typically contains numerical values and foreign keys to link to dimension tables.

On the other hand, a **dimension table** is a table that stores descriptive information about the objects, events, or entities in a business process or activity. Dimension tables are typically used to provide context and structure to the data in a fact table.

To understand this better, let's consider an example of a retail business that sells products through its online store. In this example, we can identify the following fact and dimension tables.

Fact table – sales

The sales fact table would contain quantitative information about sales transactions, such as sales revenue, quantity sold, and price. The sales fact table would typically contain foreign keys to link to dimension tables, such as product, customer, and time:

Sales ID	Customer ID	Product ID	Date	Quantity	Price	Revenue
1	1001	1	10 Apr 2022	2	50	100
2	1002	2	11 Apr 2022	1	75	75
3	1003	3	12 Apr 2022	3	20	60

Figure 2.8 – sales fact table

Apart from the preceding fact table, we can have dimension tables such as product, customer, and date tables to give us some perspective or details on every customer who bought from us and every product we sold, and some details on dates that we usually call a calendar table.

Our dimension tables will look like the following three examples.

Dimension table – product

The product dimension table would contain descriptive information about the products being sold, such as the product name, description, and category. This table would typically have a primary key, such as `Product ID`, which would be used as a foreign key in the sales fact table:

Product ID	Product Name	Product Description	Category
1	Laptop	Dell Inspiron 15	Electronics
2	Smartphone	iPhone 13 Pro Max	Electronics
3	Book	Cinderella	Books

Figure 2.9 – product dimension table

Dimension table – customer

The customer dimension table would contain descriptive information about the customers such as their names, addresses, and demographic information. This table would typically have a primary key, such as `Customer ID`, which would be used as a foreign key in the sales fact table:

Customer ID	Customer Name	Customer Address	Age
1001	Bernard	11 Sanshie	24
1002	Ferdinand	1 Abidjan	28
1003	Gina	94 Amakom	21

Figure 2.10 – product dimension table

Dimension table – date

The date dimension table would contain descriptive information about the dates, such as the date, month, year, and calendar information. This table would typically have a primary key, such as `Date ID`, which would be used as a foreign key in the sales fact table:

Date	Month	Year	Quarter
1/1/23	January	2023	1
1/2/23	January	2023	1
1/3/23	January	2023	1

Figure 2.11 – product dimension table

Now that we understand relationships, dimensions, and fact tables, let's go back to the earlier example on converting denormalized data into normalized data and apply these key concepts to that case study.

What we've created is a mockup of a relational database, a set of tables that are related to each other. To connect these tables, we need to use common columns in each set.

For each related or duplicated column, one sits in the lookup table and the other sits in the original sales table. At this point, we will call our lookup tables dimension tables. They are so-called because they give the user different ways to describe the values to be analyzed, for example, sales by city, sales by product, or sales by customer.

They are dimensional because they help us add context to our analysis and usually contain data that cannot be aggregated.

Our table of original entry is called the fact table. This is where the core activity of the business – in other words, orders and sales – is recorded. This fact table normally contains the key values that will be aggregated (for example, total sales, number of orders, etc.).

To reiterate what was covered earlier, our key columns (`Customer ID`, `Product ID`, and `City`) are present in both the dimension tables and the fact table.

In the dimension tables, the entries in these columns are unique. However, in the fact table, they can be repeated as many times as a customer orders from us. We now know the difference between dimension tables, which contain the attributes or descriptions for our key measures or calculations, and fact tables, where we store the records of the main activity of the business.

At this point, we can create a data model by connecting these tables using relationships, that is, the common column(s) that exist between each table. First, we need to understand a little bit more about primary and foreign keys. There's more on this in the next section.

Understanding the role of primary keys and foreign keys

Keys are very important in a relational database because they help create a relationship between two tables and ensure that each record in a table can be identified in a unique way. When we connect the related tables, the version of the connecting columns in the dimension tables is called the **primary key** while the version in the fact table is called the **foreign key**.

In a relational database, the primary key helps us identify a single row in a table. All primary keys must be unique in the columns where they sit. Foreign keys help connect our dimension and fact tables and, more importantly, make our fact tables accessible in our calculations. Foreign keys are typically not unique.

Going back to our mock view of our relational database, we can add primary keys and foreign keys, as shown here:

▲	W	X	Y	Z	AA	AB	AC
1							
2		Customer ID	PK	City	PK	Product ID	PK
3		Customer Name		Region		Category	
4		Segment		Country		Sub-Category	
5						Product Name	
6							
7							
8				Row ID			
9				Order ID			
10				Order Date			
11				Delivery Date			
12				Delivery Mode			
13			FK	Customer ID			
14			FK	City			
15			FK	Product ID			
16				Unit cost			
17				Quantity			
18				Selling price			
19				Discount			
20							

Figure 2.8: Assigning primary keys and foreign keys

In our data model, these primary keys will be linked to their respective foreign keys to connect all the tables.

The process of converting denormalized data into normalized data can be done effectively using Excel's Power Query. Power Query is used in Excel to connect data from many sources, and shape and transform the data for our analysis. In the next chapter, we will dive into how we can derive normalized data from our sample sales data using Power Query.

Summary

This chapter has introduced you to best practices in structuring your data for data modeling. In the real world, the data produced from most relational database management systems is already normalized. However, there will be instances where you would need to convert denormalized data into normalized data to improve calculations and reduce redundancy. After reading this chapter, you are now able to appreciate the steps you need to take to achieve this. The chapter also covered the key differences between primary keys and foreign keys and the role they play in our data model.

In the next chapter, we will learn about Power Query and how we can use this tool to shape and transform data for our data model.

Key terms in this chapter

- Data redundancy
- Normalization
- Denormalization
- Primary keys
- Foreign keys

Questions for discussion

- What are the key considerations for laying out data properly for the data model?
- When is it best to consider performing data normalization?
- List the key advantages normalized data has over denormalized data.

3

Preparing Your Data for the Data Model – Cleaning and Transforming Your Data Using Power Query

Having understood the best practices for data structuring in our earlier chapters, we will take a look at how to prepare our data for data modeling using Power Query—Microsoft Excel's data cleaning and transformation tool.

In this chapter, you will understand the architecture of the Power Query editor and data types and how to use the **Transform** and **Add Column** tabs to correct any issues with the sample sales data. You will also learn how to append and merge data from our sample sales data.

The following topics will be covered in this chapter:

- Understanding queries and connections
- An overview of the Power Query editor
- Getting your data type right
- Add Column or Transform?
- Merging and appending data using Power Query

Understanding connections and queries

Before we begin, it is important for us to understand the typical data analysis process in Microsoft Excel and the tools you can use at each stage. Data modeling, which is the main topic of this book, is part of the process and can be done with the Power Pivot tool.

However, before data gets to the data modeling stage, we may have to shape and transform it to make it easier to analyze. Not all data comes in a format ready for the data model. There are situations where you need to remove unwanted characters, split or merge columns, transpose the data, or append or merge it to make it fit to be loaded into the data model.

Microsoft Excel has a dedicated tool for this called Power Query. Power Query is Excel's data transformation and preparation engine. The tool allows you to connect to many data sources (including CSV files, the web, folders, and databases) and shape and transform the data and load it in different forms for further analysis.

Although all these transformations are code-driven using a coding language called M, the tool has a simple graphical interface that makes it easy for all users to shape and transform data as desired without writing code.

Power Query is mainly referred to as an **extract, transform, and load** (ETL) tool because it connects to your data source, transforms the data into a reusable query, and then loads it as either a table, PivotTable report, pivotchart, or connection to be used in the data model or wherever its final destination may be.

The following figure summarizes the importance of Power Query in the data analysis process in Excel.

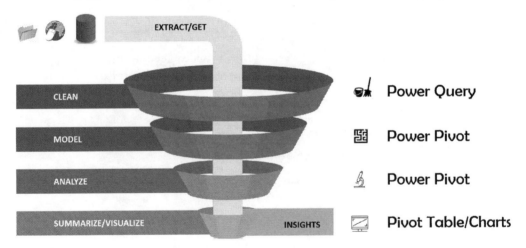

Figure 3.1 – An overview of the data analysis process in Microsoft Excel

From the preceding figure, we can appreciate the role of Power Query in getting us good data that is shaped and transformed for our data model.

Now that we know what Power Query does in the data analysis process, let us go a step further to understand some of the key concepts in the ETL process of Power Query.

Connections

Connections are links to various data sources. With Power Query, you can connect to many different sources. The following figure shows the number of connections available in Microsoft Excel at the time of writing this book:

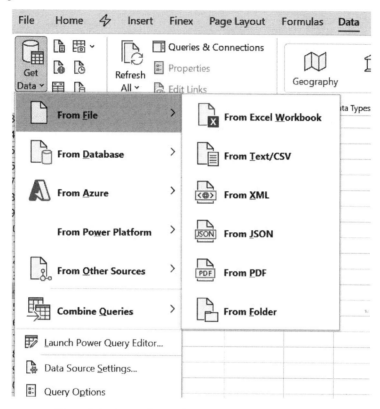

Figure 3.2 – Power Query data sources in Microsoft Excel

The main data sources here include the following:

- Excel workbooks
- Text/CSV files
- PDF
- Folders
- Web/online sources
- Access database
- Azure

Depending on the data connection type you choose, you will be guided through the steps to connect the data. Not all Excel versions support the same Power Query connectors.

For a complete list of the Power Query connectors supported by all versions of Excel for Windows and Excel for Mac, you can visit this website: `https://tinyurl.com/PQDataSources`

Now, let's talk about queries.

Queries

When you create a connection to a data source, you make the data available in Power Query's editor to be shaped and transformed. The query contains all the steps you go through to shape and transform the data. All these steps are recorded and converted into M code, which is stored in your query.

You can create as many queries as your data transformation process requires from your connections. In some cases, you can create blank queries to create dates. You can also reference or duplicate an existing query.

We will see examples of these when we go through the Power Query editor in subsequent sessions.

An overview of the Power Query editor

We will use our sales data case study to understand the various components of the Power Query editor.

The files we are going to use are in a folder that can be accessed using this link: `https://tinyurl.com/DMEFINEX`

Use this link to download a zipped file that contains one folder and five Excel worksheets as shown here:

Name	Size	Packed
..		
Main Transaction		
Finex Customer Data.xlsx	16,407	13,835
Finex Location Data.xlsx	13,253	10,782
Finex Product Data.xlsx	24,006	21,323
Finex Return Data.xlsx	268,856	253,489
Finex Store Data.xlsx	10,898	8,447

Figure 3.3 – The list of files in a zipped file

Extract the files to get access to the files.

When you open the folder, you should see a folder named **Main Transaction** that contains six files. These files are sales records from 2015 to 2020 for our sales organization, Finex Ventures.

There are five other files outside the folder, which contain information on the following:

- Customers

- Locations

- Products

- Stores

- Product returns

As we covered in an earlier chapter, this is normalized data. This data structure separates the main activities of the business from the dimensions that describe the sales. Instead of putting all the datasets into one table, this data structure is usually preferred when you are analyzing large datasets. This is to avoid data redundancy and manage the size of your data. Use the following figure as a guide to confirm that you have downloaded all the files needed in this chapter:

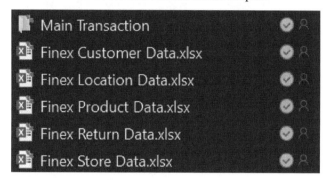

Figure 3.4 – List of files to be downloaded for the case study

Now that our files are ready, let us begin the process of using Power Query to extract, transform, and load our files:

1. Open a blank Excel workbook.

2. Go to the **Data** tab in the **Command** tabs on the ribbon and proceed to **Get Data | From File | From Excel Workbook**, as shown in the following figure:

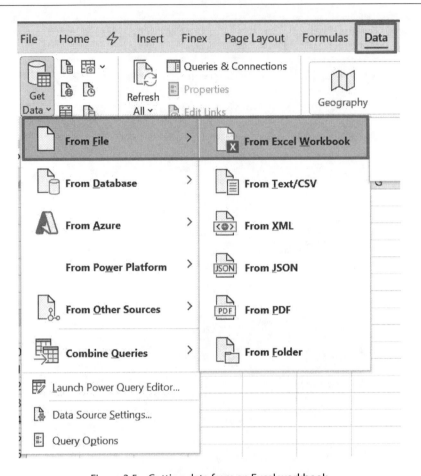

Figure 3.5 – Getting data from an Excel workbook

3. Based on where you saved the files, you can now use the navigation path to select the first file in the folder for our case study: Finex Customer Data. This brings up a navigator box that allows you to preview the content of this file.

    This step is important because it is not every worksheet in the workbook that should be committed to your final work. You can use the navigator to select only the worksheets that you want to work with.

    In our case study, we will select the customer data and ignore Sheet 1, which is empty. This allows us to preview the content of the worksheet on the right side of the navigator.

4.   After previewing, we can click on the **Transform** button located at the bottom of the navigator
     to start the data transformation process and open the Power Query editor.

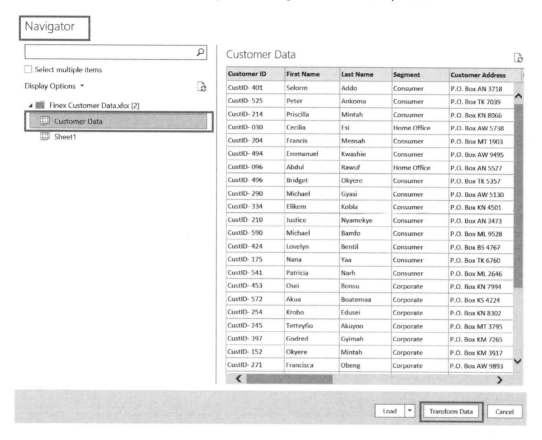

Figure 3.6 – A view of the Navigator pane for previewing data

Apart from the **Transform Data** button, there are also **Load Data** and **Cancel** at the bottom of the
screen. We could have selected **Load Data** if our data did not require any changes or transformations.
The **Load Data** button also allows us to directly add the data to the data model without transforming it.

Figure 3.7 – The Power Query editor

Meet the Power Query editor. This is the tool we are going to use to shape and transform our datasets. There are seven main components:

1. **The ribbon**: In the ribbon, you will find all the commands for shaping your data. They are grouped into tabs called **Home**, **Transform**, **Add Column**, and **View**. The **Home** tab contains a variety of commands that allow you to perform basic data transformation tasks such as filtering, sorting, grouping, splitting columns, pivoting, and managing columns and rows. The **Transform Data** tab in Power Query provides a comprehensive set of data transformation tools that allow you to reshape, clean, and manipulate your data to meet your specific needs. Under **Add Column**, all commands will result in the addition of a new column to your original query. The other tabs usually produce results that do not add new columns. It is important to know this so you know which tab to select when you are performing your various cleaning, shaping, and transformation tasks.

2. **The Queries pane**: All your queries are listed here for selection.

3. **The formula bar**: Like the formula bar in your Excel workbook, this formula bar records the M code for every activity you carry out in your Power Query. You can use the formula bar to edit and create new queries as well.

4. **Current view**: This gives you a preview of your data. Unlike your native Excel worksheet, you cannot edit cells here, but you can use the filter icons on each column to filter content and apply other transformations.

5. **Query Settings**: This allows you to rename your queries and select the **Fast Data Load** option.

6. **Applied Steps**: One of the key features of Power Query is the ability to record all steps in a data transformation process. It lists the steps in a chronological way to allow you to modify the M code as may be required.

7. **The status bar**: This bar displays information or the status of your query. In some cases, you can use the status bar to display all the items in your query or limit it to a few records. The bar also shows your processing status and the number of columns and rows in your query.

Getting your data type right

When you create your query, one of the most important steps in the transformation process is to ensure that you have the correct data type for each column. At the top-left corner of each column, there is an icon that allows you to change the data type. The following data types are available:

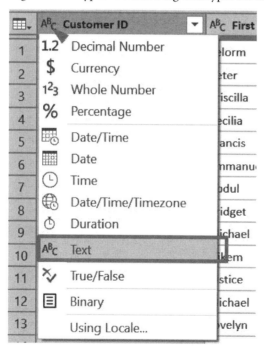

Figure 3.8 – List of data types in Power Query

Based on the settings in your Power Query, some data transformations are automatically done for some columns. When this happens, Power Query records this as a step in the Applied Steps list of the editor. An example of this is shown in the following figure:

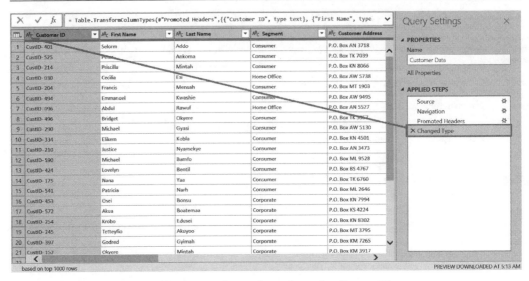

Figure 3.9 – Automatic transformation using Changed Type

In this example query, all our data types have been applied correctly apart from `Birthdate`. The correct format for the content of that column should be a date.

To do this, we do the following:

1. Select the format icon on the column.

2. Choose **Date** from the list.

3. A dialog box appears for us to choose whether we want to replace the current step in the **Applied Steps** settings or add this step as a new one.

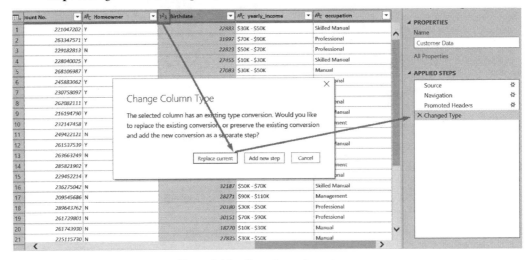

Figure 3.10 – Changing column type

This normally happens when your current step has already been executed. In this case, the **Changed Type** action already formatted the content as numbers. We will proceed to select **Replace Current** to finish the transformation.

We will add another transformation to this query in the `Bank Details` column. You will observe that there are some leading spaces in some of the bank names. To get rid of these spaces, we need to trim the content of the column.

At this point, most of the transformation steps can be accessed by right-clicking the column. In the menu that comes up, you can get access to most of the transformation steps. To trim the content, you can select **Trim** under the **Transform** menu. This step will be applied, and all the leading spaces will be removed.

This is shown in the following figure:

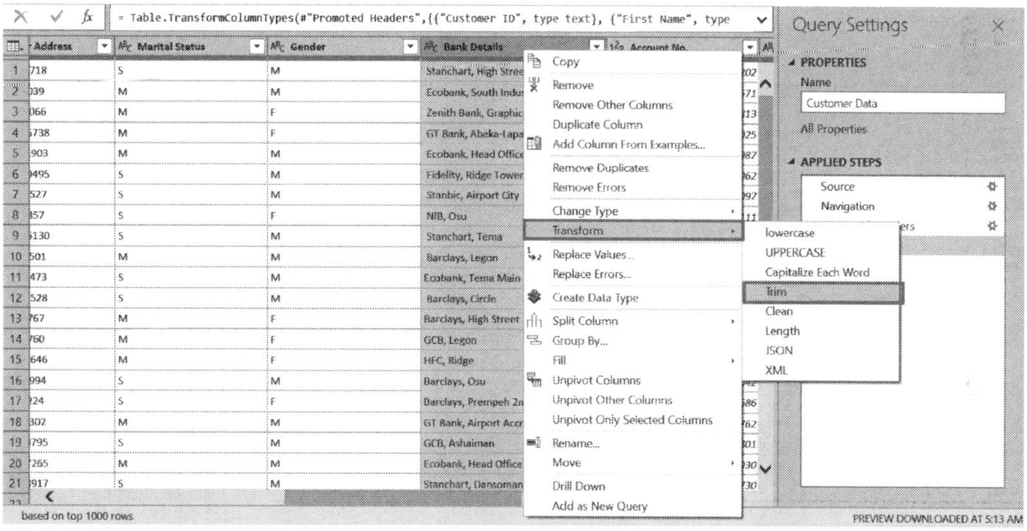

Figure 3.11 – Applying a transformation process by right-clicking on a column

At this point, we have completed all the transformation requirements for this current query. We will proceed with the rest of the files in the same manner. In the subsequent session, we will look at the key differences between the **Add Column** and **Transform** tabs in our query editor.

To bring in our next query, we can go to **Home | New Source | File | Excel Workbook** and select the next file in the folder, `Location Data`, from the same source. Using this method, we don't have to step out of our Power Query editor to query a new file. This can be seen in the following figure:

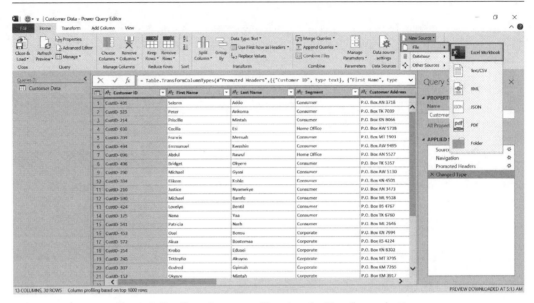

Figure 3.12 – Querying a new file using the New Source button

The new file is now added to the list in the **Queries** pane.

Can you see any transformations to be done in this new query?

Well done! Did you observe that the header row has been treated as content in row 1? See this in the following figure:

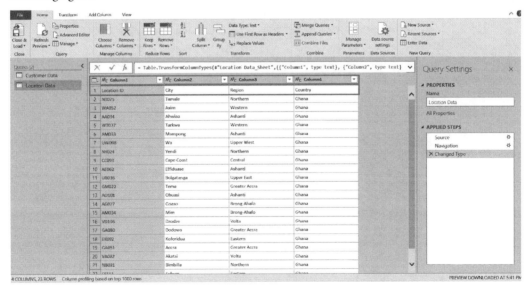

Figure 3.13 – Headers used as rows in the query editor

To fix this, we can go to the **Home** tab and select **Use First Row as Headers**.

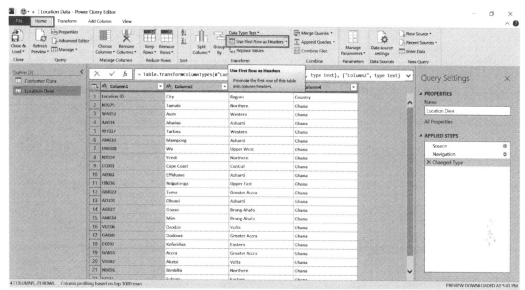

Figure 3.14 – Use First Row as Headers in the Power Query editor

Now that we are comfortable with how the transformation works, we can repeat the preceding steps to bring in the other files outside the **Main Transaction** folder. It's good if you can spot the transformations to be made in each query.

I have listed all the transformations for each file with the relevant steps and images to help you follow along. In the **Product** data, our focus is on replacing the null values with 0s to ensure completeness in the returnable list column:

1. Select the returnable list column, right-click, and select **Replace Values....**

2. In the dialog box, set **Value to Find** to null and **Replace with** to 0.

This should fill up the column with a series of 1s and 0s.

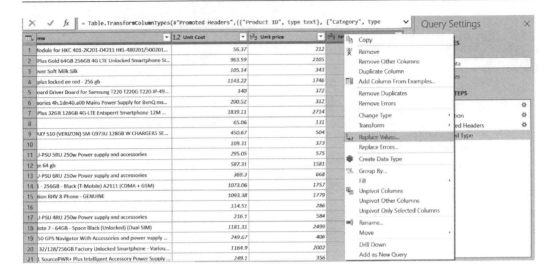

Figure 3.15 – Replacing values in the query editor

Did you notice that the green bar that shows the percentage of valid entries in the column has now been filled to 100%? Note that you can use **Column quality** under the **View** tab to review the content of each column. You can see this in the following figure:

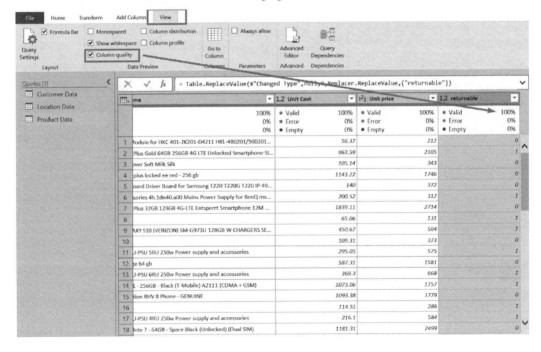

Figure 3.16 – Using Column Quality in the query editor

At this point, we have covered a few transformations to help you appreciate the importance of Power Query in shaping our data for the data model. You have learned how to do the following:

- Format data types
- Trim
- Use the first row as headers
- Replace values

There are more transformations you can do in the query editor. We will be looking at these with subsequent files.

Now let's bring in our next file, Return Transaction Data, using the New Source process. Have you noticed anything we need to fix here? It looks like all the columns are okay.

We will bring in our last file in this series, `Store Data`. Here, we need to fix two things:

- Format the `First Opened Date` and `Last Remodel Date` date columns
- Format the telephone numbers correctly to a 10-digit number

As we did earlier, we can fix the first one by clicking the format icon and selecting the date.

The second requires a leading 0 in front of each number. To do this, we can go to **Transform | Format | Add Prefix**. In the **Value** dialog box, put in 0.

This should add a leading 0 to all the phone numbers. Did you observe that the format has now changed to text? Sometimes Power Query is intelligent enough to read the content of a column and apply the right format.

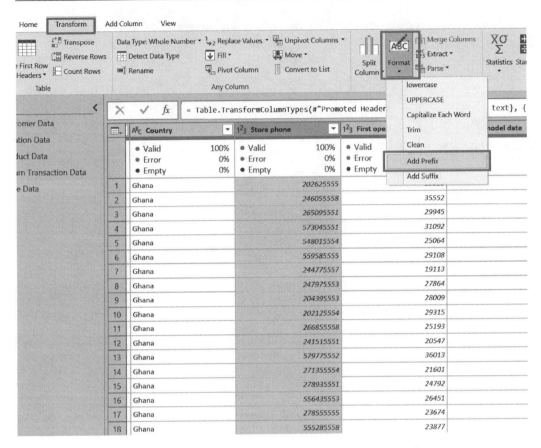

Figure 3.17 – Adding a prefix to numbers in the Power Query editor

We have completed the loading of our files outside of the **Main Transactions** folder.

Add Column or Transform?

Before we bring in our sales data, let us go back to our customer data query for one more transformation. This example will help us understand the key differences between performing a task with the **Transform** and **Add Column** tabs. In the customers query, we have the names of our customers in two columns. We want to merge these names into one column. Let's do this from the **Add Column** tab to see the results we will get.

To do this, follow these steps:

1. Go to the **Add Column** tab.
2. Select the two columns First Name and Last Name.
3. Click on **Merge Columns** in the **Add Column** tab.

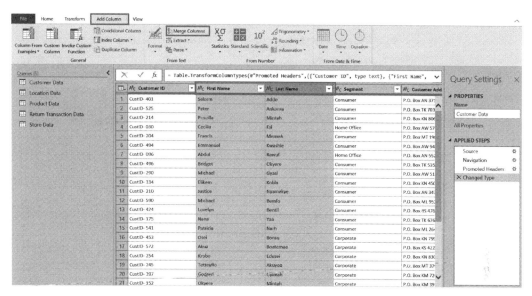

Figure 3.18 – Merging columns under the Add Column tab

4. This brings up a dialog box that requires a separator and a name for our new column.

Merge Columns

Choose how to merge the selected columns.

Separator

| Space ▼ |

New column name (optional)

| Full Name |

| OK | | Cancel |

Figure 3.19 – Selecting a separator in Merge Columns

You can select **Space** for the separator and **Full Name** for the new column name.

When you click **OK**, this will insert a new column at the end of the query called **Full Name**. Your original columns, **First Name** and **Last Name**, are still intact. This means that when we perform any activity under the **Add Column** tab, we will end up inserting a new column.

Let's reverse this step and do it under the **Transform** tab. In Power Query, if you want to undo a step, you can click on the cross icon to remove that step. If you mistakenly add a step you don't need, you can click on this cross to remove it, as shown:

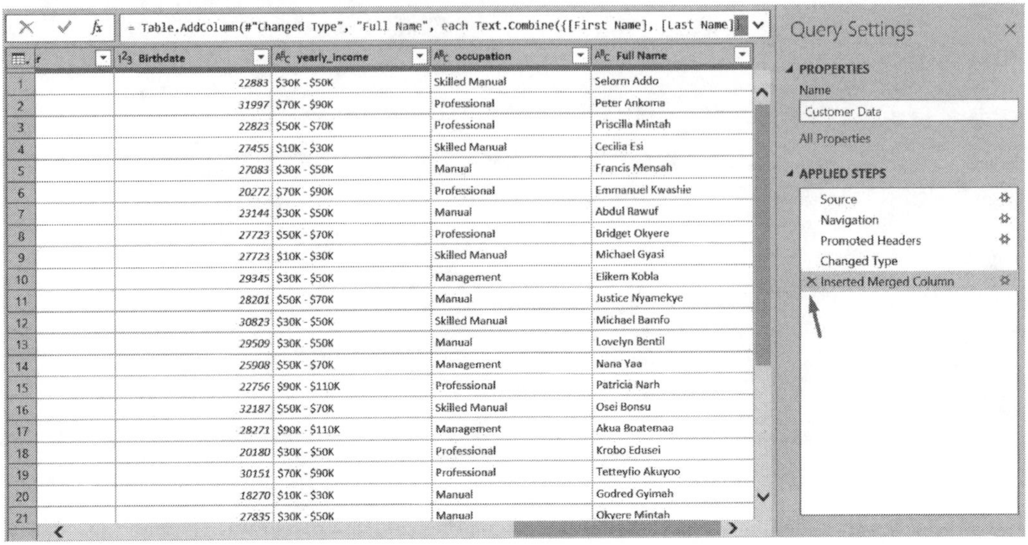

Figure 3.20 – Removing a step in Power Query

If we do this transformation under the **Transform** tab, the result, which will be a new column with the merged names, will replace the two original column names.

To do this, follow these steps:

1. Select the two columns `First Name` and `Last Name`.

2. Right-click on the two columns and click on **Merge Columns**.

3. This brings up a dialog box that requires a separator and a name for our new column. You can select **Space** for the separator and **Full Name** for the new column name.

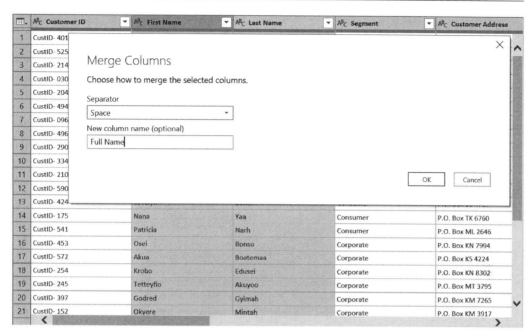

Figure 3.21 – The Merge Columns dialog box in the Power Query editor

The results can be seen in the following figure:

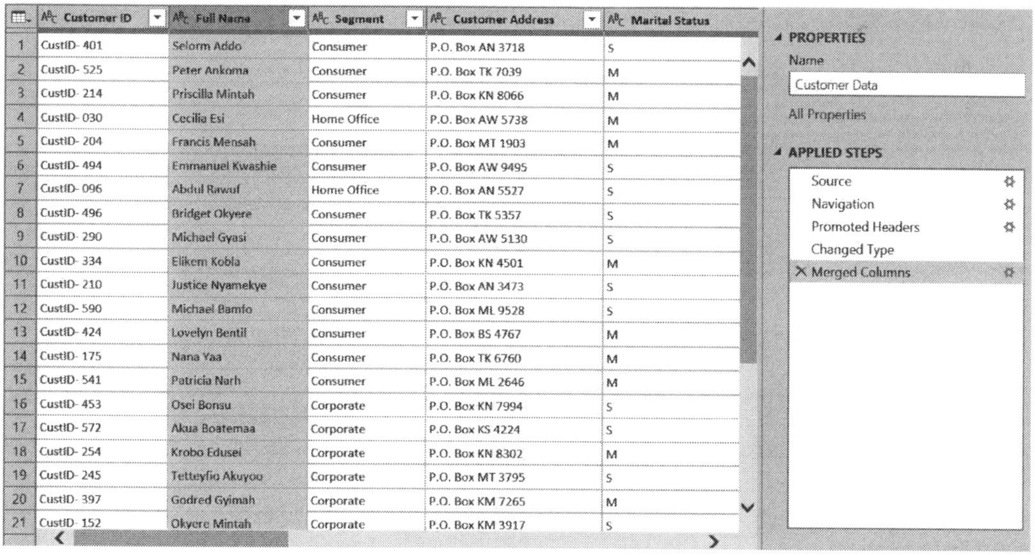

Figure 3.22 – Merging columns under the Transform tab

This works in situations where we want the new column, `Full Name`, to replace our two original columns, `First Name` and `Last Name`.

However, if we were to do the same steps under the **Add Column** tab, the new column `Full Name` would be added as a new column to our query while maintaining our two original columns. The point here is that, although there are similar items under the **Transform** and **Add Column** tabs, **Transform** will override the content of the selected column with results after the step has been executed, while **Add Column** will add the results as a new column.

Merging and appending data using Power Query

In Power Query, there are two main methods to combine data: merging and appending. When you combine to add more rows, you are appending. This is typically in situations where the tables you are combining have the same columns. When you combine to add extra columns to an existing query, you are merging. This is typically in situations where the two tables have at least one common column. The following figures summarize the difference between the two:

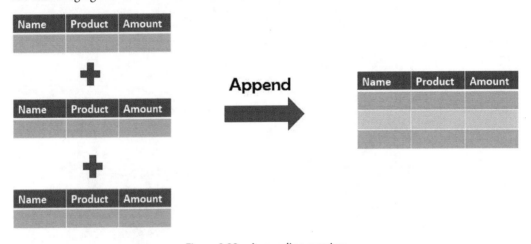

Figure 3.23 – Appending queries

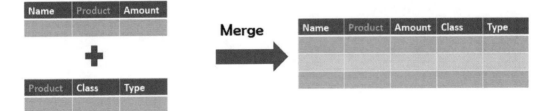

Figure 3.24 – Merging queries

With this understanding, let's proceed and append our sales records into one query:

1. Because our data is stored in a folder, this time round, we will select **Folder** when we go to **New Source**.

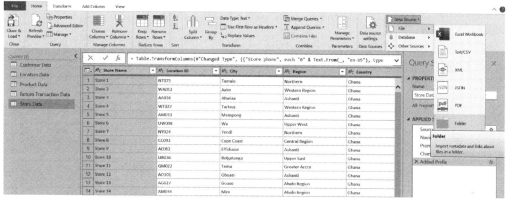

Figure 3.25 – Getting data from a folder

2. Select the folder from where it has been saved on your computer. Remember that you should select the folder icon, as shown here:

Figure 3.26 – Selecting the folder for Power Query

3. After selecting the folder, you will have a preview of all the files in the folder in the navigator, as shown in the following figure. Select **Combine & Transform Data** to combine all the files into one.

C:\Users\obeng\OneDrive\Classroom\Packt\Data\Main Transaction

Content	Name	Extension	Date accessed	Date modified	Date created	Attributes	
Binary	Finex Main Transaction Data 2015.xlsx	.xlsx	8/10/2022 7:12:20 PM	5/13/2022 7:52:19 PM	8/9/2022 4:17:48 AM	Record	C:\Users\
Binary	Finex Main Transaction Data 2016.xlsx	.xlsx	8/10/2022 7:12:54 PM	5/13/2022 7:50:20 PM	8/9/2022 4:17:48 AM	Record	C:\Users\
Binary	Finex Main Transaction Data 2017.xlsx	.xlsx	8/10/2022 7:12:57 PM	5/13/2022 7:49:25 PM	8/9/2022 4:17:48 AM	Record	C:\Users\
Binary	Finex Main Transaction Data 2018.xlsx	.xlsx	8/10/2022 7:12:57 PM	5/13/2022 7:48:33 PM	8/9/2022 4:17:48 AM	Record	C:\Users\
Binary	Finex Main Transaction Data 2019.xlsx	.xlsx	8/10/2022 7:12:58 PM	5/13/2022 7:47:38 PM	8/9/2022 4:17:48 AM	Record	C:\Users\
Binary	Finex Main Transaction Data 2020.xlsx	.xlsx	8/11/2022 3:57:51 AM	8/10/2022 7:27:04 PM	8/9/2022 4:17:48 AM	Record	C:\Users\

| Combine & Transform Data | Transform Data | Cancel |

Figure 3.27 – Combining multiple queries in the navigator

When we select **Combine & Transform Data**, Power Query applies the transformation to all the files using the first file as an example file. This is usually the first file in the list. Power Query will then combine the files automatically after the transformation. However, if we choose the **Transform Data** button instead of **Combine & Transform Data**, Power Query will open the list of files in the folder for you to make your transformations.

4. This should bring up another page in the navigator that shows you a preview of the first file in the list. Power Query profiles all the files using the first file. You have the option to change this to another file in the drop-down list. You can also click on the selected file to preview the content. After this, you can click **OK** to proceed with the appending.

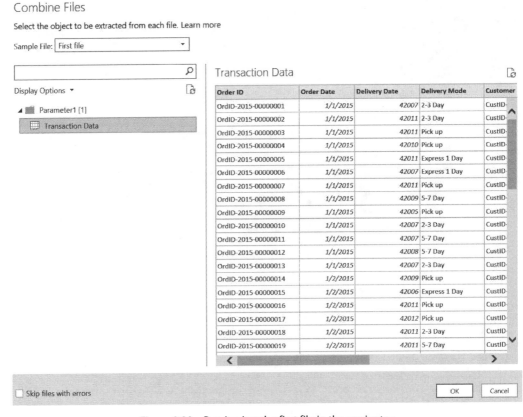

Figure 3.28 – Previewing the first file in the navigator

5. The files are now appended in the query editor. You will see some extra folders and queries in the **Queries** pane. These are called **helper queries**. They represent the steps that we executed earlier, that is, selecting, profiling, and transforming the first file to append the data.

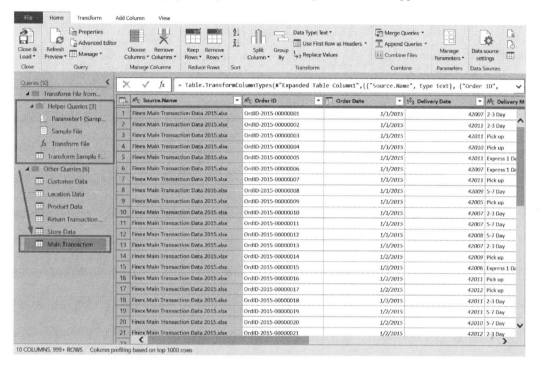

Figure 3.29 – Helper Queries in the Power Query editor

We also have the source filename as the first column of our query. This will not be useful in our analysis, but it can help you confirm whether all the files you appended are present. We will delete this for now and create a new column to help us confirm this. You can right-click this column and select **Remove**.

Can you spot any transformations?

Our delivery date has been changed to a general format. We need to transform these into dates. We can do this by selecting the column and changing the **Format** icon to a date. We can now use this column or **Order Date** to add a new Year column to our query.

This can be done under the **Add Column** tab:

1. Select any of the date columns.

2. Go to the **Date** icon.

3. Select **Year** and extract Year as a new column.

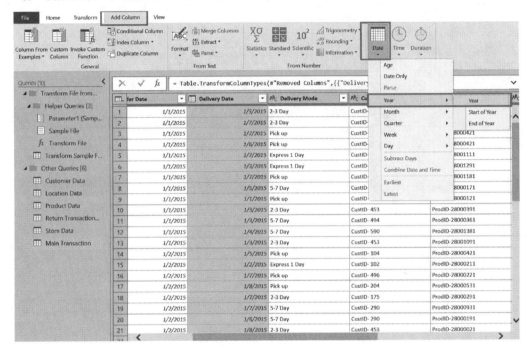

Figure 3.30 – Adding a Year column to query

You now have a new column called Year that you can use to check whether all the years are present. You can do this by selecting the filter icon on the Year column to preview the content.

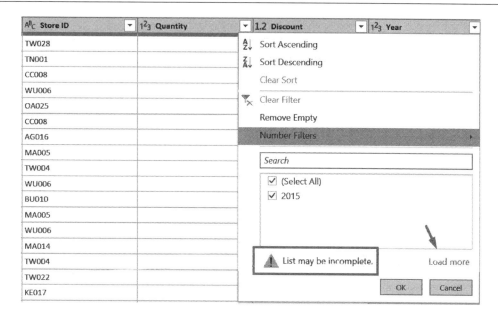

Figure 3.31 – The Load more option in Power Query

Select **Load more** to load the full year list.

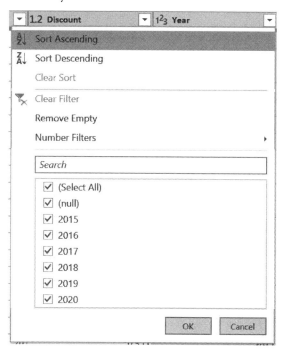

Figure 3.32 – Previewing the content of the Year column

Can you guess why we have a null value in the list?

This is coming from the empty rows from our original datasets. When we queried the data, we brought in data and empty rows in each file. At this point, we can uncheck the box against null to take off these empty rows.

A better way to do this is to select our sample file in **Helper Queries**, that is, **Transform Sample File**, and select all the content of the query by pressing *Ctrl + A*.

Go to the **Home** tab and choose **Remove Rows**. Under **Remove Rows**, select **Remove Blank Rows**.

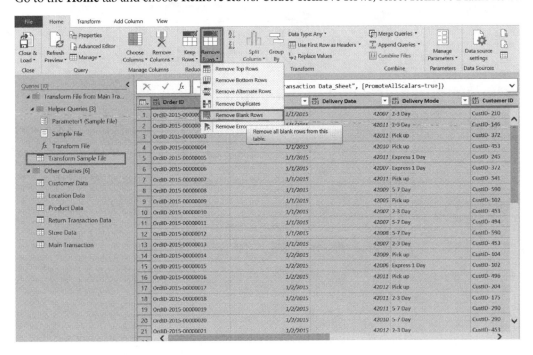

Figure 3.33 – Removing empty rows from a sample helper query

This approach will ensure that empty cells are removed before the files are appended. We are doing this on the assumption that there are no empty rows within the datasets, but the empty rows are located at the bottom of the data. This brings us to the end of our extract and transform process for all our queries.

After transforming our data, we can load it directly into our Excel worksheets as tables or to our data model to connect the different tables together.

To do this, go to **Home | Close and Load To** (from the dropdown). Take note of the difference between this and the original **Close and Load**.

If we choose **Close and Load**, the data will be loaded directly as tables into our worksheet. This is the default behavior. To get options for loading, we would rather select **Close and Load To**. This should give you a list of options for loading. Select **Only Create Connection** and **Add this data to the Data Model**.

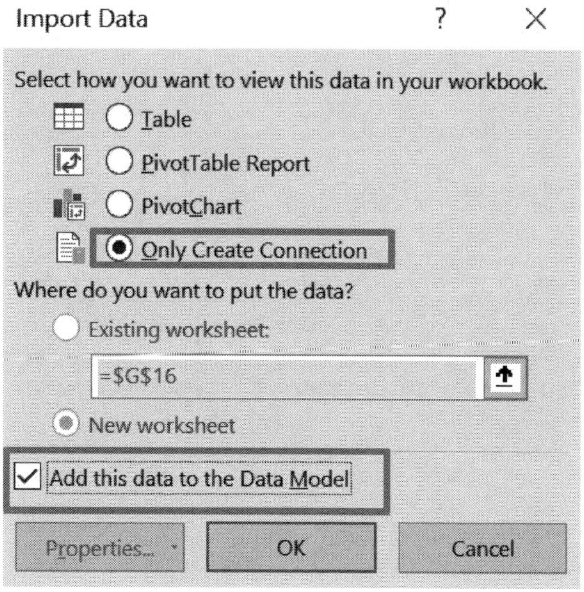

Figure 3.34 – Adding your queries to the data model

This step will now take all our queries to the data model. In the next section, we will begin our data modeling journey.

Well done making it this far. I promise it will get more exciting!.

Summary

The chapter introduced you to Power Query, the data transformation tool for extracting, transforming, and loading data to the data model. We now understand the architecture and components of Power Query. In this chapter, we used a sample case study to perform a number of transformations in the Power Query editor. We concluded the chapter by downloading all our queries into the data model.

In the next chapter, we will learn all that we can do with the data model in Power Pivot.

Data Modeling with Power Pivot – Understanding How to Combine and Analyze Multiple Tables Using the Data Model

In the previous chapters, we went through a lot of concepts to help us understand data modeling and the steps involved in extracting, transforming, and loading data into the data model.

This chapter will now focus on what goes on in Power Pivot after we load our data into the data model. You will learn how to create relationships within the data model, understand the differences between fact and dimension tables, and learn about the roles of primary and foreign keys in the data model. The chapter will also explore the advantages of using relational databases to create a data model for the subsequent calculations in the book.

The following topics will be covered in this chapter:

- Adding queries/tables to your data model

- Creating relationships using primary and foreign keys

- Adding columns to your data model

- Understanding the different types of schemas (snowflake and star)

Adding queries/tables to your data model

In *Chapter 3*, we concluded our **extract, transform, and load** (ETL) process by loading our queries into the data model.

Our transformed queries are now stored inside our Excel workbook. To find out where the queries are, you can go to **Data | Queries & Connections**. This will open the **Queries** pane to your right, as shown in the following screenshot:

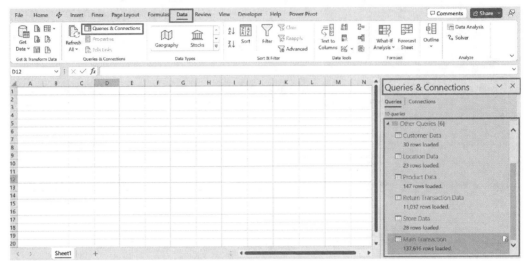

Figure 4.1 – How to display the Queries pane in Microsoft Excel

Our queries are also stored in the data model. To access the data model, you can go to **Data | Data Tools | Go to the Power Pivot Window.**

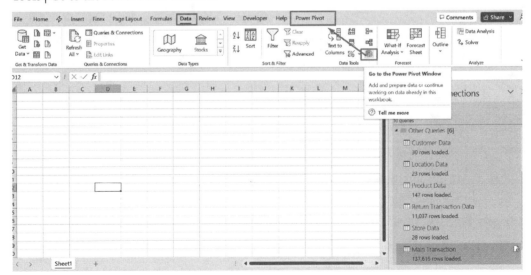

Figure 4.2 – Enabling the Power Pivot tab

If you are using Power Pivot for the first time, you will get a message box prompting you to enable Power Pivot. After a few seconds, you should see the **Power Pivot** tab in your command tabs. You can now open the **Power Pivot** window by clicking the green cube icon in the **Data Tools** group or clicking the same icon labeled **Manage** under the **Power Pivot** tab.

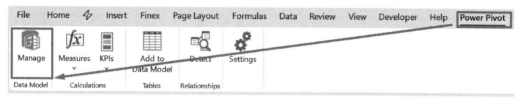

Figure 4.3 – Accessing the Power Pivot window using the Manage icon

We will explore the use of the other icons later in this section.

Clicking on the **Manage** icon opens a new Power Pivot window.

	Custom.	First Name	Last Name	Segment	Customer Address	Marital Status	Gender	Bank Details	Account No.	Homeowner	Birthdate	yearly_income
1	CustID- 401	Selorm	Addo	Consumer	P.O. Box AN 3718	S	M	Stanchart, Hig...	221047202	Y	8/25/1962 ...	$30K - $50K
2	CustID- 525	Peter	Ankoma	Consumer	P.O. Box TK 7039	M	M	Ecobank, Sout...	263347571	Y	8/8/1987 1...	$70K - $90K
3	CustID- 214	Priscilla	Mintah	Consumer	P.O. Box KN 8066	M	F	Zenith Bank, ...	229182813	N	6/26/1962 ...	$50K - $70K
4	CustID- 030	Cecilia	Esi	Home Office	P.O. Box AW 5738	M	F	GT Bank, Abe...	228040025	Y	3/2/1975 1...	$10K - $30K
5	CustID- 204	Francis	Mensah	Consumer	P.O. Box MT 1903	M	M	Ecobank, Hea...	268106987	Y	2/23/1974 ...	$30K - $50K
6	CustID- 494	Emmanuel	Kwashie	Consumer	P.O. Box AW 9495	S	M	Fidelity, Ridge ...	245883062	Y	7/2/1955 1...	$70K - $90K
7	CustID- 096	Abdul	Rawuf	Home Office	P.O. Box AN 5527	S	M	Stanbic, Airpo...	230758097	Y	5/13/1963 ...	$30K - $50K
8	CustID- 496	Bridget	Okyere	Consumer	P.O. Box TK 5357	S	F	NIB, Osu	262082111	Y	11/25/197...	$50K - $70K
9	CustID- 290	Michael	Gyasi	Consumer	P.O. Box AW 5130	S	M	Stanchart, Tema	216194790	Y	11/25/197...	$10K - $30K
10	CustID- 334	Elikem	Kobla	Consumer	P.O. Box KN 4501	M	M	Barclays, Legon	232147458	Y	5/4/1980 1...	$30K - $50K
11	CustID- 210	Justice	Nyamekye	Consumer	P.O. Box AN 3473	S	M	Ecobank, Tem...	249422121	N	3/17/1977 ...	$50K - $70K
12	CustID- 590	Michael	Bamfo	Consumer	P.O. Box ML 9528	S	M	Barclays, Circle	261537539	Y	5/21/1984 ...	$30K - $50K
13	CustID- 424	Lovelyn	Bentil	Consumer	P.O. Box BS 4767	M	F	Barclays, High...	263663249	N	10/15/198...	$30K - $50K
14	CustID- 175	Nana	Yaa	Consumer	P.O. Box TK 6760	M	F	GCB, Legon	285821902	Y	12/6/1970 ...	$50K - $70K
15	CustID- 541	Patricia	Narh	Consumer	P.O. Box ML 2646	M	F	HFC, Ridge	229452214	Y	4/20/1962 ...	$90K - $110K

Customer Data Location Data Product Data Return Transaction Data Store Data Main Transaction Calendar

Figure 4.4 – An overview of Power Pivot in Excel

This looks like your Excel worksheet, but there are key differences. Let's go through these quickly:

1. Your queries are stored with their names as separate tables in each tab.

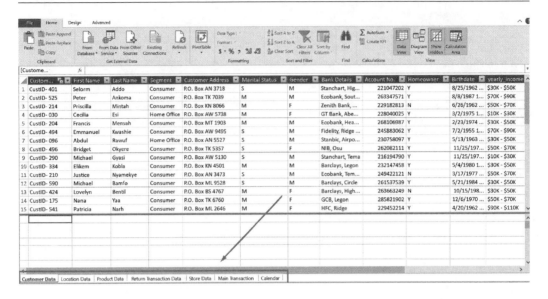

Figure 4.5 – Data tabs in Power Query

2. You can select cells, but you cannot edit them. In Power Pivot, edits and calculations are done at the column level.

3. Your screen is split into two: the data on top and a blank section called **Calculation Area** at the bottom. All our custom calculations or measures will appear in this calculation area. You can turn it off using the **Calculation Area** icon under the **Home** tab.

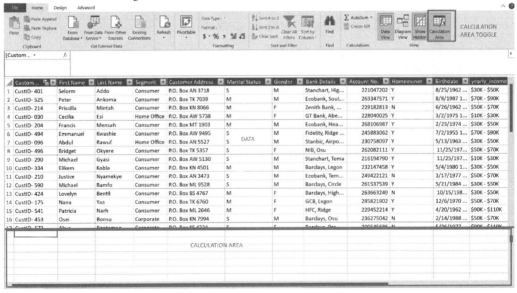

Figure 4.6 – The calculation and data segments in Power Pivot

4. You can switch between **Data View** and **Diagram View**. In **Data View**, we see all the columns and content of each table, while in **Diagram View**, we get a visual display of all the tables as separate shapes.

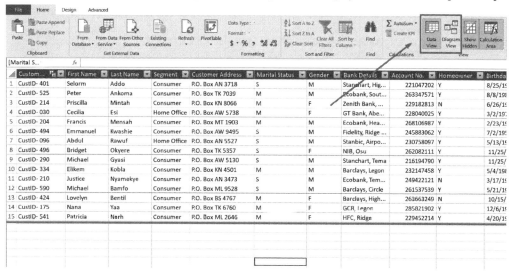

Figure 4.7 – Data View and Diagram View in Power Pivot

5. In the top-left corner of the **Power Pivot** window, you can see the **Excel** icon and the **Data Model** icon side by side. Click on the **Excel** icon to go back to your Excel worksheets and re-open the **Power Pivot** window using any of the entry methods described earlier.

Figure 4.8 – Navigation options between Power Pivot and Excel

Understanding the key features of navigating within Power Pivot will make it easier for you to create relationships, add calculated columns, and create your DAX formulas easily.

Adding columns to your data model

Before we start any activity, let us switch to the **Design** tab in the **Power Pivot** window. Here, we have some icons that can help us add new columns to our existing data. We can add a new column by selecting the **Add** icon under the **Design** menu, which will highlight the last column in our data, or by selecting this column directly.

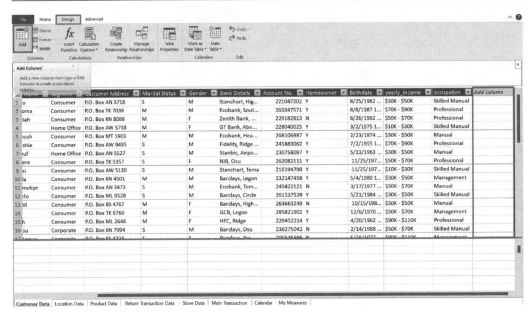

Figure 4. 9 – Adding a new column in Power Pivot

Let's try an example of adding a new column to the customer data. We want to calculate the age for each customer as a new column.

To do this, you can go to the **Customer** tab:

1. Select the last column, which will have **Add Column** as the header.

2. Type the name of the new column into the formula bar.

3. After selecting the column in the formula bar, begin the formula with the name of the column followed by a colon (:) and an equals sign (=).

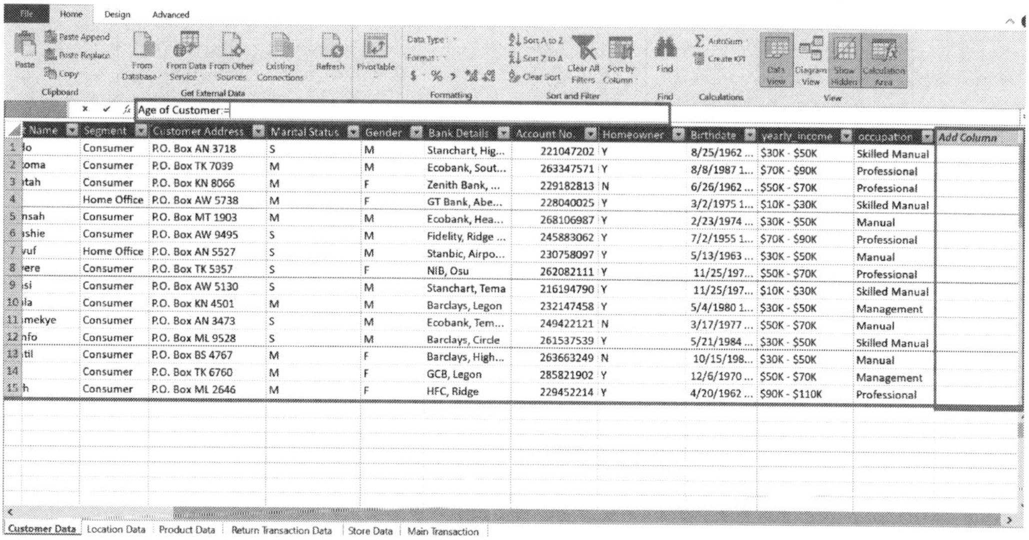

Figure 4. 10 – Creating a formula for your calculated column

Here is an example using `Age of Customer:=`.

The DAX function to calculate age is `DATEDIFF`. This is similar to what we have in native Excel, but with an extra *F*.

Complete the following formula and press *Enter*:

```
Age of Customer:=DATEDIFF([Birthdate],TODAY(),YEAR)
```

`Birthdate` in the formula is an existing column in the `Customer Data` table. When selecting an existing column in a DAX formula, you can start with the square bracket. This pulls a list of all the columns in the current dataset. You can select or press *Tab* to complete the selection process. `TODAY` is another DAX function that gives you the current date. `YEAR` is one of the many options in `DATEDIFF` if you want to return the age of the customer in `YEARS`. Other types of internal values for this parameter are `DAY`, `WEEK`, `MONTH`, `QUARTER`, and so on.

You have now created a calculated column in your data model. Ideally, calculated columns should be created in Power Query. This optimizes the performance of your datasets, especially when you have a large volume of data.

Your new calculated column should look like that in the following screenshot:

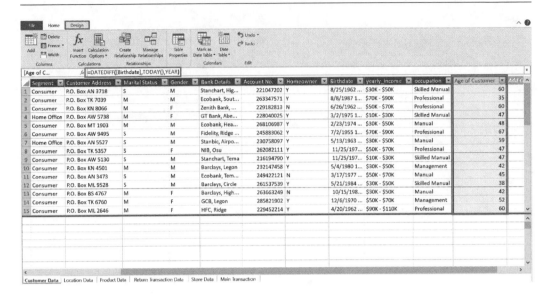

Figure 4.11 – Creating a calculated column in Power Pivot

Creating calendar tables

Another useful feature in Power Pivot is the ability to create a dynamic date or calendar table for your data model.

In our `Main Transactions` table, we have columns that contain dates (the order dates and delivery dates in the `Main Transactions` table). However, there are gaps or missing dates in these columns. These gaps will not be ideal for us to use some of the time intelligence formulas. We need to create a series of dates that begin from the earliest date in our dataset all the way to the latest date without missing a date.

Power Pivot allows us to create this by using the **Date Table** feature under the **Design** tab. This will result in the creation of a new table that contains `Date` attributes we can use in our calculations.

To do this, go to **Design | Date Table | New**.

This should give us a date table with different columns, as shown in the following screenshot:

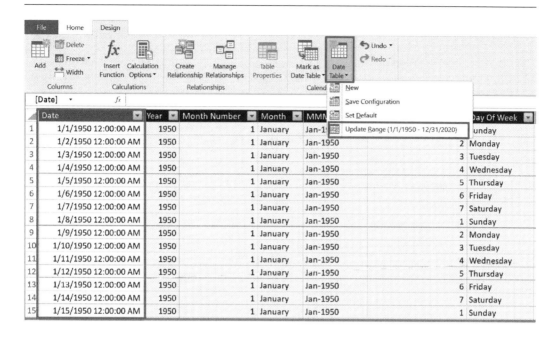

Figure 4.12 – Creating a calendar table in Power Pivot

Did you notice that our date starts in 1950? Date tables in Power Pivot scan your entire dataset for date values and start building the date series using the earliest date. Obviously, going back to 1950 to analyze transactions in our `Main Transactions` table will not be necessary. We can adjust the settings in our date table to use the earliest date in our `Main Transactions` table rather than customers' birth dates.

To do this, we can go back to **Date Table | Update Range** and change the start date from 1/1/1950 to 1/1/2020. This will update the table to create a series of dates starting from January 2020.

You can also create date or calendar tables using custom M code in Power Query. Most people who use this option prefer to create custom date columns or attributes that may not be present in the default calendar table.

As we learned earlier, we could also add new date columns using the calculated column method we covered earlier when we added age to our `Customer` table.

So far, you can appreciate how useful Power Pivot can be to the data modeling process.

In the next section, we will learn how we can connect our dimension and fact tables to complete the data model in Power Pivot.

Creating relationships using primary and foreign keys

A relationship in a data model is a connection between two entities. Entities are objects that represent real-world things, such as people, places, or things. Relationships can be one-to-one, one-to-many, or many-to-many.

A one-to-one relationship means that each entity in one table is related to exactly one entity in another table. For example, a customer table might have a one-to-one relationship with an address table. Each customer would have exactly one address.

A one-to-many relationship means that each entity in one table can be related to multiple entities in another table. For example, a product table might have a one-to-many relationship with an order table. Each product can be ordered multiple times.

A many-to-many relationship means that each entity in one table can be related to multiple entities in another table and vice versa. For example, a student table might have a many-to-many relationship with a course table. Each student can take multiple courses and each course can have multiple students.

Relationships are important in data modeling because they allow you to represent the connections between real-world things. This makes it easier to store, retrieve, and analyze data.

Here are some examples of relationships in a data model:

- A customer can have one or more orders
- An order can have one or more items
- An item can be sold in one or more stores
- A store can have one or more employees

Relationships can be represented in a data model using a variety of techniques, such as the following:

- Tables
- Columns
- Keys
- Foreign keys
- Joins

Excel offers several methods to create relationships between tables. In Power Pivot, we can use **Diagram View** to create a relationship.

When you click on **Diagram View**, you can now see all your tables. Creating relationships between these tables will help us access all the fields in our analysis and reports.

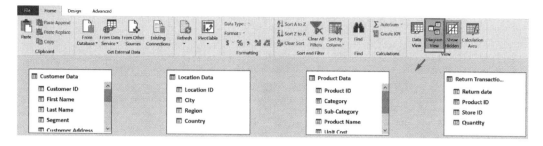

Figure 4.13 – Diagram View in Power Pivot

All the tables in **Diagram View** can be classified as either a dimension table or a fact table. The fact table contains a recording of our main activity, and it usually has the field or column we will use to create our key numerical measures. Examples include total sales, count of transactions, and so on.

On the other hand, our dimension tables include all the tables that help us describe these measures. Users of our report will rely on dimensions to get insights into our reports. After calculating Total Sales, it would be helpful for our user to see a breakdown of sales by Product, Location, Customer, Date, and so on.

Dimension tables help us view our measures from different perspectives using slicers and filters.

If you look at the list of tables, can you determine which tables should be classified as fact or dimension tables?

A fact table usually contains repetitive or duplicate data. For example, a customer can make five orders of different products in a day. All these transactions will be recorded to show the product IDs of the transactions, the dates on which the transactions were made, the store IDs, the customer IDs, and the quantity and price of the item bought stored in one record or row.

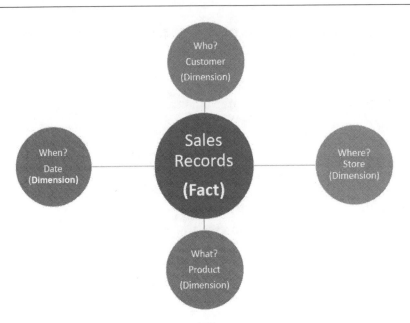

Figure 4.14 – An overview of fact and dimension tables

When a customer returns a product, we can go through a similar process to record the transaction. Here, we will record the date, product ID, store ID, and quantity. Again, in this table, we can record multiple returns in a day or within a particular period.

The Main Transactions and Return tables in our list of tables are our fact tables. The other tables that provide the details of each product ID, customer ID, location ID, and date in each transaction will be our dimension tables.

Between our two fact tables (Main Transactions and Return) and each dimension table is a common column/field that will help us connect the fact tables to the dimension tables. This common column is usually an ID field.

First, let's look at the Main Transactions table:

- Order Date and Delivery Date in this fact table can connect to the Date column in our dimension Calendar table.
- Customer ID in this fact table will connect to our Customer ID in the dimension Customer table.
- Product ID in this fact table will connect to our Product ID in the dimension Product table.
- Store ID in this fact table will connect to our Location ID in the dimension Store table.

We will then extend this relationship to the dimension Location table later. There will be more on this in the subsequent section on types of schemas.

We can create a similar relationship between our second fact table, Return, and the dimension tables:

- `Return Date` in this fact table can connect to the `Date` column in our dimension `Calendar` table

- `Store ID` in this fact table will connect to our `Location ID` in the dimension `Customer` table.

- `Product ID` in this fact table will connect to our `Product ID` in the dimension `Product` table.

Breaking down the key relationships between each set of tables this way can help you appreciate the structure of your data model. Over time and with practice, you may not have to do this every time before you connect the tables.

A primary key is a field in a table that has a unique value and is not duplicated. An example is `Product ID` in the `Product` table. A foreign key is a field in a table that references a primary key in another table and can be duplicated. An example is Product ID in the `Main Transaction` table.

When you connect two tables based on a common column, the version of the common column that is stored in the dimension table is called the **primary key**. This column should contain a unique list of the items in that column without duplicates. For example, the `Product ID` column in the Products table should not repeat the same product ID. Remember that the role of the dimension table is to help us describe our measures, so a unique value is enough to map all the details of that particular product ID.

The version of the common column in the fact table is called the **foreign key**. This column can repeat the product ID as many times as the customer buys from us or returns a product.

With this knowledge, we can now connect the various relationships by clicking and dragging each primary key to the corresponding foreign key in our Power Pivot and then create a data model that will help us access all the data from one source.

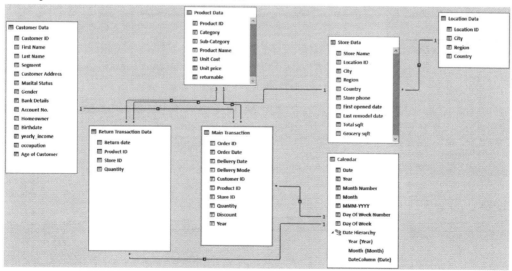

Figure 4.15 – Connecting tables using relationships to create a data model

When you use the drag-and-drop method to connect the two common columns between two tables, the column in the dimension tables is marked with 1, while the version in the fact table has a * (meaning many) with a line connector.

This is a one-to-many relationship. One unique instance of the item in the dimension table can be used to filter many instances of the same item in the fact table.

For example, when you select one of the product IDs from the Product table, the ID selected filters the fact table to give you only the rows that contain that product ID.

This type of relationship can be used to create dynamic DAX measures with filters.

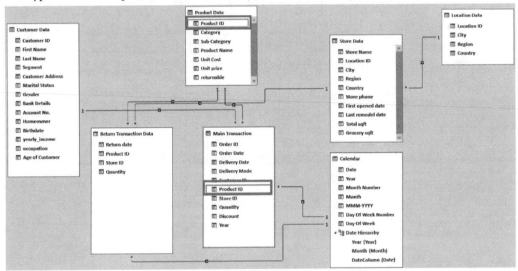

Figure 4.16 – Relationship flows in a data model

Apart from the 1 to * indicators, you will notice that there is an arrow that points toward the fact tables. This means that an item selected in the Product ID column in the Product Data table will filter rows in the fact table that contain that product ID.

Similar indicators can be seen among the tables in the data model. Remember that this is only possible when there is a unique list of IDs in the dimension tables connecting to multiple instances in the fact tables.

There are other forms of connections or relationships. We have many-to-many relationships. This type of relationship can be created between two tables with multiple instances of the same items in two common columns. This type of relationship cannot be created in the data model in Excel.

Understanding the different types of schemas (snowflake and star)

When you create a data model, the arrangement of the dimension and fact tables can help you understand how the data flows from the dimension tables to filter the fact tables containing our key measures.

At the heart of our analysis are the key measures we will calculate from our fact tables. These fact tables are normally placed at the lower section of the data model, and our dimension tables are placed on top.

In certain layouts, you can also place the fact tables in the middle surrounded by dimension tables. This type of layout where several dimension tables are connected to one or multiple fact tables placed below or at the center of the dimension tables is called a star schema.

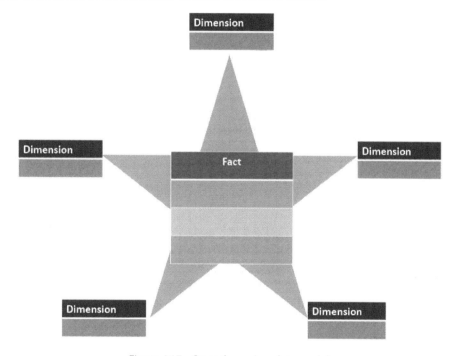

Figure 4.17 – Star schema in a data model

This is a common layout or schema for most data models. It ensures that your calculations are well optimized because it has *only dimension tables of one level.*

There are situations where a dimension table branches out into another dimension table at a second level. These second-level tables serve us sub-dimensions in the data model.

If you look at Store Data in our data model, there is a Location ID that is also present in the Location Data table. This table gives extra information on the location of each store, specifying the city, region, and country.

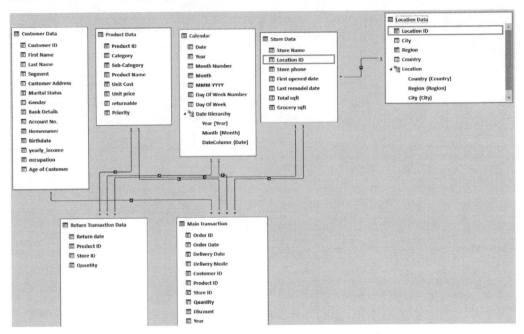

Figure 4.18 – Snowflake schema in a data model

We will connect both tables using the common `Location ID` columns. This time around, the Store table has multiple instances of Location ID while the `Location Data` table has a unique list of the IDs.

When there is a second or higher level of dimension tables, it creates a snowflake schema with multiple sub-dimensions in our data model.

A star schema has a simple and straightforward structure. It consists of a central table, called the fact table, surrounded by numerous dimension tables. Within the fact table reside the primary measurements or facts of interest, while the dimension tables hold descriptive attributes related to the facts. The dimension tables are directly connected to the fact table, forming a star-like structure.

Conversely, a snowflake schema expands upon the star schema by applying normalization to the dimension tables. This entails further breaking down the attributes within the dimension tables into additional tables, creating a more complex and hierarchical structure. These additional tables are connected through relationships, resembling a snowflake-like pattern.

Now, let's talk about the advantages of using a star schema:

- **Simplicity**: The star schema has a simple and intuitive structure. It is easier to understand and navigate, especially for beginners or users who are new to data modeling. The straightforward design allows for easier querying and analysis of data.

- **Performance**: The star schema generally offers better query performance compared to the snowflake schema. The simplified structure reduces the number of joins required to retrieve data, resulting in faster data retrieval and improved query response times.

- **Denormalization**: In a star schema, dimension tables are denormalized, meaning that attributes are stored directly in the dimension table without additional tables. This denormalization simplifies the schema and improves performance by reducing the number of table joins needed to fetch data.

- **Easier maintenance**: The star schema is easier to maintain because it has a flatter structure with fewer tables. Adding or modifying dimensions or attributes is straightforward and it has less impact on the overall schema.

When creating data models in Excel, it is advisable to use the star schema. In some cases, you can collapse the extra sub-dimension table into the dimension table it connects to by creating a hierarchy. This will help you create simpler calculations and optimize the performance of your datasets.

Creating hierarchies

Roles or positions in a typical organization can be grouped into hierarchies. Starting with the highest position, we can drill down into sub-roles or functions to get an understanding of the structure of the organization.

In data modeling, we can also group several related columns into hierarchies to help us drill down our key measures in a more structured way.

Take the geographical attributes in `Location ID`: city, region, and country. Instead of analyzing by location using three different columns, we can group all these three columns into a hierarchy and name it `Location`.

To do this, we can click on the **Create Hierarchy** icon at the top of the `Location Data` table in **Diagram View**:

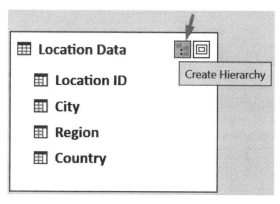

Figure 4.19 – Creating a hierarchy

Next, follow these steps:

1. Name your hierarchy Location

2. Starting from the highest level of the hierarchy, which is Country, drag each column into the Location hierarchy to create the levels in your hierarchy, as shown in the following screenshot:

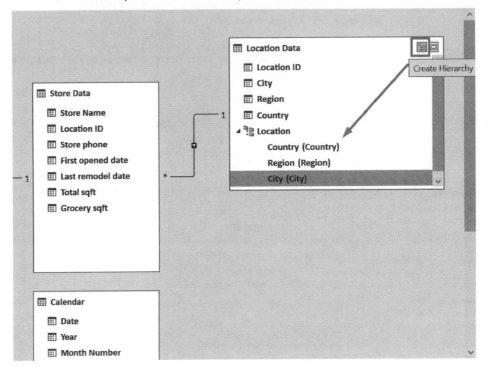

Figure 4.20 – Creating a hierarchy

When you create a hierarchy, you can use the hierarchy to drill down into measures or values in a PivotTable.

Hiding fields and tables from client tools

When you create a relationship between two tables using primary and foreign keys, duplicate fields will be listed in your pivot table fields. For example, Product ID will appear in the Product table and the fact table. Slicers, filters, or row or column fields in your pivot tables should be selected from the columns in your dimension tables. It can be confusing for your user to know which version to use to be able to employ a slicer or place in a row or column section to filter values.

Power Pivot provides a feature that allows you to hide the **Fact Table** versions of these columns. When you do this, these hidden columns will not appear in your pivot table fields list for selection.

To do this, you can select the field you want to hide in **Diagram View** by right-clicking it and selecting **Hide from Client Tools**.

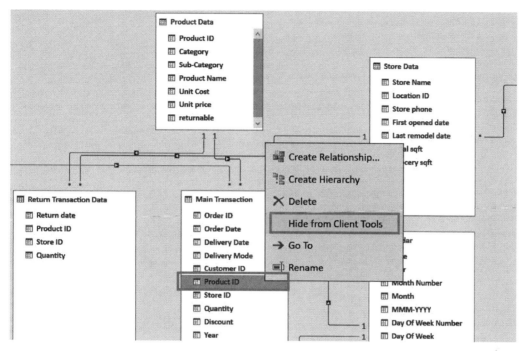

Figure 4.21 – Hiding a column with Hide from Client Tools

The same procedure can be used to hide an entire table. Some tables in your data model can be used as *helper tables* to help you calculate or simulate some dynamic measures.

You can hide this table by clicking on the header of the table in **Diagram View** and clicking **Hide from Client Tools**. The table will not appear in your **Pivot Tables** field list.

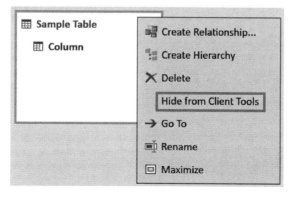

Figure 4.22 – Hiding tables in the data model

You have successfully created a data model that will now be the basis for all our calculations and analysis for our final sales dashboard.

In the next chapter, we will start creating some key measures in our data model using DAX to help you aggregate some key insights from our data.

Summary

The chapter introduced you to Power Pivot, the main authoring tool or environment for data modeling in Excel. You have now learned some of the key features in Power Pivot that can help you view all your tables in **Diagram View**, create relationships between tables, and add calculated columns.

We also covered how we can use Power Pivot to create and modify calendar tables for our data model. You now understand the key differences between dimension and fact tables and the role of primary and foreign keys in creating relationships in the data model.

In the next chapter, we will get hands-on with some DAX measures. The chapter will introduce you to some useful DAX functions and help you master syntax in creating powerful formulas in your data model.

Part 2:
Creating Insightful Calculations from your Data Model using DAX and Cube Functions

This part is tailored to provide you with a comprehensive understanding of how DAX and Cube Functions can be used to create sophisticated calculations in Excel, thereby adding a new dimension of analysis to your data models. This section serves as a primer on how to create both measures and calculated columns using DAX. The section starts with the basics of DAX, helping you to understand the syntax and fundamental concepts. This chapter presents Cube Functions as a flexible alternative for incorporating calculations into your data model. You will be guided through the process of using these functions to retrieve data from Power Pivot, offering a different approach compared to DAX. The section also compares and contrasts Cube Functions with DAX, helping you understand when and how to use each effectively.

This section has the following chapters:

- *Chapter 5, Creating DAX Calculations from your Data Model*
- *Chapter 6, Creating Cube Functions from your Data Model*

5

Creating DAX Calculations from Your Data Model – Introduction to Measures and Calculated Columns

We are halfway through our journey to creating a dynamic sales dashboard that will give users insights into our sales business. After extracting, transforming, loading, and modeling our data, we now have to **measure** our sales performance. To do this, we need to calculate some key metrics. These metrics will help us create visualizations using some of the various dimensions in our data model.

In this chapter, you will learn the key differences between **measures** and **calculated columns**, understand the various ways to create a **Data Analysis Expressions** (**DAX**) measure in Excel, master some key DAX functions and concepts, and apply these to our final sales dashboard.

The following topics will be covered in this chapter:

- DAX as a calculated column or measure
- Creating your first measure—where to go
- Common DAX functions (time intelligence, FILTER, CALCULATE, and so on)
- Understanding row and filter contexts
- Editing your DAX formulas

DAX as a calculated column or measure

After creating our data model, we need to calculate some key numbers to track performance. There are some basic calculations we can create from the columns with values in our data model, using functions such as SUM, AVERAGE, MAX, MIN, and so on.

For example, we can find the total quantity of products sold by summing all the values in the **Quantity** column of our **Main Transaction** table.

There are measures we can create by simply dragging existing columns or fields to the **Values** section of a PivotTable. These measures are called **implicit measures**, while the ones we create with formulas that can be accessed and reused in any part of our data model are called **explicit measures**. Explicit measures can be created using DAX. DAX is the formula language of a data model. In the data model, we can create two types of DAX calculations: **calculated columns** and **measures**.

In an earlier chapter, we learned how to create calculated columns. In this chapter, we will learn about explicit measures.

Let's look at some key features of explicit measures:

- They can be **reused** in several ways in our data model. For example, if I calculate **total sales** for a particular product, I can use that measure in multiple visuals in my final dashboard.

- You can apply a **permanent number format** to a measure such that it uses that format when you apply the measure in your dashboards or reports.

- Existing measures can be used to **create other complex measures**.

- In a PivotTable, we can use explicit measures only in the **Values** section, as seen here:

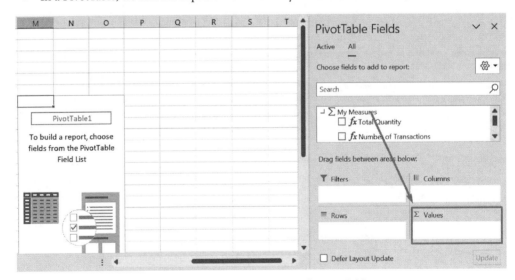

Figure 5.1 – The Values section of a PivotTable

Creating your first measure – where to go

Before we create our first measure, it would be a good idea to store all our measures in one table. This will make it easier to organize our measures and separate them from other fields in our data.

To create such a measures table, follow these steps:

1. Select an empty cell in your worksheet.

2. Copy the empty cell and click on the **Manage** button, as shown in the following screenshot:

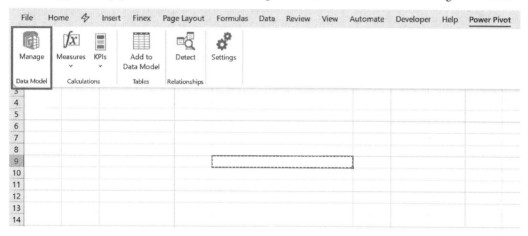

Figure 5.2 – Creating a table for measures

3. This should open the **Power Pivot** window.

4. Click on **Paste** under the **Home** tab:

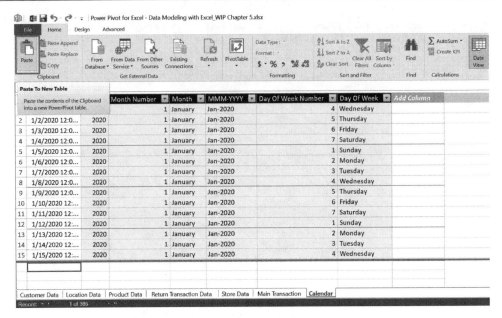

Figure 5.3 – The Paste dialog box in Power Pivot

This brings up the following **Paste Preview** dialog box:

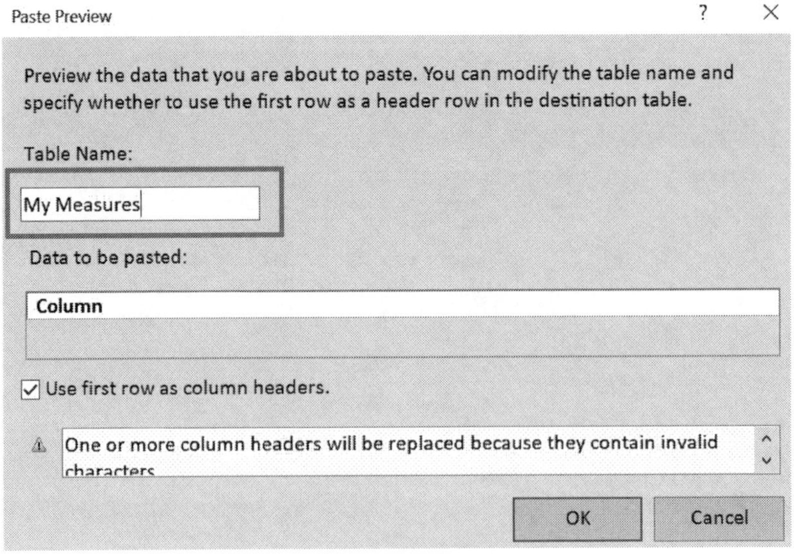

Figure 5.4 – Naming your measures

You can now assign a new name to the table. In my case, I named it **My Measures**. Click **OK** to finish the process.

You should now find a new table pasted in your data model called **My Measures**. This is the table we will assign all our measures to.

My Measures shows up as an empty tab in your **Data View** with a single column. It would be useful to right-click on this column and select **Hide from Client Tools**:

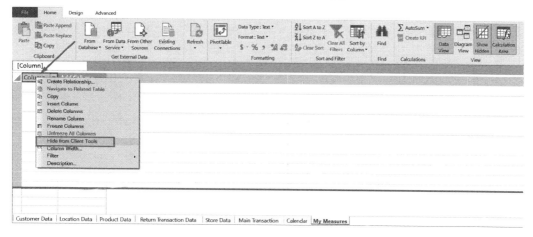

Figure 5.5 – Hiding columns in a table

This ensures that your measures table moves up in the list of tables in your PivotTable. This is shown in the following screenshot:

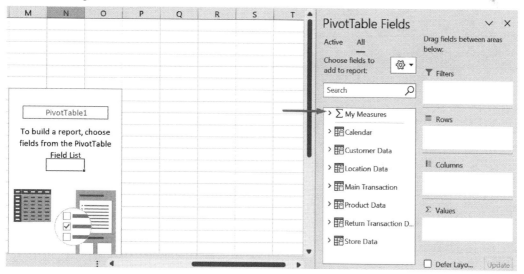

Figure 5.6 – The measures table in the PivotTable

After creating this measures table, we will create our first measure, **Total Quantity**, which will sum the quantity of products sold during the period.

To do this, go to the **Power Pivot** tab | **Measures** | **New Measure…**:

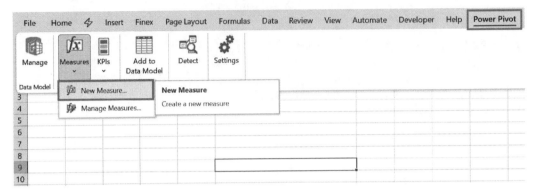

Figure 5.7 – Creating a new measure using the Power Pivot tab

Clicking on **New Measure…** will bring up the following dialog box:

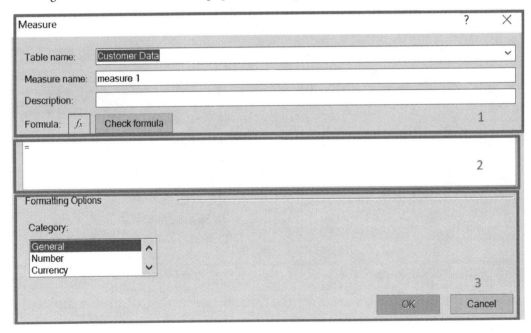

Figure 5.8 – The Measure dialog box

The dialog box is categorized into three main areas.

The first part contains information on the measure. This includes the following categories:

1. **Table name**: This shows the name of the table in your data model that is hosting your measure. Every measure gets assigned to a table you specify. We have already created a table for our measures, **My Measures**, so we will select it from the dropdown.

    My Measures appears in the list of table names for selection, as shown next:

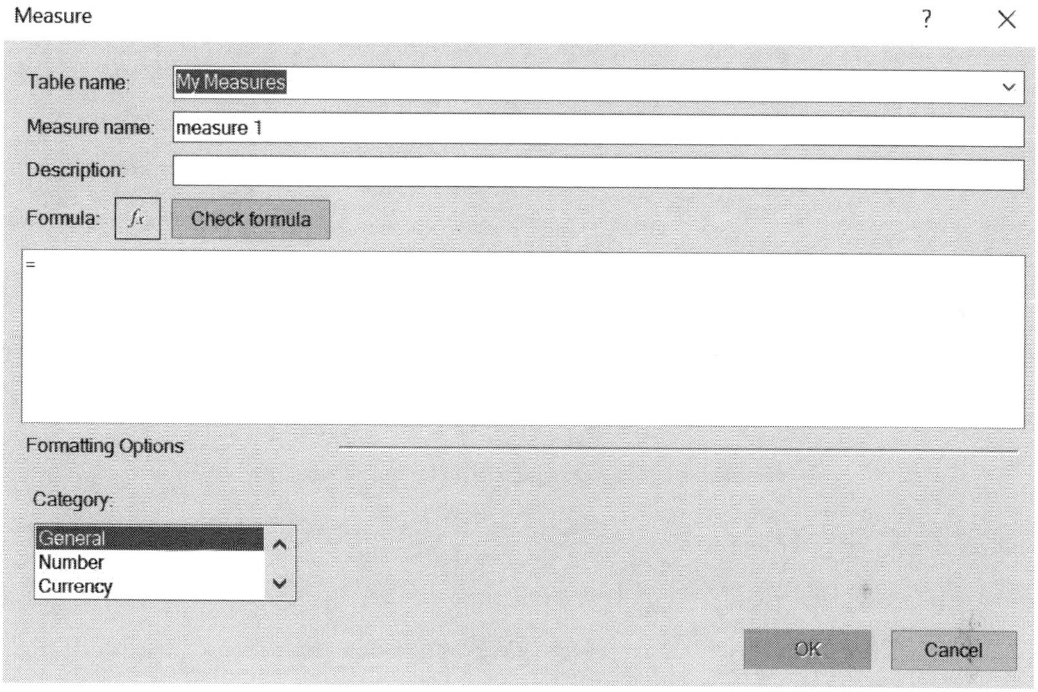

Figure 5.9 – Selecting the My Measures table

You can use **Measure name** to assign a name to your explicit measures. Here, you can provide an optional description of your measure in the **Description** field.

2. The second segment of your **Measure** dialog box helps you create your formula or DAX measure. The process starts with an equals sign, and then you can type the syntax for your formula. The **fx** button against the **Formula** field allows you to explore the DAX functions library, and **Check formula** is a very important button that helps you check the accuracy of your formulas. Ideally, you should always click on this button to validate your formulas.

    We will now create our first measure, **Total Quantity**. This will sum up the quantity of all items sold in our data model. In our data model, these values sit in our **Main Transaction** table.

    Our formula will be like a regular SUM formula in Excel. DAX formulas, in most cases, are like regular Excel formulas.

    Our completed formula will be entered into the dialog box, as shown next:

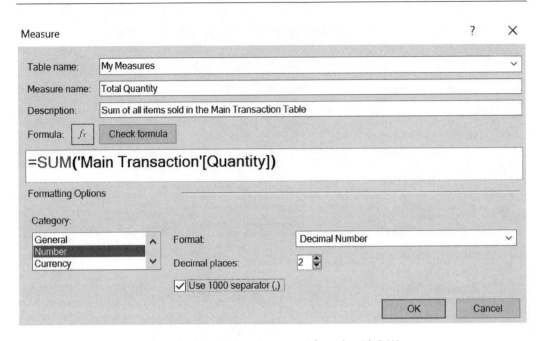

Figure 5.10 – Creating a basic SUM formula with DAX

A few notes on the preceding screenshot:

- The name of the measure is **Total Quantity**.

- In the **Description** field, we have given some details on what the measure is calculating. This can be useful to help your users understand complex formulas.

- The formula starts with SUM and uses the table name and the column reference of the **Main Transaction** table to sum up items in the **Quantity** column.

  When you are referencing a column in your DAX formulas, the standard rule is to use the fully qualified name—that is, Table[Column]. In our case, the name of the table is **Main Transaction** and the column name is **Quantity**, so we reference the column as Main Transaction[Quantity]. The table name needs to be encapsulated in single quotes if it contains a space. This will normally be done automatically, but it's good to know this in case your formula returns an error.

  You will get guidance when you are writing DAX formulas with in-built IntelliSense to help you input the requirements of the function accurately.

- In the formatting options, the format category is set to **Number** and two decimal places. This will format the measure accordingly.

- You can now click on the **Check formula** button to validate the formula:

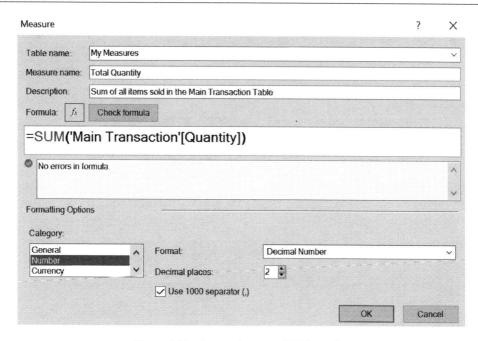

Figure 5.11 – Formatting your DAX formulas

After a **No errors in formula** confirmation message, you can now proceed and click **OK**.

To find your measure, you can go to the **Power Pivot** tab | **Measures** and click on **Manage Measures…**:

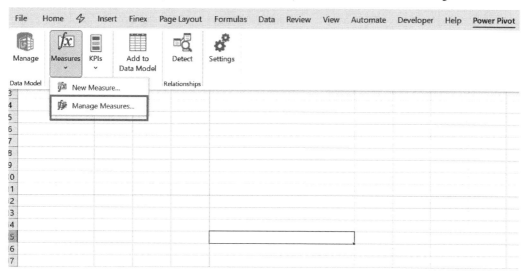

Figure 5.12 – Locating your measures

This opens up a dialog box that lists all your measures, as shown next:

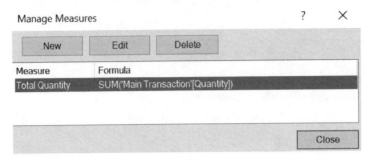

Figure 5.13 – Display of current measures

From here, you can add new measures, edit existing measures, or delete them. You can also find your measures in your **Power Pivot** window. These measures will be stored in the calculation area of the table they have been assigned to, as shown next:

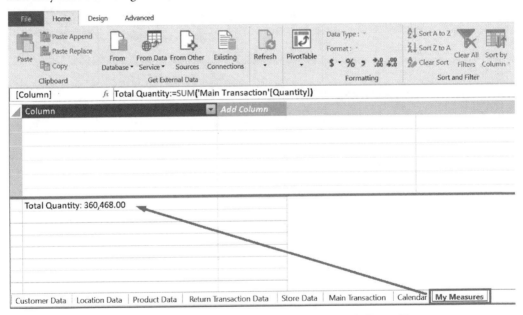

Figure 5.14 – Alternative display of current measures in Power Pivot

Common DAX functions (time intelligence, FILTER, CALCULATE, and so on)

There are over 250 DAX functions. We will not be covering all these functions in this book, but we will use and apply the most common functions to our sales dashboard.

Earlier, we calculated our first DAX formula using SUM. SUM falls under the category of DAX functions called **aggregation functions**. They are responsible for computing scalar values, such as sums, averages, minimums, maximums, and counts, across all rows within a column or table in our data model.

Here are some other categories of DAX functions and what they can be used to calculate:

- **Filter functions**: These functions assist in fetching specific data types, searching for values in related tables, and applying filters based on associated values. Lookup functions operate by utilizing tables and their relationships. Filtering functions provide the ability to modify the data context, enabling the creation of dynamic calculations. This includes functions such as CALCULATE, FILTER, ALL, SELECTEDVALUE, and others.

- **Financial functions**: These functions are employed within formulas designed for financial computations, including calculations such as **net present value (NPV)** and **rate of return (RoR)**. For instance, functions such as PMT, FV, IPMT, and similar tools are utilized for these purposes.

- **Information functions**: These functions examine a table or column that is given as an argument to another function and determine whether the value corresponds to the anticipated type. For instance, when you use the ISERROR function, it will yield TRUE if the value you're referring to contains an error.

- **Logical functions**: These functions provide details about values within an expression. For instance, the TRUE function informs you whether an expression being evaluated yields a TRUE value. This includes functions such as IF, IFERROR, SWITCH, AND, OR, and others of similar nature.

- **Math and trig functions**: DAX mathematical functions share similarities with Excel's mathematical and trigonometric functions. Nevertheless, there are distinctions in the numeric data types employed by DAX functions. This is evident in functions such as MROUND, DIVIDE, and RANK, where variations may arise.

- **Parent and child functions**: These functions aid users in handling data organized in a parent/child hierarchy within their data models. Examples of such functions include PATH and PATHITEM.

- **Relationship functions**: These functions are designed to oversee and apply relationships between tables. For instance, you have the capability to designate a specific relationship for use in a calculation. This involves functions such as RELATED, RELATEDTABLE, and USERELATIONSHIP.

- **Statistical functions**: These functions compute values associated with statistical distributions and probability, such as standard deviation and the count of permutations. Examples include MEDIAN, RANKX, and similar functions.

- **Table manipulation functions**: These functions either provide a table or modify existing ones. For instance, you have functions such as GROUPBY, SELECTCOLUMNS, and SUMMARIZE.

- **Text functions**: These functions enable you to retrieve a portion of a string, search for specific text within a string, or combine different string values. There are also additional functions designed for managing date, time, and number formats. Examples include CONCATENATE, LEFT, MID, and RIGHT.

- **Date and time intelligence functions**: These functions assist in generating calculations that leverage pre-existing knowledge about calendars and dates. Through the integration of time and date ranges with aggregations or calculations, you can establish insightful comparisons across equivalent time frames for metrics such as sales and inventory. Examples include SAMEPERIODLASTYEAR, DATESYTD, DATEADD, and similar functions.

We will now go through simple examples of how we can use some basic DAX functions to create an insightful report using some case studies.

Case study 1: *Create a report that summarizes the number of transactions, return rate, and unique products for each store.*

The preceding report will require us to use the following DAX functions:

- COUNTROWS: This is part of the group of counting functions that are mostly used to count the rows in a table. However, if you want to count the items in a specific column, then use COUNTA instead on the column.

- DIVIDE: Used for division when the denominator is an expression that could return 0 or BLANK. The function allows you to assign an alternative value to the resulting error.

Let's proceed to calculate the number of transactions.

We will do this using COUNTROWS.

To create a new measure, we will go to the **Power Pivot** tab | **Measures** | **New Measure...**:

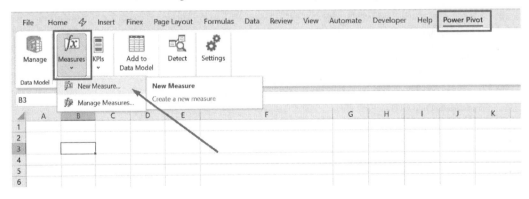

Figure 5.15 – Starting a new measure

This opens our **Measure** dialog box. As indicated earlier, all measures will be stored in the **My Measures** table we created. So, we select this and proceed with the name of our measure:

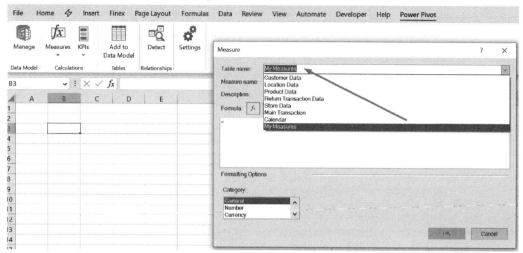

Figure 5.16 – Selecting a table to host your measure

The name of the measure is **Number of Transactions**. We will assign this to the **Measure Name** dialog box and proceed to write the formula.

All DAX functions have unique requirements. Some functions require table inputs while others require column inputs. In some cases, you will need to input an expression, which could be a simple calculation or referencing an existing measure.

For COUNTROWS, which requires a table name, we will input the name of the table, **Main Transactions**. When you use COUNTROWS with table names, ensure that there are no blank rows and that the granularity of the records is one row per transaction. Otherwise, you will get an inflated count if there are blank rows present in the dataset.

Our completed formula looks like this:

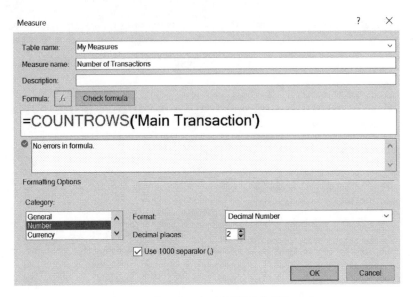

Figure 5.17 – Creating the COUNTROWS function

You can now proceed to check the formula and click **OK** to complete this step.

We can calculate the number of transactions that were returned using the same method.

To do this, we will start a new measure and assign it to the measures table, as we did earlier.

The completed **Measure** dialog box for this formula is shown here:

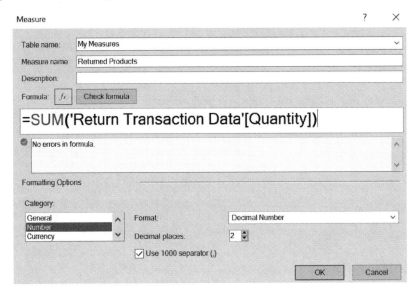

Figure 5.18 – Creating the total quantity formula

The name of the measure is **Returned Products**. We used SUM on the Product [Quantity] column of the **Return Transaction Data** table. This sums up all items that were returned.

Now that we have **Returned Products** and **Total Transactions**, we can simply calculate the **Return Rate** value by dividing the two measures.

This is a job for DIVIDE. It is more suitable for this type of math operation because it has an optional requirement to provide a value when there are no transactions for a particular store. This way, we avoid using an IFERROR function to handle errors.

We will go through the steps to create a new measure. When writing the formula for DIVIDE, we can easily call existing measures by using a square bracket ([):

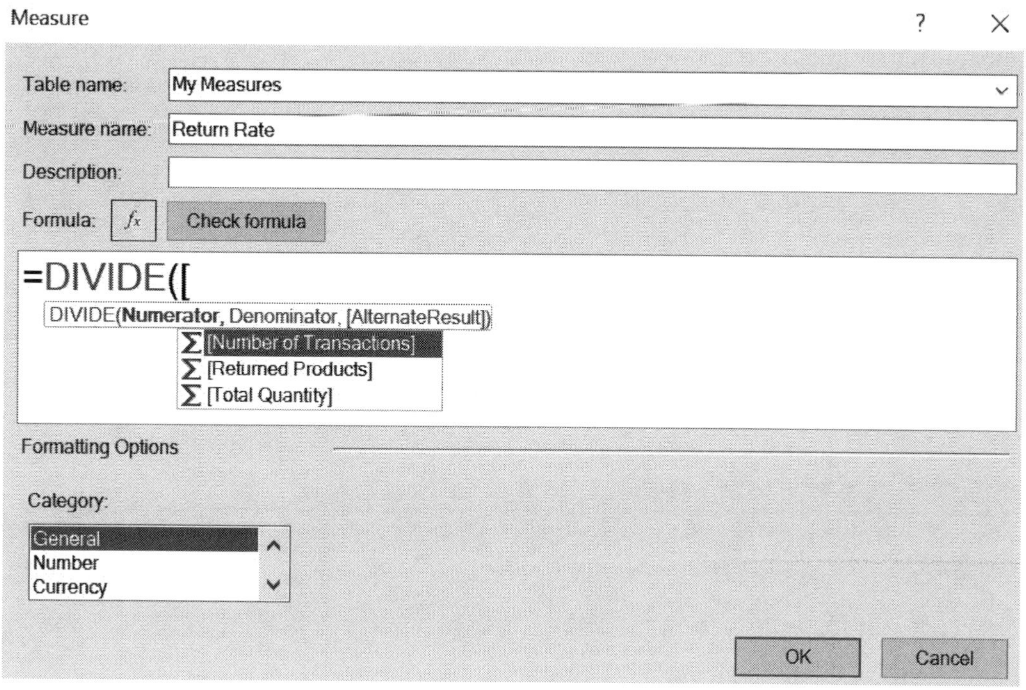

Figure 5.19 – Using the DIVIDE function

It makes it easy to reference measures when you are creating formulas.

Our completed formula is shown next:

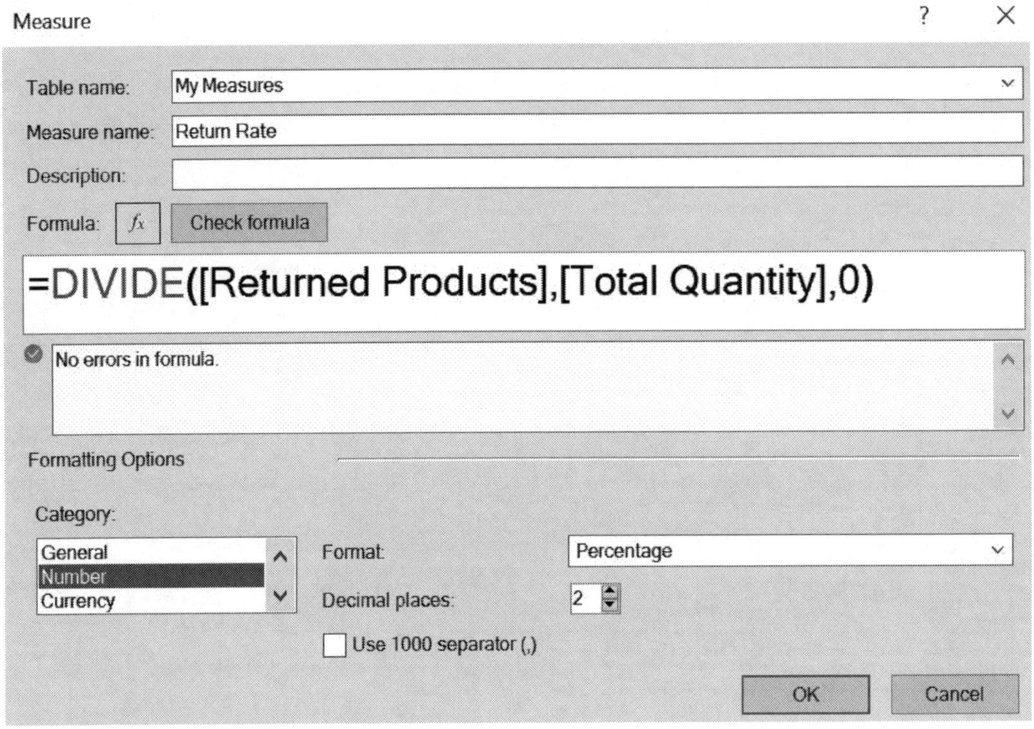

Figure 5.20 – The completed DIVIDE formula

Let's break this down.

The DIVIDE formula has three arguments:

- **Returned Products**, which is the numerator
- **Total Quantity**, which is the denominator
- 0 as an alternate result if there is an error

You will also notice that the number format has been changed to **Percentage** in the **Format** option.

We will now conclude this case study by creating a summary report with the PivotTable. The report will analyze all stores by **Number of Transactions**, **Returned Transactions**, and **Return Rate**.

Back in our worksheet, we can insert a PivotTable directly from the data model by going to **Insert | PivotTable**:

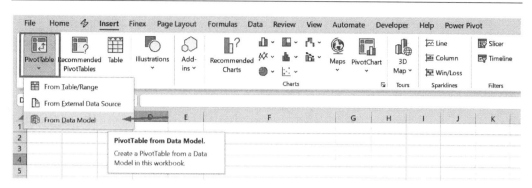

Figure 5.21 – Inserting a PivotTable from the data model

We will choose **Existing Worksheet** in the options to place the PivotTable in the current worksheet:

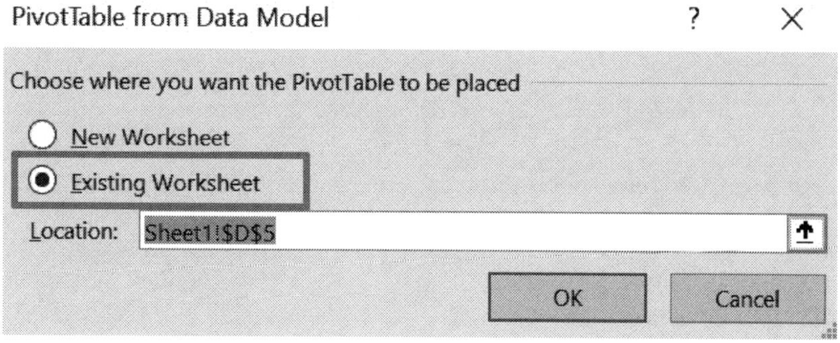

Figure 5.22 – Choosing an existing worksheet

When the PivotTable is created, you will see a list of your tables and measures in the PivotTable field to your right:

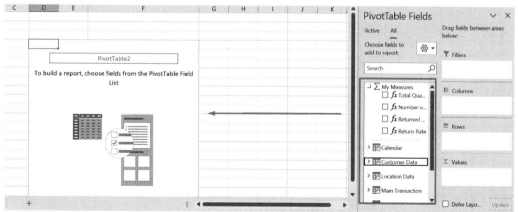

Figure 5.23 – PivotTable fields

We can now create our summary report by dragging **Store Name** in the store data to the **Rows** section. Then, drag the measures—**Total Quantity**, **Number of Transactions**, **Returned Items**, and **Return Rate**—to the **Values** section.

Our completed PivotTable report will look like this:

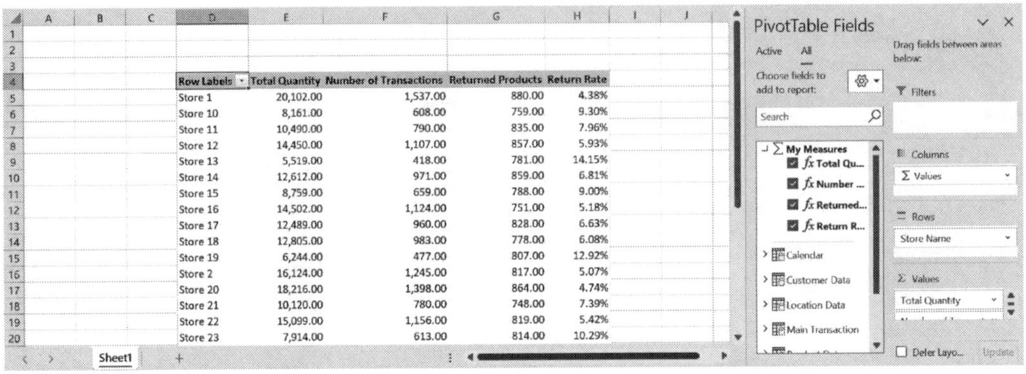

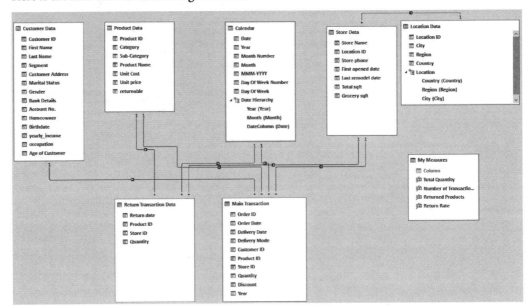

Figure 5.24 – A PivotTable report showing different values

It is possible to have one of the columns display the same values. This happens when the tables involved in the report are not connected to the data model. This is a good time to check and audit all the connections in your data model to ensure that the relevant tables are connected.

Here is the final data model in **Diagram View**:

Figure 5.25 – The data model in Diagram View

You will notice that the table we created to host our measures sits disconnected to the right. This is fine. Our **My Measures** table cannot be connected to any table because there are no primary and foreign keys we can use to connect to the other tables.

You can use **Diagram View** as a guide to correct your model if needed.

Back to our summary report. We can apply some formats to make our store report look more presentable.

We can achieve this by using **Conditional Formatting | Data Bars** to help us visualize which store has the highest return rate.

To do this, you can select any cell in the **Return Rate** column in the PivotTable. Right-click and sort from the largest to the smallest.

We now have the return rates sorted in descending order:

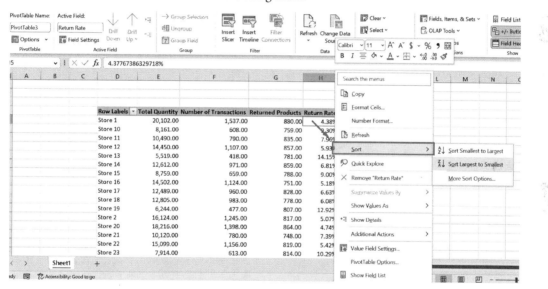

Figure 5.26 – Sorting a PivotTable column

Select this column, and under the **Home** tab, go to **Conditional Formatting | Data Bars | Solid Fill** and select the red bar option. This will now highlight the **Return Rate** column with red data bars:

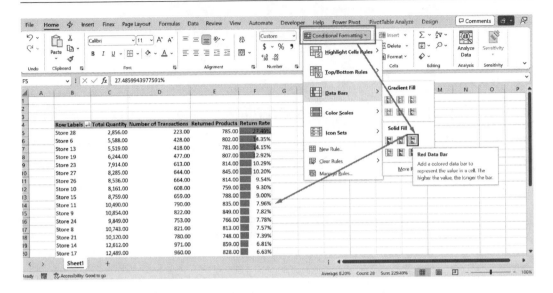

Figure 5.27 – Applying conditional formatting

From the report, we can see **Store 28** has an unusually high number of returned products. This is an insight that must be investigated.

Hopefully, this case study has given you a good introduction to how you can use basic DAX functions to get quick insights from your data.

We will now move on to *case study 2*.

Case study 2: *Create a report showing the total quantity of priority products that were returned.*

The shop's criteria for identifying priority products are as follows:

- The product should be electronic

- The price of the product must be more than 500

- The product must be returnable

In a previous chapter of the book, we used DATEDIFF, a DAX function to calculate the ages of our customers. In creating the report for this case study, we are going to use a set of logic functions, IF and AND, to create another calculated column in the **Products** table using the preceding conditions.

We will start off by going to the **Products** table in the data model. The last column in this table is the **returnable** column.

You can select the idle column next to this column and proceed to write the IF statement in the formula bar, as shown next:

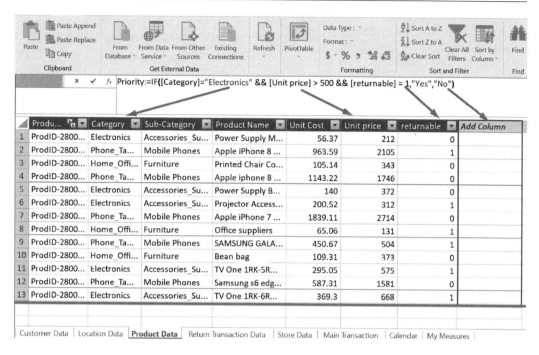

Figure 5.28 – Creating a calculated column with IF

Let's break down the steps in the preceding screenshot:

1. The formula begins with `Priority:=`. This is a way to include your column header names in your formula. The alternative is to proceed without the name and start directly with an equals sign. You can edit the name of the column afterward.

2. The `IF` statement has three `AND` arguments. In regular Excel formulas, we would have written this using the `IF(AND(logic1,logic2,logic3)…)` approach. However, in DAX, we are only limited to two logical conditions if we use `OR` or `AND`. The alternative is to input each condition and separate the statements with a double pipe (`||`) for `OR` statements and a double ampersand (`&&`) for `AND` statements.

The three `AND` statements as indicated previously are shown here:

```
=IF(
[Category] = "Electronics" &&
[Unit price] > 500 &&
[returnable] = "1", meaning the product is marked returnable
```

If any of the previous statements are `True`, the result should be **Yes**; otherwise, it should be **No**, as shown in *Figure 5.28*.

The conditions can be linked to the columns in the **Products** table. These have been marked with red arrows in *Figure 5.28*; that is, **Electronics** for the category and >500 in the **Unit price** column, and then [returnable]=1.

3. The final values for True (**Yes**) and False (**No**) have been included in the last section of the formula.

When you press *Enter*, this should now give you a new column with a series of **Yes** and **No** outputs, as shown next:

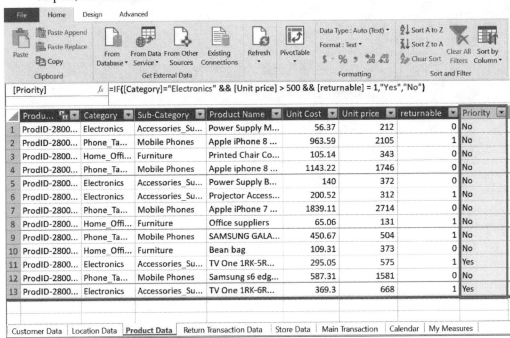

Figure 5.29 – Showing the results of the calculated column

This new calculated column is now available in the **PivotTable Fields** list.

We can right-click and add a slicer to our earlier report to give further information on the return rate of our priority products:

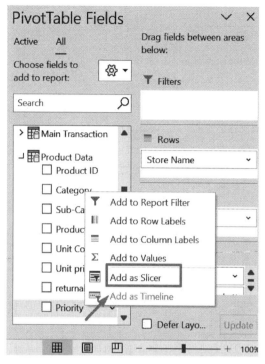

Figure 5.30 – Adding a slicer in a PivotTable

We now have an interactive report that gives us further information on our priority products when we select **Yes**:

Row Labels	Total Quantity	Number of Transactions	Returned Products	Return Rate
Store 28	421.00	33.00	77.00	18.29%
Store 13	491.00	38.00	86.00	17.52%
Store 19	707.00	57.00	89.00	12.59%
Store 6	607.00	49.00	71.00	11.70%
Store 26	871.00	69.00	84.00	9.64%
Store 9	1,002.00	77.00	80.00	7.98%
Store 11	1,205.00	94.00	89.00	7.39%
Store 24	1,089.00	84.00	77.00	7.07%
Store 10	954.00	72.00	67.00	7.02%
Store 27	1,069.00	85.00	73.00	6.83%
Store 22	1,639.00	126.00	107.00	6.53%
Store 21	1,041.00	81.00	66.00	6.34%
Store 8	1,108.00	88.00	68.00	6.14%
Store 23	1,115.00	87.00	68.00	6.10%
Store 12	1,269.00	101.00	74.00	5.83%
Store 15	1,209.00	92.00	70.00	5.79%
Store 3	1,794.00	131.00	102.00	5.69%
Store 18	1,620.00	130.00	90.00	5.56%

Priority: No / Yes

Figure 5.31 – Interacting with slicers

From the report, **Store 28** still dominates our list of priority products returned, and management may have to take a look at this.

So far, we have looked at some basic DAX functions. Let's switch to the most widely used function in DAX, CALCULATE. To help us properly understand this function, we will apply it to *case study 3*.

Case study 3: *Calculate the total quantity of products purchased by our professional customers.*

If you are familiar with PivotTables, we can easily calculate this by creating and moving a few fields around to obtain a final value. However, calculating these measures directly gives you more flexibility with your dashboards and reports.

The CALCULATE function modifies filters that have been applied to an expression or a calculation.

The syntax looks like this: CALCULATE (<expression>[, <filter1> [, <filter2> [, ...]]])

The expression used as the first parameter can be an existing measure we have created already, such as Total Quantity, or a new calculation.

The filters after this expression can be a Boolean filter expression (that is, statements evaluating to TRUE or FALSE); for example, Customer_Data[Occupation] = "Professional".

If we used the preceding filter with our original expression/measure **Total Quantity**, we would be calculating something similar to SUMIFS in Excel where the criteria for summing will be only rows in the **Occupation** column that contain **Professional**.

But CALCULATE does more than just summing. It can modify any calculation that is used as an expression in the first part of the function.

Let's create the measure for our case study using CALCULATE.

To create this measure, first go to **Power Pivot | Measures | New Measure**.

The completed **Measure** dialog box is shown next:

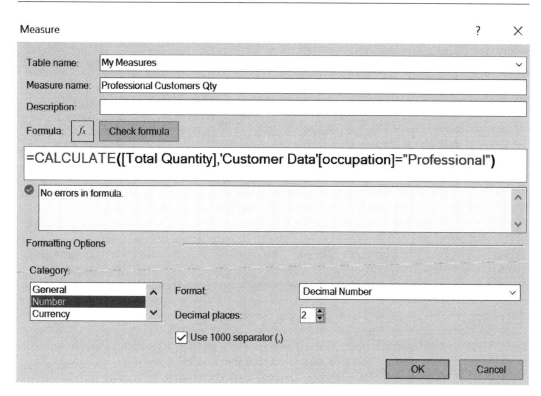

Figure 5.32 – Creating a formula with CALCULATE

The preceding formula takes **Total Quantity** as an expression and filters that expression to only customers who have **Professional** in the **Occupation** column in the **Customers** table.

This is a basic example of how to use the CALCULATE function, but it can be applied to more advanced scenarios to help us get specific calculations.

We can add this new measure to our earlier PivotTable by selecting the measure from the list of measures shown in the PivotTable. This is shown next:

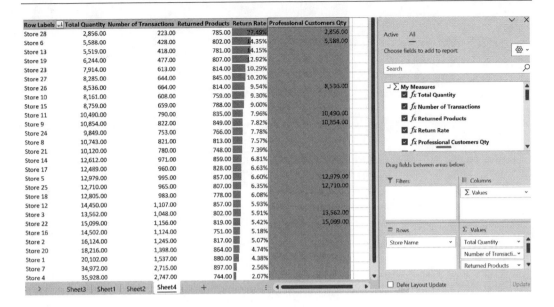

Row Labels	Total Quantity	Number of Transactions	Returned Products	Return Rate	Professional Customers Qty
Store 28	2,856.00	223.00	785.00	27.49%	2,856.00
Store 6	5,588.00	428.00	802.00	14.35%	5,588.00
Store 13	5,519.00	418.00	781.00	14.15%	
Store 19	6,244.00	477.00	807.00	12.92%	
Store 23	7,914.00	613.00	814.00	10.29%	
Store 27	8,285.00	644.00	845.00	10.20%	
Store 26	8,536.00	664.00	814.00	9.54%	8,536.00
Store 10	8,161.00	608.00	759.00	9.30%	
Store 15	8,759.00	659.00	788.00	9.00%	
Store 11	10,490.00	790.00	835.00	7.96%	10,490.00
Store 9	10,854.00	822.00	849.00	7.82%	10,854.00
Store 24	9,849.00	753.00	766.00	7.78%	
Store 8	10,743.00	821.00	813.00	7.57%	
Store 21	10,120.00	780.00	748.00	7.39%	
Store 14	12,612.00	971.00	859.00	6.81%	
Store 17	12,489.00	960.00	828.00	6.63%	
Store 5	12,979.00	995.00	857.00	6.60%	12,979.00
Store 25	12,710.00	965.00	807.00	6.35%	12,710.00
Store 18	12,805.00	983.00	778.00	6.08%	
Store 12	14,450.00	1,107.00	857.00	5.93%	
Store 3	13,562.00	1,048.00	802.00	5.91%	13,562.00
Store 22	15,099.00	1,156.00	819.00	5.42%	15,099.00
Store 16	14,502.00	1,124.00	751.00	5.18%	
Store 2	16,124.00	1,245.00	817.00	5.07%	
Store 20	18,216.00	1,398.00	864.00	4.74%	
Store 1	20,102.00	1,537.00	880.00	4.38%	
Store 7	34,972.00	2,715.00	897.00	2.56%	
Store 4	35,928.00	2,747.00	744.00	2.07%	

Figure 5.33 – Using a calculated measure in a PivotTable

From the report, it is clear that not all stores sold to our professional customers.

Understanding row and filter contexts

Before we move on to the next set of DAX functions, let's take a moment to understand the concepts of row and filter contexts.

Understanding this will help you write better DAX formulas.

In Excel, calculations in tables are mostly done in the current row and copied down. When we create calculations that operate on values in every single row of our tables, we are using a row context. What this means is that each row calculates differently based on its unique values. We used row contexts when we created a calculated column for the ages of our customers. The DATEDIFF function runs an operation on the date of birth of each customer "row by row" to return the corresponding age for each customer.

Calculated columns automatically compute within an existing row context. However, when we create measures, this behavior is not there by default, and we need to find some creative ways to select rows for our calculations. This is normally achieved using an iterator function—a function that can scan over a table and create calculations based on the rows. Examples of these functions are SUMX, RANKX, MAXX, and so on. With these functions, we are able to get aggregated calculations after the iterator has calculated "row-by-row" values. This will be the subject of our next deep dive into DAX functions.

Filter contexts, on the other hand, are a set of filters that are applied when you calculate a value or create a table. Remember how we used CALCULATE earlier? We took an existing measure and applied an (Occupation = "Professional") filter to give us the total quantity of our professional customers.

DAX calculations respond to filters from the PivotTable when we create our reports. We can directly apply these filters in measures as we create them.

Take a look at this highlighted value in the PivotTable report shown next:

| Total Quantity | Category | | |
Store Name	Electronics	Home_Office	Phone_Tablets
Store 1	7,120.00	5,785.00	7,227.00
Store 10	3,284.00	2,260.00	2,617.00
Store 11	4,159.00	2,841.00	3,490.00
Store 12	5,299.00	4,235.00	4,916.00
Store 13	1,750.00	1,785.00	2,034.00
Store 14	4,855.00	3,676.00	4,081.00
Store 15	3,472.00	2,425.00	2,862.00
Store 16	5,486.00	4,216.00	4,800.00
Store 17	4,787.00	3,480.00	4,222.00
Store 18	4,531.00	3,486.00	4,788.00
Store 19	2,397.00	1,718.00	2,129.00
Store 2	5,953.00	4,504.00	5,667.00
Store 20	7,038.00	5,077.00	6,101.00
Store 21	3,681.00	2,912.00	3,527.00
Store 22	5,644.00	4,199.00	5,256.00
Store 23	2,932.00	2,240.00	2,742.00
Store 24	3,504.00	2,942.00	3,403.00

Figure 5.34 – Understanding filter contexts

The number represents the total quantity of products sold that belong to the Home_Office category and **Store 15**.

We can directly create this value as a measure using CALCULATE, as shown next:

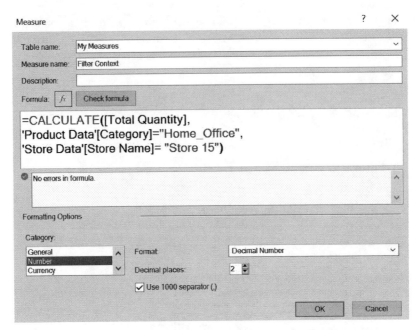

Figure 5.35 – Understanding filter contexts with CALCULATE

With filter contexts, the value or numbers you see depends on the filter constraints that have been applied to the value or numbers. This powerful feature allows us to modify calculations and drill down numbers to answer specific questions.

We can break down this new measure by month in a PivotTable, as shown next:

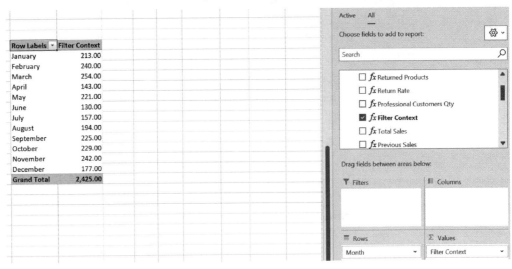

Figure 5.36 – Using a calculated measure with a filter context in a PivotTable

When we calculate in Excel, we reference values from cells to create other formulas. DAX measures cannot reference cells, so we rely on row and filter contexts to create flexible calculations in the data model.

The next set of DAX functions we are going to look at are iteration functions. These functions rely on row contexts to calculate values. We'll cover this in *case study 4*.

Case study 4: *Calculate the total sales for each store using* SUMX.

To calculate total sales, we need to multiply the price and quantity sold for each transaction at a row level first and then sum these values up to get our total sales.

SUMX does exactly this in one step. Let's look at how this works. Our SUMX formula in the **Measure** dialog box will look like this:

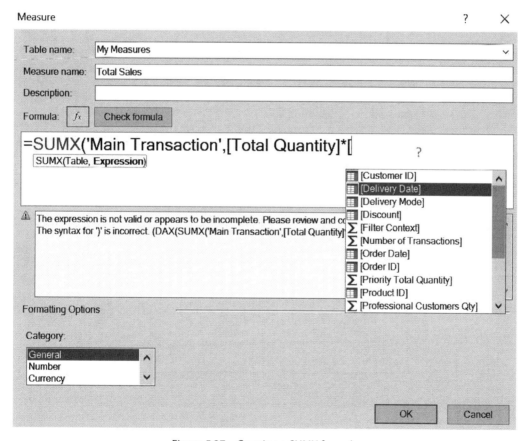

Figure 5.37 – Creating a SUMX formula

Let's try to break down the preceding incomplete formula and find out why we have an error.

The SUMX function requires a table. This is the table containing the rows for which the expression will be evaluated. For example, multiply each quantity by price. After inputting the table name, which is **Main Transaction**, we can now input the formula, `Price x Quantity`, for each transaction before summing up these values. We can call the **Quantity** column from the **Main Transaction** table, but we hit a block because we cannot find a **Price** column in the same table.

The solution is to look up the price for each transaction from the `Product_Data` table. We can now use another DAX function called RELATED to do this for each transaction. RELATED acts like a lookup function to bring the corresponding price for each transaction from a related table, which is our `Product_Data` table. Our updated DAX formula will now look this:

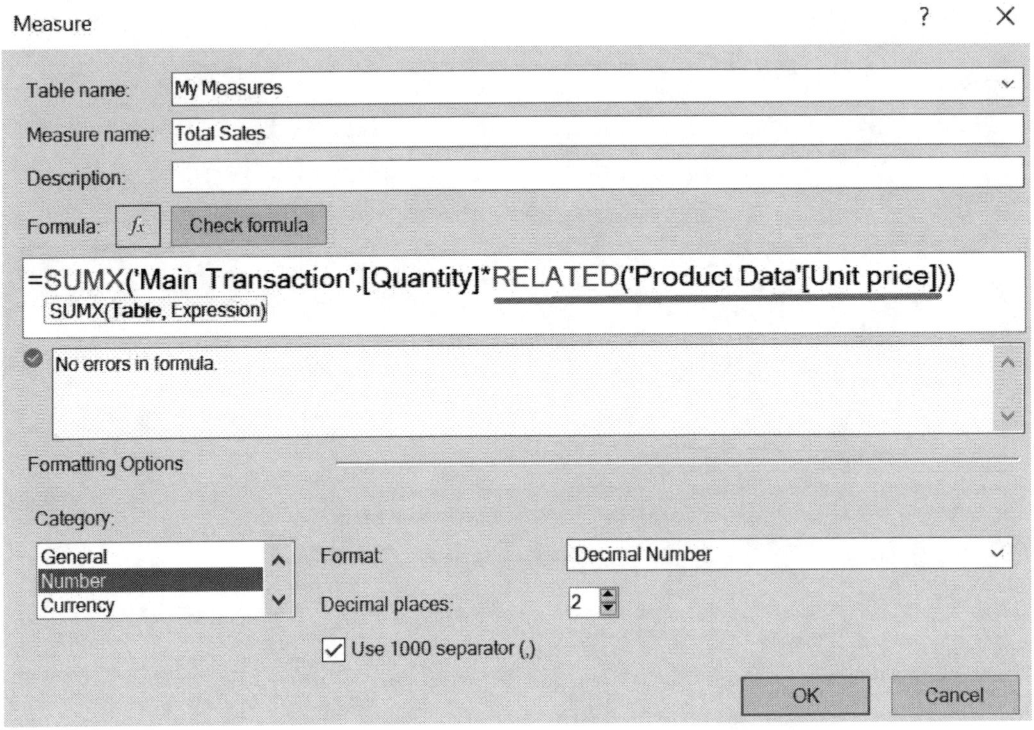

Figure 5.38 – Creating a SUMX formula with RELATED

RELATED now completes this formula by bringing the related price for each transaction.

We can now create our final report in the PivotTable by dragging **Total Sales** to the **Values** section and **Store Name** to **Rows**.

Our final report looks like this:

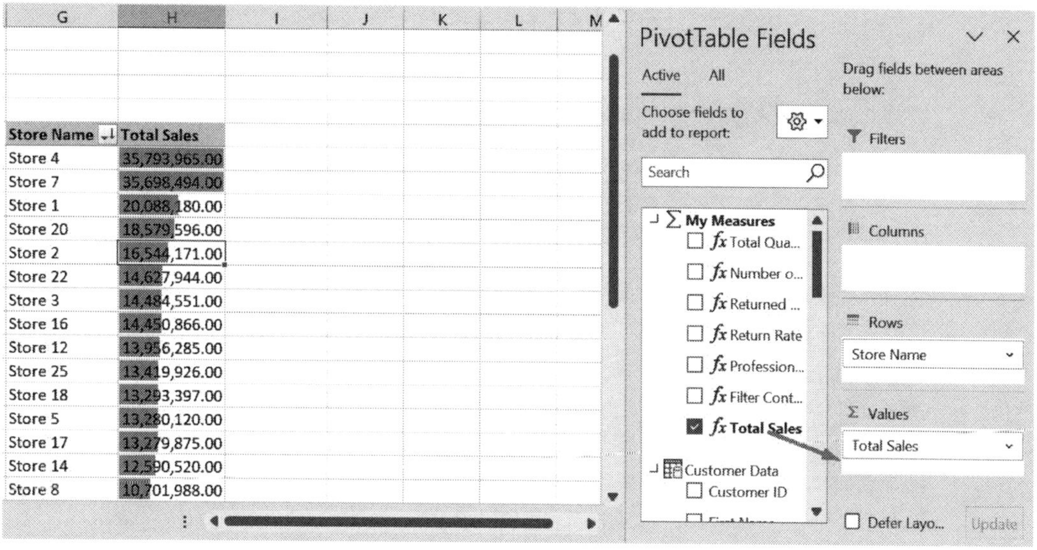

Figure 5.39 – Displaying total sales in the PivotTable

We have sorted the values in descending order and applied conditional formatting as we did in our earlier case study.

Now, let's look at our last case study.

Case study 5: *Create a report that compares the previous year's sales to the current year's sales.*

To answer this, we need to use time intelligence DAX functions, which give date or period perspectives from our **Calendar** table. This set of functions allows us to create time comparisons for our measures. For accurate calculations, we use the CALENDAR function and the CALCULATE function to calculate the following:

- Previous period (for example, SAMEPERIODLASTYEAR or DATEADD)

- Performance to date (for example, DATESYTD or DATESMTD)

- Running total (for example, DATESINPERIOD)

Let's now calculate last year's sales using CALCULATE and SAMEPERIODLASTYEAR. We learned earlier in the chapter that CALCULATE modifies existing measures with filters.

So, we can take **Total Sales** and use CALCULATE to modify this measure to give us last year's values. Our complete formula will look like this:

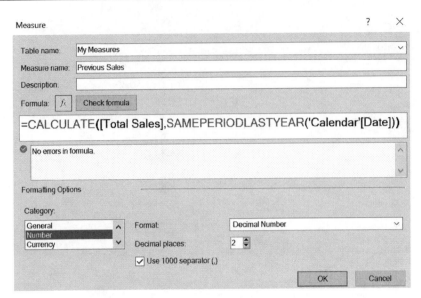

Figure 5.40 – Calculating sales for a previous year

The formula uses CALCULATE with our current **Total Sales** column and modifies this measure using SAMEPERIODLASTYEAR on the **Calendar Date** column.

We can now create a simple summary of all sales and compare them to previous sales by year.

To do this, we can go to the PivotTable, drag the **Year** column into the **Rows** section, and then drag **Total Sales** and **Previous Sales** into the **Values** section. Our report looks like this:

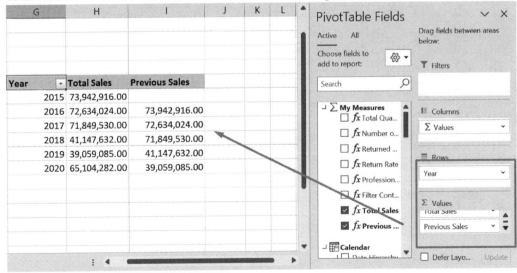

Figure 5.41 – Displaying sales for a previous year using PivotTables

Editing your DAX formulas

You may need to go back to your DAX formulas to make changes. You can easily edit current measures by going to the **Power Pivot** tab | **Measures** | **Manage Measures…**, as seen here:

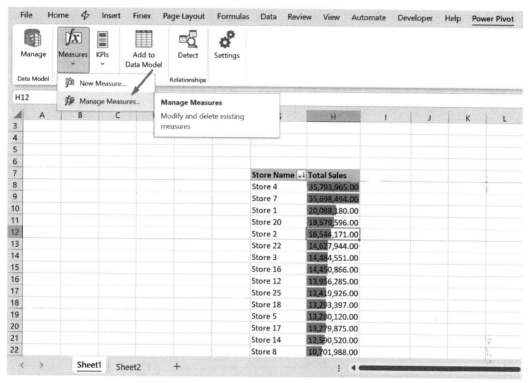

Figure 5.42 – Editing your measures

Select the measure you want to edit from the list and click on **Edit**. This brings you to the **Manage Measures** dialog box. You can make your changes from here:

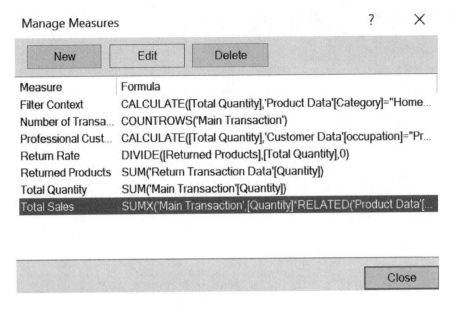

Figure 5.43 – The Edit button in the Manage Measures dialog box

Summary

It's been an exciting journey and introduction to the world of DAX.

We started by understanding the difference between a calculated column and a measure. We explored the **Measure** dialog box and how the different components can help us create effective DAX formulas.

You are now familiar with some basic DAX functions including SUM, COUNTROWS, CALCULATE, SUMX, RELATED, and some time intelligence functions. You now know how to edit your measures and create simple summary reports using PivotTables.

This is a scratch on the surface of DAX. We will go into more specific calculations in subsequent chapters.

6

Creating Cube Functions from Your Data Model – a Flexible Alternative to Calculations in Your Data Model

In the previous chapter, we learned how we could create measures to analyze data using DAX. These measures will be used to create PivotTable reports that will drive some of the key numbers and visuals in our final dashboard. However, there may be situations in our data analysis where we need to get calculations from our data model without using a PivotTable. Cube functions allow us to create flexible calculations to get or retrieve data from our data model so that we can have a more integrated and interactive dashboard.

This chapter covers the use of cube functions in Excel, which are a flexible alternative to calculations in your data model. The chapter will also cover the basics of cube functions and how to use them in your data model, as well as advanced techniques such as using dynamic array formulas and adding slicers to your cube formulas.

We will cover the following main topics:

- What are cube functions?
- When do we use cube formulas?
- Exploring cube functions in Microsoft Excel
- Spilling cube functions with dynamic array formulas

What are cube functions?

Cube functions are a set of advanced Excel functions that allow you to perform calculations and data analysis from your data model. These functions are designed to work with a data model that is based on a cube, which is a multi-dimensional representation of your data. Cube functions allow you to create flexible calculations and analyses from your data model and express them directly in cells in your worksheet without using PivotTables.

When do we use cube formulas?

Cube formulas should be used when you need more flexibility in your calculations beyond what PivotTables give you. After creating measures, the only way to give expression to the measures in your worksheet is to create PivotTables and drag those measures into the VALUE section of the PivotTable. With cube formulas, your measures do not always have to sit in PivotTables. We can get the measures directly in cells from the data model and use them in calculations in our worksheet.

As an example, if I want to call or see the **Total Sales** measure we calculated earlier in a cell, we can use CUBEVALUE to retrieve this measure directly from the cube or data model. I used the word "retrieve" because these measures are already calculated and stored by dimensions and hierarchies in the cube. When we use cube formulas, we are essentially using a combination of expressions to retrieve a specific measure or dimension we need from the data model.

We can only use cube formulas in Excel when our data has a connection to a **SQL Server Analysis Services (SSAS)** data source or through a data model in Power Pivot. When we create a data model in Excel, we create an **online analytical processing (OLAP)** database. OLAP databases allow us to quickly analyze data from multiple sources and usually contain fact and dimension tables. We defined these tables in an earlier chapter.

When we create a PivotTable, it connects to the data model using a language called **Multidimensional Expressions (MDX)**. MDX is a query language for the OLAP database. You really don't need to know how to write MDX to get your calculations. All these happen in the background when you create your data model using Power Pivot and generate your summaries using PivotTables. The process looks like that shown in the following diagram:

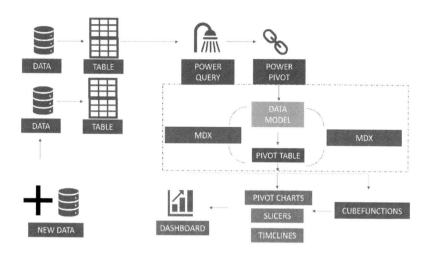

Figure 6.1 – The MDX query and the data model connection

When we create PivotTables from OLAP data models, it has some key differences from regular PivotTables:

- We are not able to drill down beyond 1,000 rows. In regular PivotTables, you can double-click on a value to drill down to see details of records that make up the value. This is limited in OLAP data models. You will normally see this expression (in the following screenshot) when you drill down:

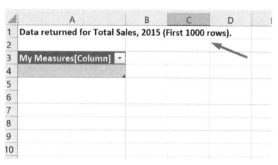

Figure 6.2 – Drilling down on data model PivotTables

- We are also unable to use the **Show Report Filter Pages** option. This feature in regular PivotTables allows you to create separate filtered reports based on the field you drag into the **Filter** section of your PivotTable.
- The menu to create calculated fields and calculated items is deactivated in the PivotTable settings:

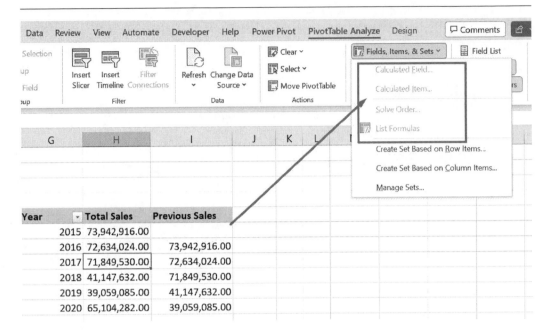

Figure 6.3 – Calculated fields and items in data model PivotTables

On the other side of the coin, there are features in data model PivotTables that are not present in regular PivotTables. These features offer us more flexibility in creating or getting calculations from the data model. The summary reports we get from regular PivotTables do not allow us to insert rows and columns. We can achieve this flexibility if we convert our PivotTable reports into cube formulas. The good thing about cube formulas is that they respond to slicers that you have in your report. So, without PivotTables, your calculations can still be sliced and filtered.

Cube formulas are particularly useful when working with large datasets, as they can handle a large amount of data and perform calculations quickly. Cube formulas are also useful when working with data that has multiple dimensions, such as time, location, product, and so on.

Let's look at an example. In our previous chapter, we created a summary PivotTable report that compared previous sales to current sales:

Year	Total Sales	Previous Sales
2015	73,942,916.00	
2016	72,634,024.00	73,942,916.00
2017	71,849,530.00	72,634,024.00
2018	41,147,632.00	71,849,530.00
2019	39,059,085.00	41,147,632.00
2020	65,104,282.00	39,059,085.00

Figure 6.4 – Inserting rows in PivotTables

If we wanted to insert a row after the first 3 years to calculate a subtotal, the structure of the PivotTable would not allow this. However, by converting this PivotTable report into cube formulas, we will be able to convert this "rigid" report into a "flexible" one that will still respond to our slicers and updates.

PivotTable reports that are created from the data model can be converted to cube formulas. To do this, select **PivotTable > PivotTable Analyze > OLAP Tools > Convert to Formulas**:

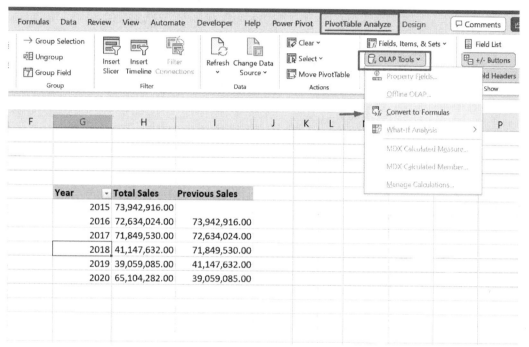

Figure 6.5 – Converting PivotTables to cube formulas

This now converts the PivotTable report into cube formulas.

We can now insert a row after 2017 and create a direct subtotal formula for the first 3 years, as shown next:

Year	Total Sales	Previous Sales
2015	73,942,916.00	
2016	72,634,024.00	73,942,916.00
2017	71,849,530.00	72,634,024.00
	=SUM(H8:H10)	
2018	41,147,632.00	71,849,530.00
2019	39,059,085.00	41,147,632.00
2020	65,104,282.00	39,059,085.00

Figure 6.6 – Calculating within your converted PivotTable

If we had inserted a slicer in this PivotTable before converting to cube formulas, the slicers would still be able to filter these sales numbers. We will look at this example later in the section.

You also realize that after converting the PivotTable report to cube formulas, we can see editable formulas in each cell now. This means we can directly write these formulas ourselves from the data model. This will also be covered in the next section as we explore some key cube functions in Excel.

Exploring cube functions in Microsoft Excel

There are currently seven cube functions in Excel. We will take a quick look at five of these functions and then proceed to create examples with each function. We will use the data model we created in our earlier chapter.

Of the seven cube functions, three of them are used often and serve as building blocks for the rest. These are CUBEVALUE, CUBESET, and CUBEMEMBER:

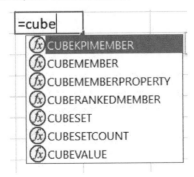

Figure 6.7 – List of cube functions in Microsoft Excel

The remaining are CUBERANKEDMEMBER, CUBESETCOUNT, CUBEMEMBERPROPERTY, and CUBEKPIMEMBER.

To help you understand how these cube functions work, it is important to know that all the functions work in a similar way by retrieving aggregated values or attributes from the data model, which we will refer to here as a cube.

Because of this, all the functions start with the same argument, `"ThisWorkbookDataModel"`:

Year	Total Sales	Previous Sales
2015	=CUBEVALUE("ThisWorkbookDataModel",$G8,H$7)	
2016	CUBEVALUE(**connection**, [member_expression1], [member_expression2], [member_expression3], ...)	
2017	71,849,530.00	72,634,024.00
	218,426,470.00	
2018	41,147,632.00	71,849,530.00
2019	39,059,085.00	41,147,632.00
2020	65,104,282.00	39,059,085.00

Figure 6.8 – Exploring the syntax of cube functions

To help us understand the application of cube functions, we will create measures for the following in our data model:

- Revenue

- Cost

- Profit

- Profit margin

After creating these measures, we will retrieve them from the data model using some of the aforementioned cube functions to create different reports. Let's start with our **Revenue** measure. This measure will be calculated by multiplying the quantity sold in the **Main Transaction** table by the unit price for each product in the **Product Data** table. We will also apply the discount rate in the **Main Transaction** table as well.

To create this measure, we go to the **Power Pivot** tab and click on **New Measure…**, as shown here:

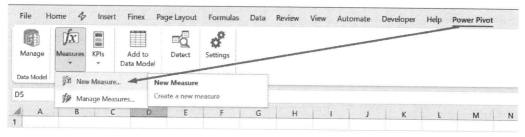

Figure 6.9 – Creating a new measure

This brings us to the **Measure** dialog box. In our previous chapter, we learned how to use this dialog box to create measures.

Our completed measure will look something like this:

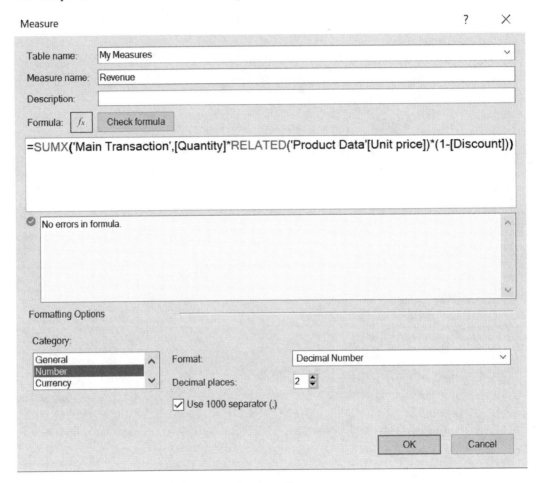

Figure 6.10 – Creating a Revenue measure

SUMX is the main function here that multiplies and sums the quantity sold in each transaction by the relative price from the product data. This price is then multiplied by the corresponding discount rate in each transaction to give us our total revenue.

We will repeat the same process for cost in calculating our next measure.

The completed Cost measure is shown next:

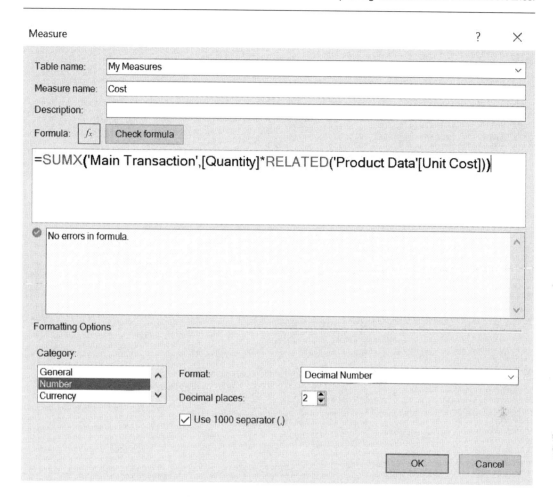

Figure 6.11 – Creating a Cost measure

This is similar to the **Revenue** measure we calculated previously but without the **Discount** column. The formula will give us our total cost by multiplying the unit cost for each product by the quantity sold.

Next is our **Profit** measure. This will be calculated by subtracting the total cost from the total revenue. The completed measure looks like this:

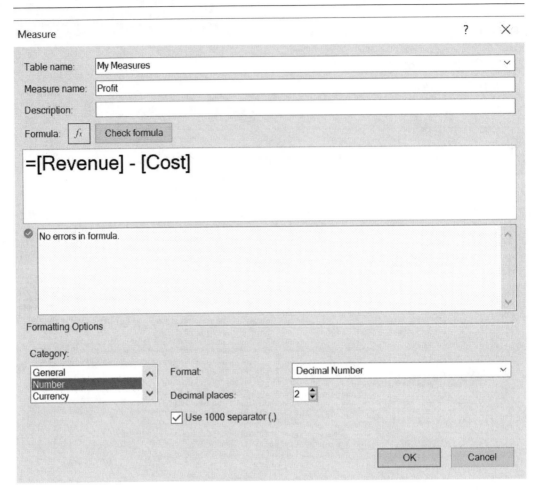

Figure 6.12 – Creating a Profit measure

We will complete this list of measures with our **Profit Margin** measure. The profit margin will be calculated by dividing profit by revenue.

We can use the DIVIDE function for this. This function is normally preferred when it comes to dividing numbers because it provides an argument to input a value when there is an error in the division.

The completed measure is shown next:

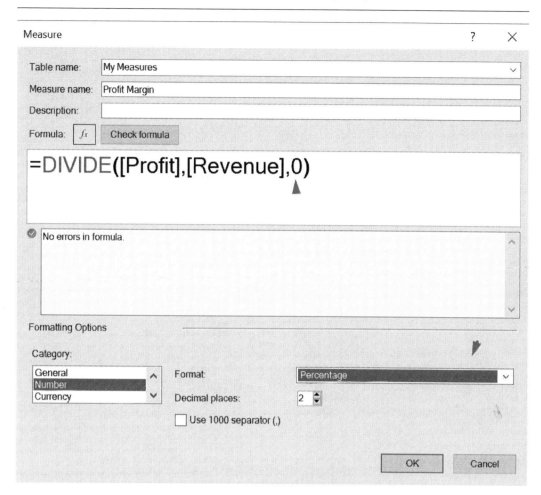

Figure 6.13 – Creating a Profit Margin measure

Note the use of the alternative result argument to return zero. This is important because you may end up with errors when there is no value for the denominator. Instead of returning an error, zero will be returned as an alternative result.

This measure has also been formatted as a percentage because we want to see **Profit Margin** show up in our final dashboard as a percentage value.

Now that we have calculated these four measures, let's apply our cube functions to retrieve them from our data model, starting with CUBEVALUE.

CUBEVALUE

The CUBEVALUE function is used to return an aggregated value from our data model based on a set of expressions:

Figure 6.14 – The syntax of the CUBEVALUE function

The arguments begin with the name of our connection, which is our data model. We will reference the data model with a starting double quotes, and this will bring up the default input ThisWorkbookDataModel, as shown next:

Figure 6.15 – Accessing the data model in a cube function

After we close our quotes, we can now proceed to pull or retrieve the measure or attribute we need from our data model using a structured reference.

As we indicated earlier, all measures are pre-calculated and stored in the data model, and by providing the right coordinates, we can retrieve our measures and filter them with a set of attributes or dimensions from our data model.

This is essentially how cube formulas work.

To retrieve our **Revenue** measure from our data model, we will add Measures as the first set of our expressions, as shown next:

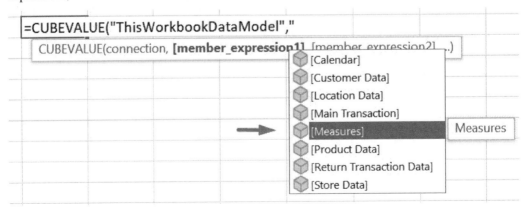

Figure 6.16 – Referencing your measure dimension in a cube function

`Measures` is stored here as part of the list of dimensions we can go into and retrieve values from our data model. In the preceding list, you see that all the tables we created in our data model are listed as "sides" of the cube.

If we go into any of these sides of the cube, we can drill down to get a specific item from the dimension by bringing in a dot (.). This is shown next:

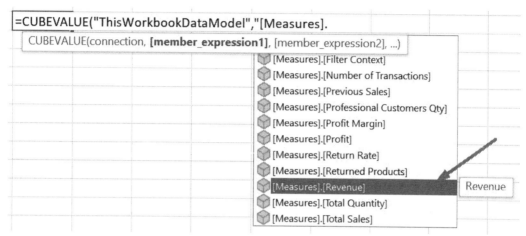

Figure 6.17 – Referencing your Revenue measure in a cube function

By selecting `[Measures] . [Revenue]`, we can now pull the **Revenue** measure we calculated earlier into a cell. Our completed formula looks like this:

Figure 6.18 – Referencing your complete Revenue measure using CUBEVALUE

We will use the same approach to retrieve the other measures we calculated –that is, **Cost**, **Profit**, and **Profit Margin**:

Measure	Value
Revenue	330,084,566.89
Cost	177,220,943.35
Profit	152,863,623.54
Profit Margin	46%

Figure 6.19 – List of measures created by the CUBEVALUE function

Our completed list of measures we retrieved using the CUBEVALUE function is shown in *Figure 6.18*.

We did this without a PivotTable.

We can proceed to filter these values by adding a slicer or an extra dimension to this formula using any of the dimension tables in our data model.

Let's add a slicer to filter these values by product category.

Adding slicers to your cube formulas

We can insert a slicer from the data model by going to **Insert** > **Slicer** > **Data Model**:

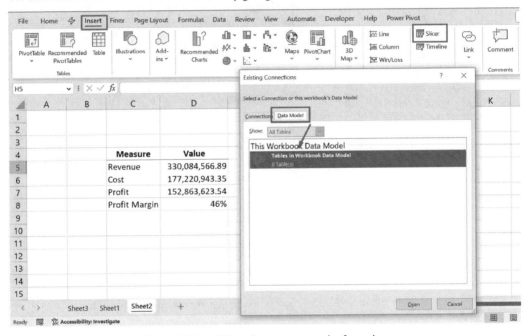

Figure 6.20 – Adding slicers to your cube formulas

This will open up the list of tables in our data model. We can now select **Category** from the **Product Data** table:

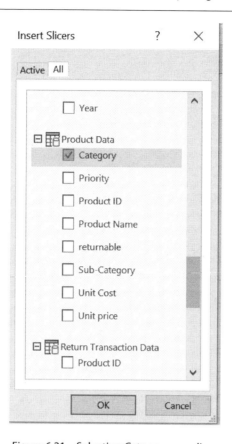

Figure 6.21 – Selecting Category as a slicer

This now inserts a slicer listing unique product categories:

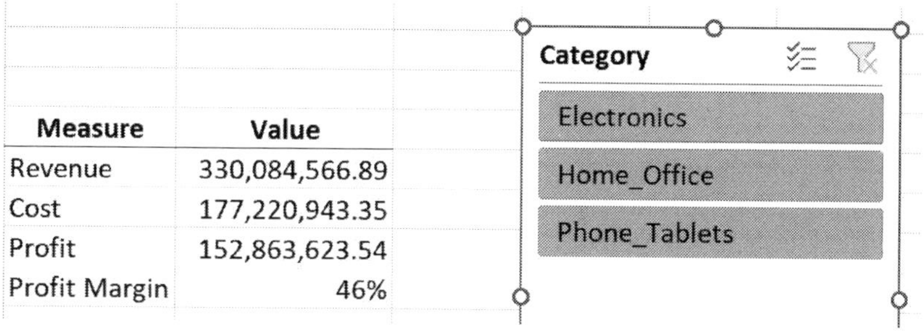

Measure	Value
Revenue	330,084,566.89
Cost	177,220,943.35
Profit	152,863,623.54
Profit Margin	46%

Category

- Electronics
- Home_Office
- Phone_Tablets

Figure 6.22 – Slicers to filter your cube formulas

We can now filter our values by adding the name of the slicer to our original CUBEVALUE formula. Names of slicers usually start with a Slicer prefix followed by the name of the attribute it was created from. So, the name of this slicer will be Slicer_Category.

This `Slicer_Category` slicer will be added as a second expression in our formula to filter our original measure. The formula is shown next:

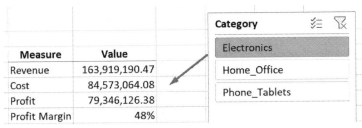

Measure	Value
Revenue	=CUBEVALUE("ThisWorkbookDataModel","[Measures].[Revenue]",Slicer_Category)
	CUBEVALUE(connection, [member_expression1], [member_expression2], [member_expression3], …)
Cost	
Profit	152,863,623.54
Profit Margin	46%

Figure 6.23 – Inserting the slicer name to filter your cube formulas

If we do these for the rest of the measures, our slicer is now able to filter these values when we select a particular category:

Measure	Value
Revenue	163,919,190.47
Cost	84,573,064.08
Profit	79,346,126.38
Profit Margin	48%

Category

Electronics

Home_Office

Phone_Tablets

Figure 6.24 – Clicking the slicer to filter your cube formulas

Let's explore more cube functions by looking at CUBEMEMBER.

CUBEMEMBER

A CUBEMEMBER function returns an item from a column in the tables in our data model. From our earlier example, we were able to use a slicer to drill down our measure by selecting a particular product category from the slicer.

If we wanted the revenue for a particular product category – for example, **Electronics**, we could use CUBEMEMBER to extract this value and then directly create our formula on this "member."

The syntax or argument for a CUBEMEMBER function begins with a reference to the data model followed by an expression to bring in the location of the particular item we need from our data model.

To get the **Electronics** category using CUBEMEMBER, our formula will be as follows:

=CUBEMEMBER("ThisWorkbookDataModel","[Product Data].[Category].[Electronics]")
CUBEMEMBER(connection, **member_expression**, [caption])

Figure 6.25 – The CUBEMEMBER syntax

You are already familiar with the first part of the formula. The second part of the formula, which has been highlighted, shows the path to **Electronics** in our data model. We start with the table name, which is **Product Data**, then drill down to the **Category** column, and then input the name of the item in our column, which is **Electronics**. This returns **Electronics** in the cell as a CUBEMEMBER function. With this, we can calculate the total revenue for electronics by referencing this result in a CUBEVALUE formula.

To calculate the total revenue for electronics, our formula will be this:

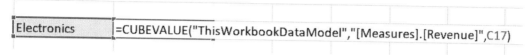

Figure 6.26 – Referencing a CUBEMEMBER function in a CUBEVALUE formula

By referencing this cell that contains the **Electronics** member in the CUBEVALUE formula, we get the same results we had from our earlier example when we used a slicer on **Electronics**:

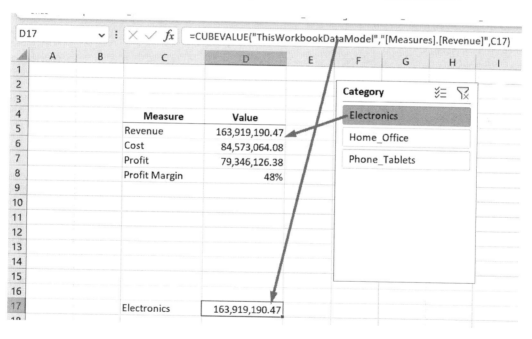

Figure 6.27 – Comparing formulas with and without the slicer

CUBESET

CUBESET represents the entire list of items in a column. It is a collection of **members**. If **Electronics** from our earlier example is a CUBEMEMBER, then the column it can be found in – that is, **Category** in the **Product Data** table – is a CUBESET.

We can use the CUBESET function to return and store all items in a column. We do this so that we can rank or spill the content of the CUBESET function in other calculations.

Let's look at how this works.

We want to create CUBESET formulas for the following columns:

- **Regions**
- **Product** sub-category
- **Months**

We will be using the content in each column to create visuals in our final dashboard.

The arguments for a CUBESET function require the following:

- Connection – This is a reference to the data model. We get this by typing "ThisWorkbookDataModel".
- Set expression – This will be a reference to the column that we want to create a set out of. The syntax is usually in this format [Table].[Column].children. This gives us access to all the items in that column.
- Caption – This is an optional input to give the set a name. If you don't provide this, the cell for the results will be blank but will still contain our results. It is advisable to give it a caption so that you clearly know which set you are calculating.
- Sort_order – This allows us to sort the items in the set in a particular order. There are six order options to choose from.
- Sort_by – This feature allows you to rank or sort items based on an existing measure. For example, you can order your **Product** categories by revenue. **Revenue** will be a measure in your data model.

Let's create our first CUBESET formula for regions.

The completed formula is shown here:

CUBESET	
=CUBESET("ThisWorkbookDataModel","[Location Data].[Region].children","Regions",2,"[Measures].[Revenue]")	
CUBESET(connection, **set_expression**, [caption], [sort_order], [sort_by])	

Figure 6.28 – The CUBESET syntax for region values

The main argument here is the reference to our **Location Data** table to get our **Regions** column. We add `children`, which is a native MDX syntax to bring a unique list of items into that column.

The next argument, `"Regions"`, is the caption we give to the formula. The `"2"` after `"Regions"` is the option for sorting the set of members in descending order. We want this sorted by revenue, so we add the **Revenue** measure as well. We calculated this measure earlier.

When you press *Enter*, you will only see **Region** in the cell. However, the formula contains 10 unique regions. We will learn how to count and extract these regions later.

Let's repeat the same process for **Month** and **Product** sub-categories:

=CUBESET("ThisWorkbookDataModel","[Calendar].[Month].children","Months")
CUBESET(connection, **set_expression**, [caption], [sort_order], [sort_by])

Figure 6.29 – The CUBESET syntax for month values

In this formula, we omitted the optional sorting arguments because our month list is already sorted by month values in the data model. We did this in an earlier chapter.

The final formula for returning a set of **Product** sub-categories is shown next:

=CUBESET("ThisWorkbookDataModel","[Product Data].[Sub-Category].children","Sub-Category",2,"[Measures].[Revenue]")
CUBESET(connection, set_expression, **[caption]**, [sort_order], [sort_by])

Figure 6.30 – The CUBESET syntax for sub-categories' values

We have now completed the list of sets we will be using in our final dashboard.

Now, let's move on to confirm how many items we have in each set. We will do this with another cube formula called CUBESETCOUNT.

CUBESETCOUNT

This formula simply counts the number of items in a CUBESET formula. It requires only one argument, and that is a reference to the set.

We can now proceed and count the number of items in each set. The first formula for returning the number of regions is shown next:

CUBESET	CUBESETCOUNT
Regions	=CUBESETCOUNT(C21)
Months	
Sub-Category	

Figure 6.31 – The CUBESETCOUNT syntax

Our previous CUBESET calculations have now been used as labels in the preceding screenshot. By referencing these sets, we now have a count of the list of items in each set:

CUBESET	CUBESETCOUNT
Regions	10
Months	12
Sub-Category	13

Figure 6.32 – Count of items in each cube set

This completes our CUBESETCOUNT formula. It will be useful to see all items in each set visibly displayed in our worksheet. We can retrieve these values using another cube function called CUBERANKEDMEMBER.

CUBERANKEDMEMBER

This function returns a single item from a set based on an ordered ranking. In simple terms, if we reference a set and provide a rank or position, the function returns the item in that position.

From our **Regions** CUBESET calculation, we can return the first region in the list using the following formula:

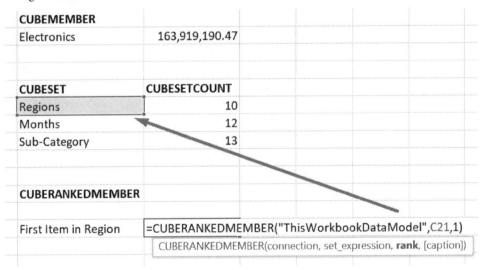

Figure 6.33 – The CUBERANKEDMEMBER syntax

This formula makes reference to the set that we calculated for **Regions** and returns **Northern**. **Northern** is ranked number one in terms of revenue, and that is why it shows up here.

In the same way, we can return the first items for **Month** and **Sub-Category**.

The full report is shown here:

CUBERANKEDMEMBER	
First Item in Region	Northern
First Month	January
First Sub-Category	Television

Figure 6.34 – Extracting first items from a list of cube sets

Beyond returning the first items in each set, we can combine CUBERANKEDMEMBER with a dynamic array formula, SEQUENCE, in Microsoft Excel to spill all the content in the cube set.

Let's explore this in the next section.

Spilling cube functions with dynamic array formulas

We have already calculated CUBESETCOUNT formulas that gave us the number of items in each set.

Excel's SEQUENCE function returns a sequence of numbers when you input the number of rows or columns required. We are going to use the results from our CUBESETSETCOUNT function to indicate the number of rows required. An example is shown next:

	X ✓ fx	=SEQUENCE(D21)							
	C		D	E	F	G	H	I
	CUBEMEMBER								
	Electronics		163,919,190.47						
	CUBESET		**CUBESETCOUNT**						
	Regions		10			⬅	=SEQUENCE(D21)		
	Months		12				2		
	Sub-Category		13				3		
							4		
							5		
	CUBERANKEDMEMBER						6		
							7		
	First Item in Region		Northern				8		
	First Month		January				9		
	First Sub-Category		Television				10		

Figure 6.35 – Using SEQUENCE to spill numbers

We take advantage of this spilling feature of SEQUENCE and input this formula into our CUBERANKEDMEMBER function so that instead of returning the *n*th item, it will return all the items in the set based on the numbers in the SEQUENCE formula.

Our completed formula to return all the items in the **Regions** column looks like this:

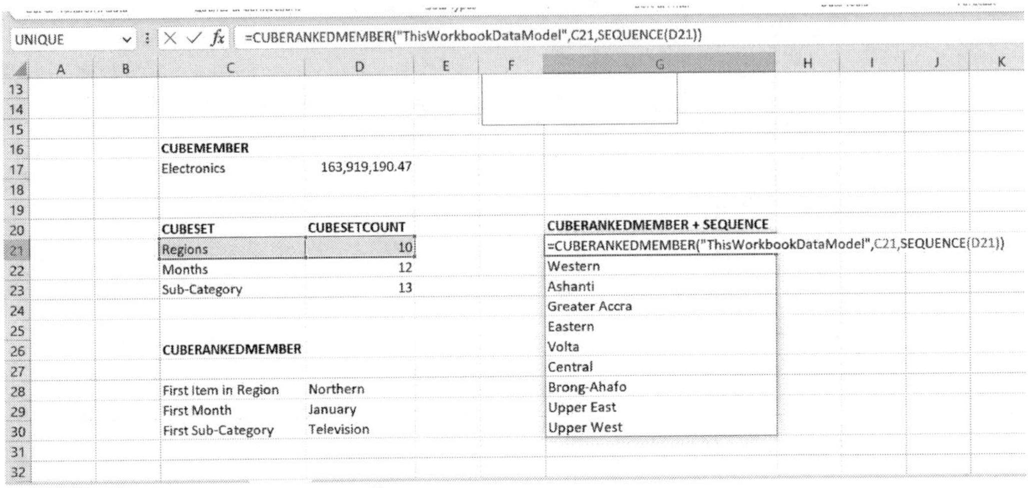

Figure 6.36 – Combining SEQUENCE with CUBERANKEDMEMBER to spill cube members

You now know how to create measures using DAX, create summary reports using PivotTables, and directly retrieve values from the data model using cube functions.

You will find out in the next chapter that mastering DAX measures, PivotTables, and cube functions gives you a wide range of options to create insightful and interactive dashboards in Microsoft Excel.

Summary

In this chapter, we explored a flexible option to bring or retrieve your measures from your data model using cube formulas. You know that cube formulas are a flexible way to create summary reports for your dashboards when PivotTables do not give you the flexibility you want.

In this chapter, we learned about the key differences between regular PivotTables and data model PivotTables and understood how an MDX query works to retrieve information from our data model.

We explored definitions and examples of five cube functions: CUBEVALUE, CUBEMEMBER, CUBESET, CUBESETCOUNT, and CUBERANKEDMEMBER, and how we can use them in our dashboards. You know now that it is possible to add dynamic array functions to cube functions to make your formula output more dynamic.

We will put all these together to create an interactive dashboard in the next chapter.

Part 3:
Putting it all together
with a Dashboard

This part is dedicated to teaching you how to effectively communicate insights from your data models by creating interactive and visually appealing dashboards. It covers the entire process, from conceptualization to deployment, ensuring that you can not only analyze your data but also present it in a meaningful and impactful way. *Section 3* will equip you with the knowledge and skills needed to transform your data models into compelling dashboards, thereby completing the data analysis and presentation loop in Excel.

This section has the following chapters:

- *Chapter 7, Communicating insights from your Data Model using Dashboards*
- *Chapter 8, Visualization Elements for your Dashboard*
- *Chapter 9, Choosing the right Design Themes*
- *Chapter 10, Publication and Deployment*

7

Communicating Insights from Your Data Model Using Dashboards – Overview and Uses

We have done a lot of data transformations and calculations in our previous chapters. It is now time to communicate insights to our users using dashboards in Excel. In today's data-driven world, the ability to effectively communicate insights derived from data analysis is crucial. Dashboards in Excel allow users to transform raw data into compelling visual representations, making it easier to convey complex information to various stakeholders.

This chapter covers the use of dashboards in Excel for communicating insights from your Data Model. Dashboards are a powerful tool for visualizing data and presenting insights in an easy-to-understand format. This chapter will discuss the basics of dashboards, including what they are and how they can be used. It will also cover important factors to consider when laying out your dashboard and common dashboard elements. In the next chapter, we will then apply these concepts to build our custom dashboard for this book.

We will cover the following main topics:

- What are dashboards?
- Factors to consider when laying out your dashboard
- Common dashboard elements
- Making your dashboard interactive

What are dashboards?

A dashboard is a visual representation of data that is designed to provide an overview of **key performance indicators** (**KPIs**) and other important information. Dashboards can be used to present data in a variety of formats, including charts, graphs, and tables. They are typically used to communicate insights from data to stakeholders, such as managers and executives, in an easy-to-understand format.

Dashboards in Excel are dynamic visual interfaces that consolidate and display key information in a concise and visually appealing manner. By leveraging Excel's extensive data manipulation capabilities and charting features, we can create interactive dashboards that enable the exploration and analysis of complex datasets. The primary objective of a dashboard is to provide a comprehensive overview of key metrics, trends, and patterns, enabling users to make informed decisions quickly. The following is a sample **Personal Finance Dashboard** to help a user compare **Actual** and **Budget** transactions:

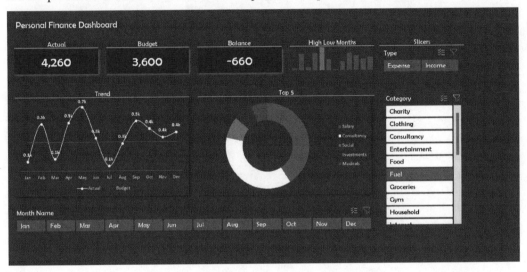

Figure 7.1 – Sample financial dashboard

At a glance, you can easily know how much was spent in **Actual** terms and compare this number with the budgeted values and the balance for the period. The dashboard also shows a trend chart that compares actual and budget values for the year displayed with a line chart. To the right is a doughnut chart showing the **Top 5** expenses or income items.

You will notice that apart from charts, there are other elements in this dashboard such as slicers, which help the user filter some of these indicators by **Category**, **Month**, and **Type**. Slicers make your dashboards interactive.

Apart from slicers, we have also used sparklines to highlight the high and low months within the period. This sparkline responds to slicer selections and will display the high and low months for expenses, income, category, and month. All these elements come together to help the user get insights into their personal finances. That is the objective of dashboards. We will be building a similar dashboard with our data in the next chapter. This chapter will help us lay a good foundation for this exercise.

Let's now look at some factors to consider when laying out and creating your dashboard.

Factors to consider when laying out your dashboard

Before we dive deep into creating our own dashboards, let's talk about various factors that may influence the choice of the elements on your dashboards.

When laying out your dashboard, there are several important factors to consider to ensure that it is effective in communicating insights from your data.

These factors include the following:

- The purpose and audience
- Clarity and simplicity
- Hierarchy and organization
- Consistency and visual harmony
- Interactivity and user controls
- Data visualization techniques
- Accessibility and documentation

Let's now explore these in detail.

Purpose and audience

Before designing your dashboard layout, clearly define its purpose and identify the target audience. Understand what insights or information the dashboard needs to communicate and who will be using it. Tailoring the layout to the specific needs and preferences of the audience will enhance the dashboard's relevance and usability.

The following is an example of an HR dashboard:

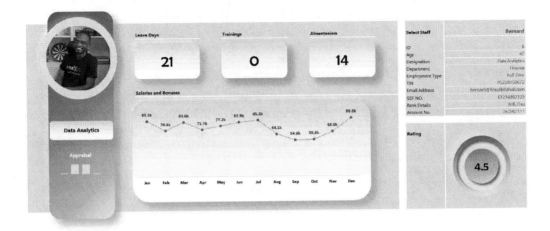

Figure 7.2 – Sample HR dashboard

It has been built with a typical HR manager in mind. The goal is to boldly display some of the key HR indicators that any HR manager can use to make strategic decisions on staff management. The dashboard displays an image of each staff member when the name of the staff member is selected and shows their bio details. There is also a prominent display of the rating of the staff member below the staff bio.

The dashboard also displays the **Appraisal** trend, leave days, and absent days for the selected staff member. At the heart of the dashboard is a trend of salaries and bonuses for the selected staff member. For an HR manager, this dashboard provides a lot of insights. You will notice that the choice of colors and the level of detail shown provide all the key insights an HR manager may need.

If you were to design this for a financial analyst, more details and indicators may be required. Starting your dashboard with an understanding of your audience and the purpose is a crucial first step because not all dashboards are the same.

Clarity and simplicity

A well-designed dashboard should be visually clear and easy to understand. Avoid cluttering the layout with excessive information or unnecessary visual elements. Use a clean and intuitive design, ensuring that the most critical insights are prominently displayed. Keep in mind that simplicity aids comprehension and facilitates efficient decision-making.

From the dashboards you have seen so far, you will notice that the choice of the elements of the dashboard makes it easy for the user to focus on the key indicators. Your average dashboard user is already overwhelmed with so much data, so it is easier if your design is clear and less noisy.

Hierarchy and organization

Organize the elements of your dashboard in a logical hierarchy to guide the user's attention and facilitate comprehension. Group related information together and use clear headings and titles to provide context. Arrange the visual elements in a structured and intuitive manner, ensuring that users can quickly locate the information they need.

Account	Actual	Budget	Spent	Status	Jan	Feb	Mar	Apr	May	Jun	Jul	Aug	Sep	Oct	Nov	Dec
Revenue	14,914,931	16,894,800	88%	●	2,343,596	7,106,193	650,169	441,284	1,947,291	1,559,325	610,987	2,237,241	522,984	1,628,078	464,061	442,152
Cost of Sales	6,960,035	7,802,400	89%	●	85,935	167,773	254,227	341,450	429,625	520,483	609,861	701,747	807,630	905,187	1,013,206	1,123,709
Commissions	156,000	156,000	100%	●	2,000	4,000	6,000	8,000	10,000	12,000	14,000	16,000	18,000	20,000	22,000	24,000
Conferences	986,655	1,014,000	97%	●	10,000	34,800	45,820	56,320	67,170	78,570	89,070	99,520	109,760	120,340	131,543	143,643
Training	21,304	31,700	68%	●			3,087	1,087	1,087	1,087	2,217	2,217	2,217	2,217	-4,043	4,043
Employee Benefits	7,560	7,800	97%	●	80	180	280	380	480	580	680	780	880	980	1,080	1,180
Equipment	108,400	234,000	46%	○			5,000	5,000	5,000	9,000	9,000	9,000	12,850	12,850	27,850	
Marketing Materials	29,299	39,000	75%	●		2,174	2,174	2,174	2,174	2,174	2,174	2,913	2,913	3,477	3,477	3,477
Office Supplies	20,000	15,600	128%	●					2,500	2,500	2,500	2,500	2,500	2,500	2,500	2,500
Professional Services																
Rent	600,000	273,000	220%	●	50,000	50,000	50,000	50,000	50,000	50,000	50,000	50,000	50,000	50,000	50,000	50,000
Subscriptions	41,600	44,000	95%	●					5,200	5,200	5,200	5,200	5,200	5,200	5,200	5,200
Vehicles	936,000	1,029,600	91%	●	12,000	24,000	36,000	48,000	60,000	72,000	84,000	96,000	108,000	120,000	132,000	144,000
Telephone	5,345	3,900	137%	●	419	419	419	419	419	419	419	419	419	524	524	524
Travel	32,913	6,000	565%	●								5,652	5,652	5,652	5,652	5,652
Utilities	17,574	23,400	75%	●			854	854	1,516	1,719	1,719	1,970	1,970	2,240	2,240	2,491
Salaries & Wages - Staff	3,418,200	3,720,600	92%	●	42,200	84,400	126,600	168,800	211,000	253,200	295,400	337,600	379,800	464,200	506,400	548,600

Figure 7.3 – Example Actual v Budget dashboard

Figure 7.3 is a typical financial dashboard. Financial dashboards normally display a lot of numbers. However, you realize that grouping elements together and using clear headings and titles makes it easy for the user to clearly understand the indicators.

Consistency and visual harmony

Maintain consistency in the design elements throughout the dashboard. Choose a cohesive color palette, font styles, and sizes that are visually pleasing and harmonize with your organization's branding, if applicable. Consistency enhances the dashboard's professional appearance and fosters a sense of coherence.

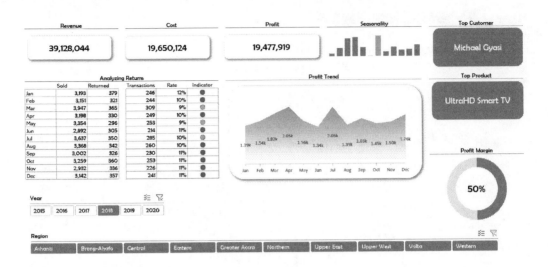

Figure 7.4 – Example Sales dashboard

In this dashboard, notice that the font type and colors have been deliberately chosen to harmonize the presentation. Simple elements such as the consistent use of font type, color, and effects can give your dashboard a clear presentation.

Interactivity and user controls

Integrate interactive features and user controls to enhance the usability of the dashboard. Utilize Excel's features, such as drop-down lists, checkboxes, and slicers, to enable users to filter and drill down into specific data subsets. Interactive controls empower users to explore the data and customize their viewing experience, increasing engagement and usefulness.

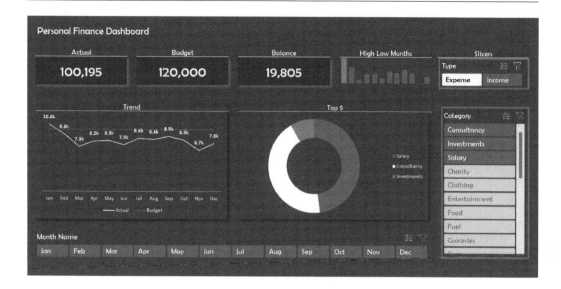

Figure 7.5 – Using slicers in your dashboard

In this dashboard, the slicers on the right can help your users drill down on specific **Expense** or **Income** categories. Adding slicers and other interactive elements provides an opportunity for your users to filter the elements in your dashboard for more insights.

Data visualization techniques

Select appropriate data visualization techniques that effectively represent the insights and trends you want to communicate. Choose the most suitable chart types, such as line charts, bar charts, or pie charts, based on the nature of your data and the key messages you want to convey. Use labels, legends, and tooltips to provide additional context and ensure clarity.

In Excel, you can use the data validation feature to explain some components or fields in your dashboard.

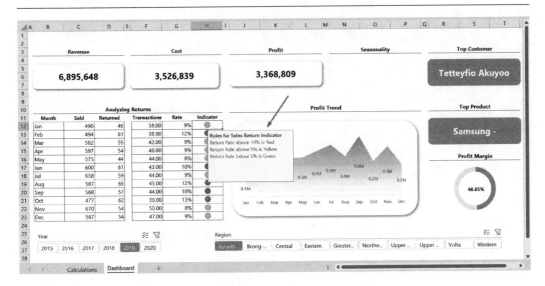

Figure 7.6 – Using tooltips in your dashboard

In *Figure 7.6*, we have used the data validation feature to provide some context for the icons in the indicator **field**.

You can do this by selecting the cell, going to **Data** > **Data Validation**, and typing the tip for your user in the following dialog box:

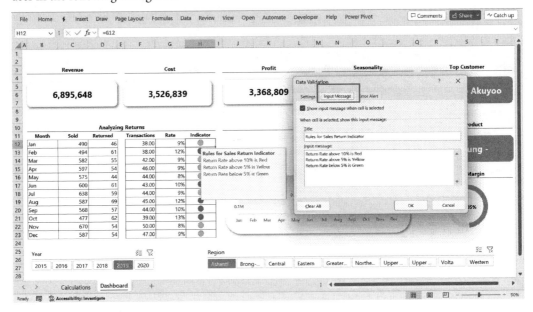

Figure 7.7 – Working with the Data Validation dashboard

When a user selects the cell, the message in the yellow box will appear and provide extra information on that component of your dashboard.

Accessibility and documentation

Consider accessibility requirements when designing your dashboard. Ensure that the layout adheres to accessibility standards, such as providing alternative text for images and using high-contrast color combinations for better readability. Additionally, document the dashboard's functionality, data sources, and any instructions or assumptions to help users understand and interpret the insights accurately.

A simple guide or notes to the dashboard can be helpful to you and your user:

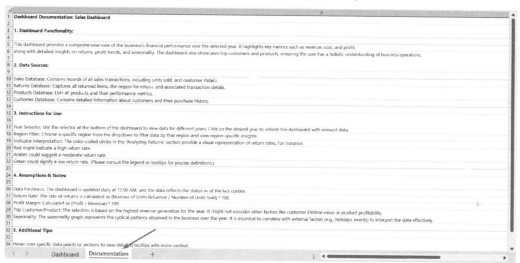

Figure 7.8 – Example documentation for a dashboard

By considering these factors when laying out your dashboard in Microsoft Excel, you can create a visually appealing, user-friendly, and impactful tool for effectively communicating insights from your Data Model.

Building on these factors, we can now explore some common dashboard elements that can be used as inputs to create insightful dashboards. Let's look at some of these elements in the next section.

Common dashboard elements

In Excel, creating a dashboard isn't just about presenting numbers. It's also about telling a story and making that story interactive and engaging. The dataset in our Data Model already contains valuable information on customers, products, stores, locations, sales, and returns. Think of each piece as a chapter of your story.

Let's dive into how you can use the dataset you already have to craft this story with some common dashboard elements.

PivotTables

PivotTables provide a powerful way to summarize and analyze large datasets dynamically. PivotTables are normally used to stage the summary reports that most of the charts in our dashboard are created on. This is very useful because if there are changes in your source data, the summary reports will also be updated after clicking on refresh. Most charts in your Excel dashboard will be driven by a PivotTable.

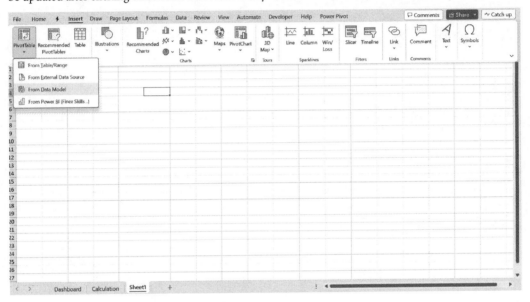

Figure 7.9 – Inserting a PivotTable from the Data Model

Let's build a simple PivotTable that shows total profit by store. If this is an indicator you want to visualize in your dashboard, then the journey begins with a PivotTable.

We go to **Insert** > **Pivotable**, and here we have the option to insert a PivotTable directly from our Data Model.

When we choose this option, we can insert a PivotTable in the same worksheet or in another worksheet.

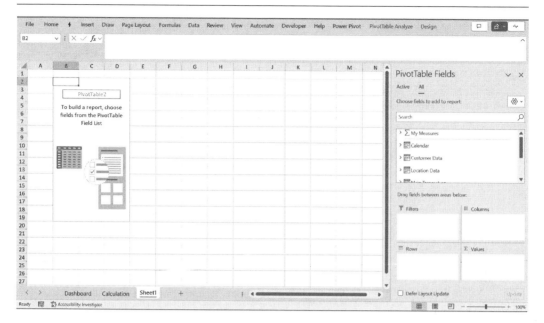

Figure 7.10 – Overview of the PivotTable fields

After we insert a PivotTable, we get access to **PivotTable Fields**, which lists all the tables in our Data Model and our measures at the top. With the different fields or columns in our tables and measures, we can create a summary table using the following areas:

- **Filters**
- **Columns**
- **Rows**
- **Values**

In a PivotTable, these terms are used to organize and analyze data from a spreadsheet or database in a structured way:

- **Rows**: The **Rows field** in a PivotTable determines how the data is organized vertically. When you place a **field** in the **Rows** area, it creates a unique list of values from that **field** and displays them as rows in the PivotTable. Each row represents a category or group based on the values in that **field**. For example, if you drag the **Category field** into the **Rows** area, each row will represent a different product category:

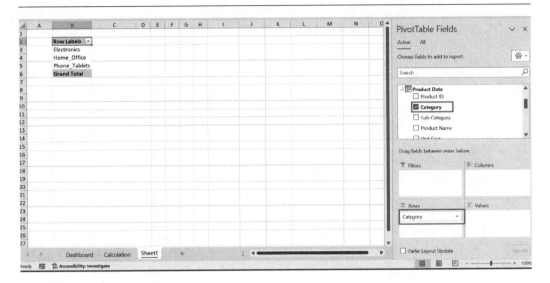

Figure 7.11 – Moving the Category **field** to Rows

- **Columns**: The **Columns field** in a PivotTable determines how the data is organized horizontally. Like the **Rows** area, when you place a **field** in the **Columns** area, it creates a unique list of values from that **field** and displays them as columns in the PivotTable. Each column represents a different category or group based on the values in that **field**. For example, if you have a **Year** field in the **Columns** area, each column will represent a different year.

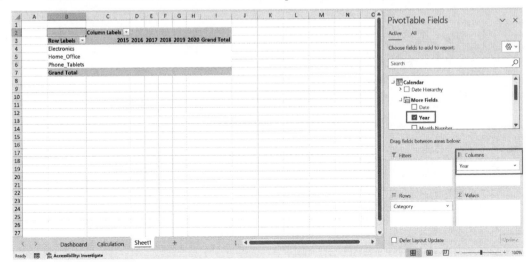

Figure 7.12 – Moving the Year **field** to Columns

- **Values**: The **Values field** in a PivotTable is where you specify the data you want to aggregate or analyze. This **field** typically contains numerical data that you want to perform calculations on, such as sums, averages, counts, or other mathematical operations. For example, if you want to see the total profit for each product sub-category, you will place the Profit measure in the **Values** area:

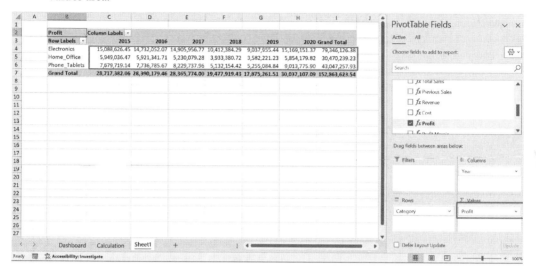

Figure 7.13 – Moving the Profit **field** to Values

- **Filters**: Filters allow you to narrow down the data displayed in your PivotTable based on specific criteria. You can add **field**s to the **Filters** area, and then you can select one or more values from those **field**s to filter the data.

    For dashboards, we normally use slicers instead of filters to do this. We will talk about slicers in a subsequent section.

    From this summary table, we can insert a chart that will be placed in our final dashboard. You may need to make some modifications such as taking off the Grand Total, as you don't want this to be part of your chart. There are many options and settings like this that you may want to consider as you work through customizing the design of your dashboard for your audience.

PivotTables are an integral part of the dashboard process. Let's build on this and insert a chart.

Charts

Charts are essential visual elements for presenting data in a concise and understandable manner. Excel offers a wide range of chart types, including column charts, line charts, pie charts, bar charts, scatter plots, and more. These visual representations help illustrate trends, comparisons, and patterns within the data.

Let's explore some common chart types and their appropriate use cases along with simple examples:

Chart type	Description	Practical use
Column chart	Displays data in vertical bars.	Comparing monthly sales for different products or showing returns per store.
Line chart	Shows trends over a series of points (usually time).	Showing monthly sales trends across the year or tracking product sales trajectory over time.
Pie Chart	Representing parts of a whole.	Displaying sales distributions of each product as a percentage of total sales.
Bar chart	Like a column chart, but the only difference is orientation. Bar charts plot with horizontal bars from left to right.	Comparing categories with long names, e.g., sales across stores with long names.
Area chart	Similar to a line chart but with the area below the line filled in.	Showing cumulative sales of a product over time.
Scatter plot	Plots two variables as points on a graph	Analyzing the relationship between two variables, e.g., advertising expenditure and sales revenue.
Doughnut chart	Similar to a pie chart but with a hole in the center.	Visualizing sales distributions across regions or product categories.
Radar/spider chart	Plots data points on axes that radiate out from a center point.	Assessing product performance based on attributes such as quality, price, and user reviews.
Combo chart	Combines two or more chart types into one. A common combination is a line and column chart.	Showing the number of products sold and average sale price over time on the same graph.
Histogram	Shows the distribution of a single variable.	Analyzing frequency distribution of sales values.
Waterfall chart	Shows the cumulative effect of a series of positive and negative values.	Representing inflows and outflows such as financial data.
Funnel	Shows progressively smaller stages in a process.	Showing data values with progressively decreasing proportions.

Figure 7.14 – Using the Recommended Charts feature

For the dataset we have, appropriate charts might be column, line, pie, bar, and scatter plots, given the nature of the data (sales, returns, products, etc.). However, you can be more creative and use other custom charts as long as they meet the end goal and clearly have a purpose. Apart from these charts, we can create a combo chart by combining more than one chart. Combo charts allow us to create cross-functional charts.

Let's create a chart out of this PivotTable by going through the following steps:

1. Stand in any cell in the PivotTable and navigate to **Insert** > **Recommended Charts**.

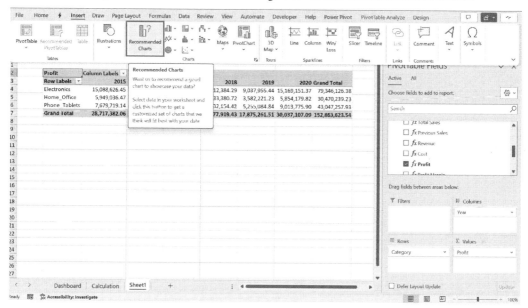

Figure 7.15 – Using the Recommended Charts feature

Using the **Recommended Chart** approach can help you choose an appropriate chart for your data. You will see all the different charts listed on the left side of the dialog box. From here, you can preview how your chart will look by clicking on any of the charts available.

2. We will select the **Column** chart.

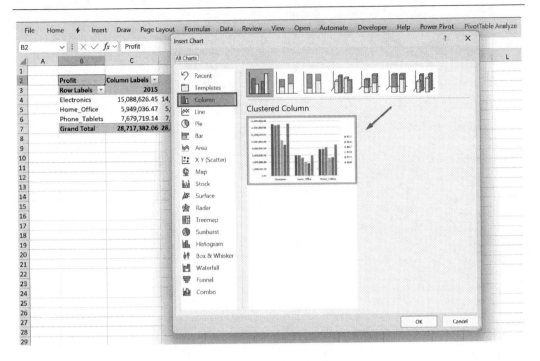

Figure 7.16 – Selecting the Column chart

This gives us the following chart:

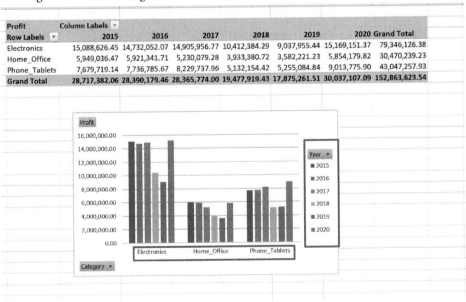

Figure 7.17 – Comparing the categories and series in the chart

3. You notice that there are six bars representing each year in our dataset plotted over three categories. This appears clumsy. However, we can switch things around by selecting the chart and going to **Design** > **Switch Row/Column**.

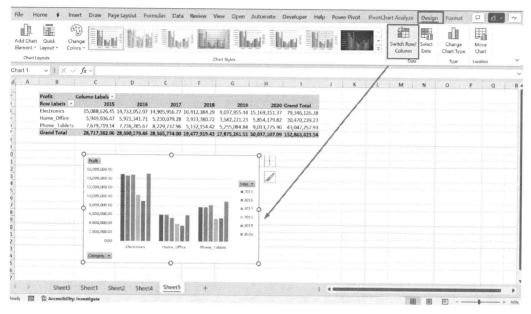

Figure 7.18 – Switching the categories and series in the chart

The resulting chart gives us the performance of the various product categories across the years:

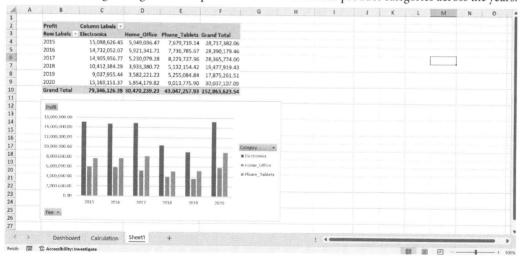

Figure 7.19 – Final column chart

We can now use this chart as one of the inputs of our dummy dashboard. You can insert a new worksheet and name it `Dashboard`. Afterward, you can cut and insert the chart into the new worksheet as follows:

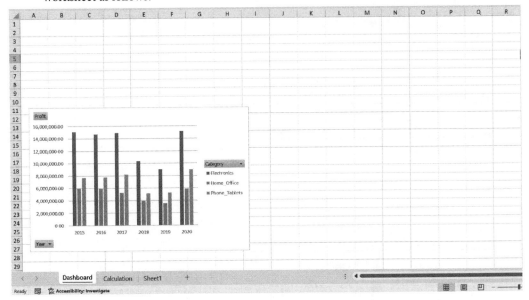

Figure 7.20 – Inserting the first chart into your dashboard

To practice, can you use the same process to create a PivotTable and insert a line chart in our dummy dashboard to show the total number of returns for each year? We created a measure for this named `Returned Products`. When you are done, your final chart should be placed to the right of our combo chart:

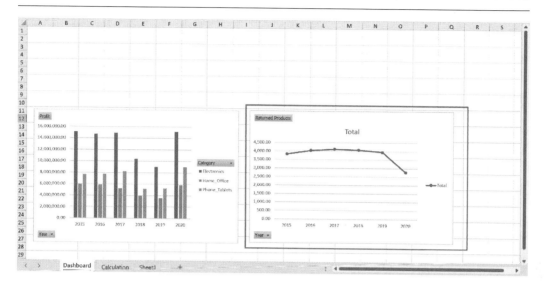

Figure 7.21 – Inserting a line chart in your dashboard

Here are a few points to help you go through this:

- Insert a new PivotTable from the Data Model and place it next to the current PivotTable. When creating multiple PivotTables in the same worksheet, it is important to anticipate situations where the column or row **fields** will have more unique items added to the source table in the future. For instance, we can have more product categories, and this will extend the current PivotTable downwards. If that is the case, you should place new PivotTables to the right and not below the current PivotTable.

  Best practice tip: The ideal situation will be to place new PivotTables in a new worksheet. We will discuss this again in the next chapter.

- The **fields** you will be using for the values and columns areas of the PivotTable are the Returned Products measure and Year from the calendar table.

- Afterward, insert a line chart on the PivotTable. Cut and place it in the dashboard.

Apart from charts and PivotTables, let's look at other elements in Excel we can use to create our dummy dashboard.

Text boxes and labels

These are your story's narrators. Text boxes and labels allow you to provide explanatory or descriptive text within the dashboard. You can use them to provide titles, headings, captions, or annotations that provide context and guide the users' understanding of the data presented.

For instance, a label above your returns trend chart can read Annual Returns Trend.

To insert a text label, go to **Insert** > **Text** > **Textbox** to select and draw the shape of the textbox. We will place this textbox on top of our trend chart. After you insert the textbox, you have the option to edit the textbox with the text you want as a label.

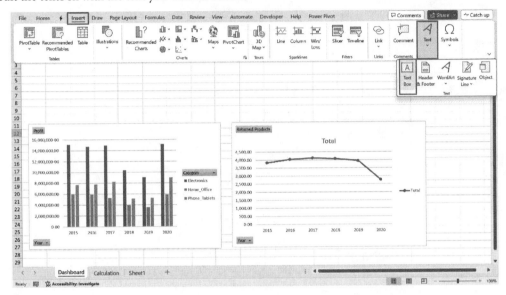

Figure 7.22 – Adding textboxes as captions

In the following screenshot, we have applied text labels to our charts to make it easier for our users to know the purpose of the charts:

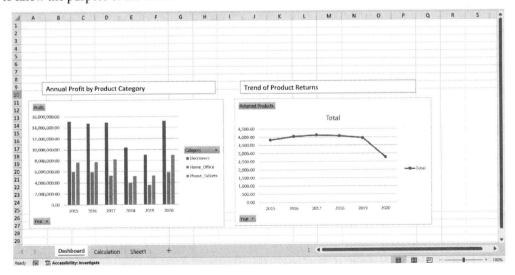

Figure 7.23 – Textboxes as captions in your dashboard

We will be discussing how to properly format these dashboard elements in the next chapter. For now, what is important is that you know where to find and apply these dashboard elements.

Images and shapes

Excel also supports the inclusion of images and shapes in dashboards. You can insert company logos, product images, icons, or illustrations to enhance the visual appeal and branding of the dashboard. Shapes, such as arrows, callouts, or boxes, can be used to draw attention to specific areas or highlight important information.

Apart from that, we can also use shapes to display key numbers in our dashboard. Shapes are similar to textboxes, but they have extra formatting features we can use to make our dashboards more elegant, such as rounded corners for rectangles, and gradient color fills and shadows.

Let's insert some shapes into our dummy dashboard to show total revenue, total cost, and total profit on top of our charts.

Navigate to **Insert** > **Illustrations** > **Shapes** > **Rectangle: Rounder Corners**.

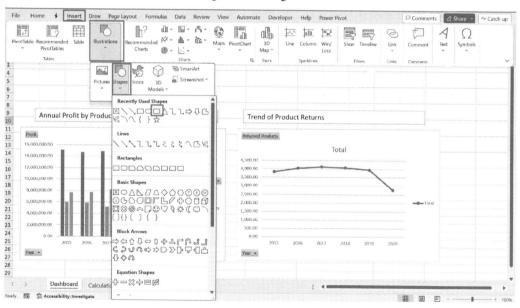

Figure 7.24 – Locating shapes

Select this shape and draw it on top of our Annual Profit chart:

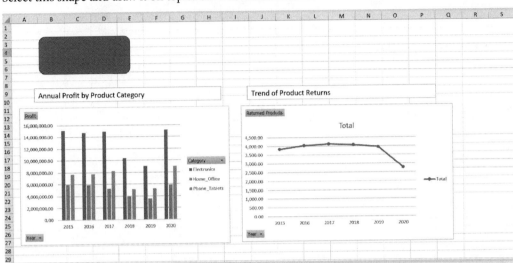

Figure 7.25 – Inserting shapes

We can now insert our total revenue measure in this shape. But first, we need a dedicated PivotTable that will host our total revenue measure.

As I mentioned earlier, most of the elements, especially the key numbers and charts in your dashboard, will be driven by supporting PivotTables.

Let's proceed and create a new PivotTable from the Data Model. Alternatively, you can copy and paste one of the existing PivotTables and modify the **field**s. Our new PivotTable will have only the Revenue measure in the **Values** section:

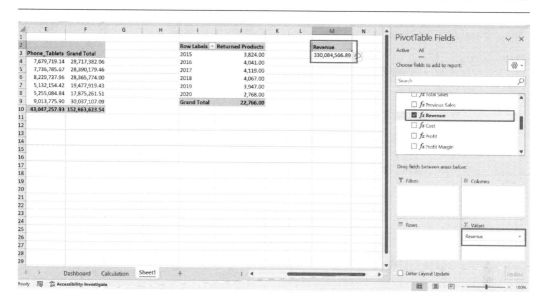

Figure 7.26 – Inserting the Revenue measure into the Values section

We can now reference this value in our shape in the dashboard. Before we do this, we must turn off the GETPIVOTDATA function in the PivotTable. This feature renders all references to PivotTable as GETPPIVOT formulas. These formulas cannot be referenced into shapes, so we need to turn the feature off to get a more direct reference to the cell.

We will get into the details in the next chapter when we design the dashboard for this case study.

To turn off this feature, go to **PivotTable** > **PivotTable Analyze** and then turn off **Generate GetPivotData**.

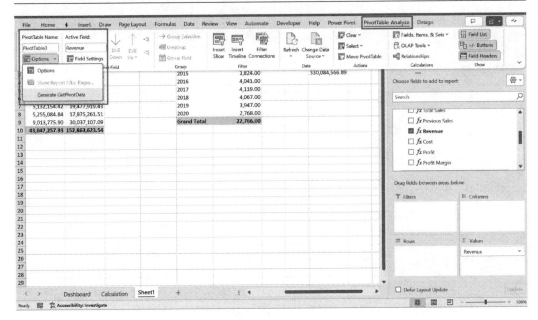

Figure 7.27 – Deactivating the GETPIVOTDATA feature

Now that we can select the shape in our dashboard, type an equals sign in the formula bar and then navigate to the sheet that contains our PivotTables and reference the Revenue measure in the PivotTable. Press *Enter* after selecting the value and you will get the number in the shape, as shown in *Figure 7.28*.

At this point, we can format the text to make it bigger, change the font color to white, and center align the text. In the next chapter, we will discuss how to use themes to make these formats easier.

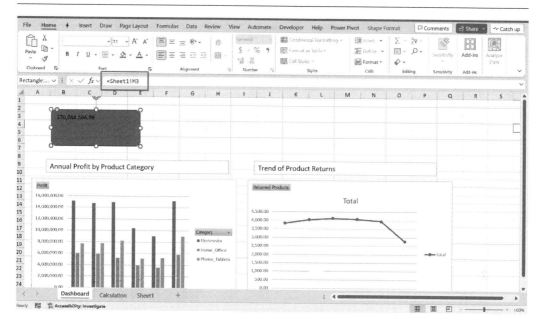

Figure 7.28 – Referencing the Revenue value

Our formatted text looks like that in the following screenshot:

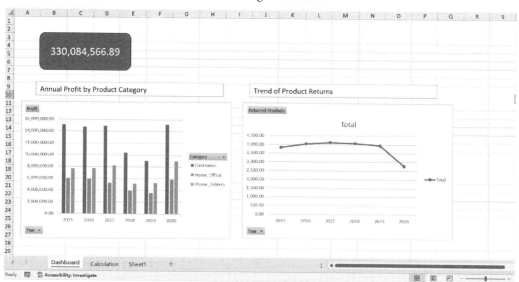

Figure 7.29 – Formatting the Revenue value

Practice

Repeat the process of displaying measures using shapes. Create two more shapes to display the cost and profit measures. After completing this task, your dashboard should be like this:

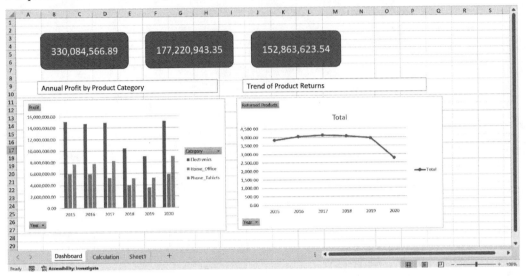

Figure 7.30 – Duplicating and creating two other shapes with values

Here are a few points to help you through this:

- You can duplicate the existing PivotTable that is currently showing Revenue by copying and pasting the PivotTable to the right

- Change the measure in the **Value** section of the duplicated PivotTables to Cost and Profit, respectively

- Afterward, you can also duplicate the current textbox for Revenue and use the referencing method we used earlier to reference your new measures: Cost and Profit

We will now proceed and add sparklines, another dashboard element, to our practice dashboard. But first, let's understand what they are.

Sparklines

Sparklines are compact, inline charts that provide a visual representation of trends or patterns within a specific data range. These mini charts are typically placed within cells and allow for quick data analysis at a glance. Excel supports different types of sparklines, such as line sparklines, column sparklines, and win/loss sparklines.

You can find **Sparklines** on the **Insert** tab:

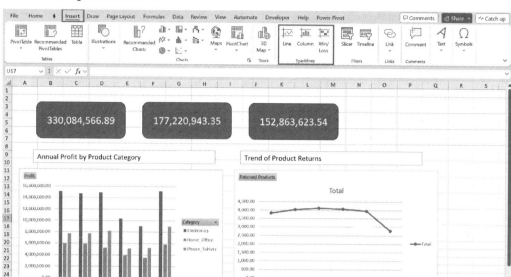

Figure 7.31 – Locating Sparklines

In our example, we can use sparklines to visualize sales, returns, or profit trends. As indicated earlier, sparklines are mini charts that are placed in cells. Consequently, we will need PivotTables to drive these charts. Let's now create a PivotTable that gives the trend of Annual Profit.

We can duplicate the Profit PivotTable and drag the Month **field** under our calendar to the **Rows** section to give us the following PivotTable:

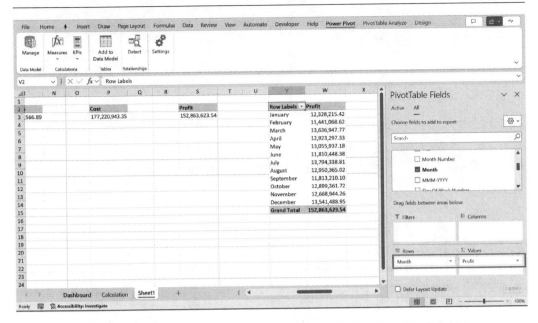

Figure 7.32 – Creating a PivotTable summary report with Month and Profit fields

We will plot the sparkline using only the values section. We will reference these numbers in another range of cells because sparklines cannot be inserted directly on PivotTables. Leave a blank column and reference the first value, which is the profit for January, and copy down.

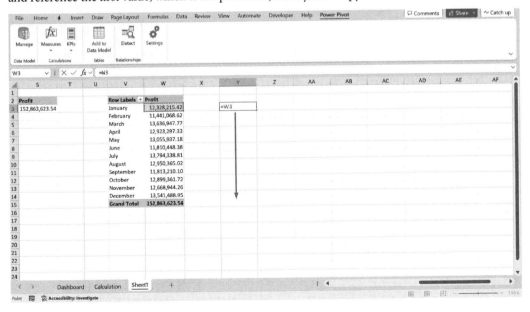

Figure 7.33 – Dragging down for values in mirrored range

After this, we can go back to our dashboard and select a cell we can use to insert the sparkline. In my case, I am inserting this from cell O3 and inserting a column sparkline:

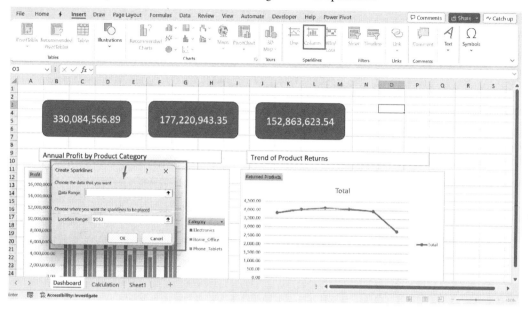

Figure 7.34 – Inserting the data range for your sparkline

In the **Data Range field**, select the up arrow icon and select the range that corresponds to the Profit values we referenced from the PivotTable. After pressing **OK**, you should see the sparkline appear in the cell you initiated the process from.

To enlarge the sparkline, we will highlight a wider range around the initial cell and merge the cells:

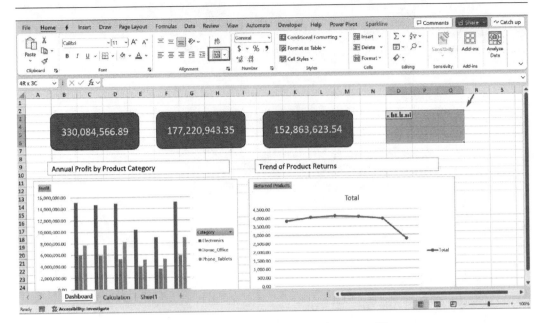

Figure 7.35 – Expanding the range of your sparkline

You should now see a clearer display of the sparkline:

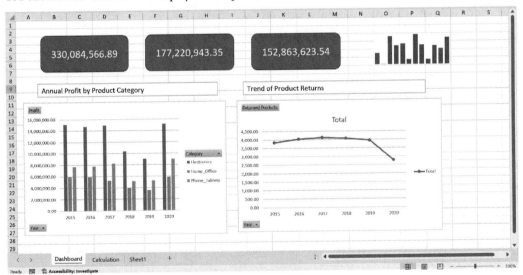

Figure 7.36 – Merging the range for your sparkline

Our practice dashboard is now taking shape. At this point, we can put some labels on top of these new elements in our dashboard using textboxes:

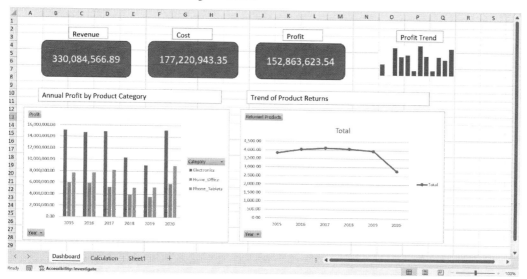

Figure 7.37 – Adding captions to your shapes

We will be discussing the most effective way to format all these elements in a later chapter. For now, the goal is to understand what these elements are and how we can use them to create an insightful dashboard for our users.

We will now look at other elements you can use for creating dashboards.

Conditional formatting

Conditional formatting allows you to highlight specific data based on predefined rules or conditions. It enables you to apply colors, data bars, icon sets, or color scales to cells or ranges, making it easier to identify trends, variances, or outliers within the data. Conditional formatting enhances the visual impact and emphasis on important data points.

You can find the option to apply conditional formatting on the **Home** tab in the **Styles** group.

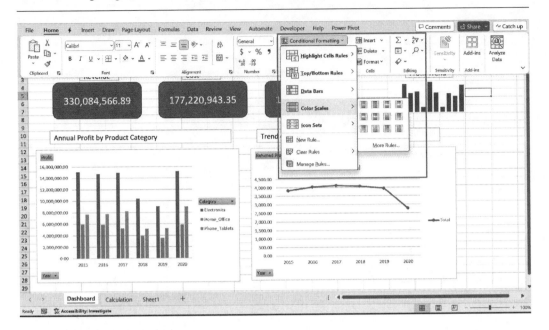

Conditional formatting is usually applied directly to values in a cell or a range. We will apply conditional formatting in our case study dashboard in the next chapter.

Making your dashboard interactive

While the elements described are very useful in creating dashboards, the key objective is to engage your reader. Your dashboards should have options for them to interact with the data, explore different scenarios, and come away with insights that matter to them.

Excel offers several features and techniques to make dashboards interactive. Here are some ways you can make your Excel dashboards interactive.

Slicers

Slicers are interactive controls that allow users to filter and slice the data displayed in a dashboard. By connecting slicers to tables or PivotTables, users can easily select specific data subsets or filter by various criteria, such as dates, categories, or regions. Slicers provide a user-friendly way to explore data and customize the dashboard's view.

Let's proceed to add a `Region` slicer to our dashboard. The objective is to make the user see the key indicators on the dashboard filtered by the selected region in the slicer.

You can insert slicers standing in any cell in the dashboard. Navigate to **Insert** > **Slicers**.

This opens a dialog box where you can switch to the Data Model to select the table that contains the particular **field** you want to insert the slicer from:

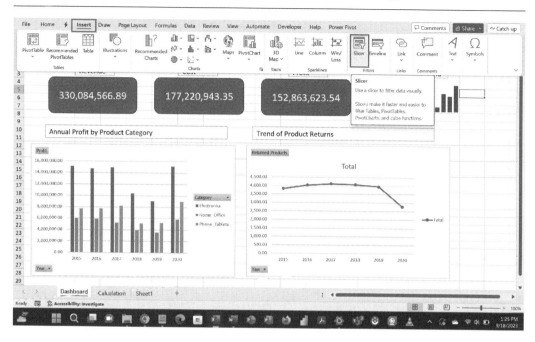

Figure 7.39 – Locating the Slicer feature

In our case, we will locate Location Data and select Region:

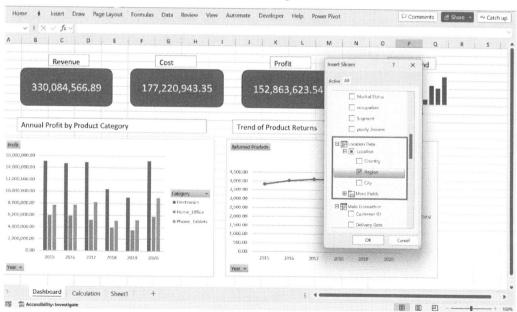

Figure 7.40 – Inserting a slicer from the Region **field**

This now brings up the slicer for `Region`, as shown:

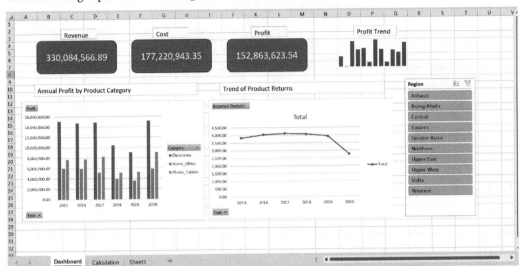

Figure 7.41 – Positioning your slicer in the dashboard

We have placed this on the right side of the dashboard to make it user-friendly. The placement and style of the slicers depend on the design of your dashboard. In the next chapter, we will learn different ways to style and customize your slicers.

Selecting any region from this slicer will not filter our indicators because the slicer is currently not connected to any of the PivotTables in our dashboard.

We can connect the slicer to the PivotTables by right-clicking on the slicer, going to **Report connections** and selecting the PivotTables we want to connect to the slicer.

Note that if you connect a slicer to a PivotTable in your dashboard, all charts and other visual elements connected to that PivotTable also get filtered.

This is what makes your dashboard interactive.

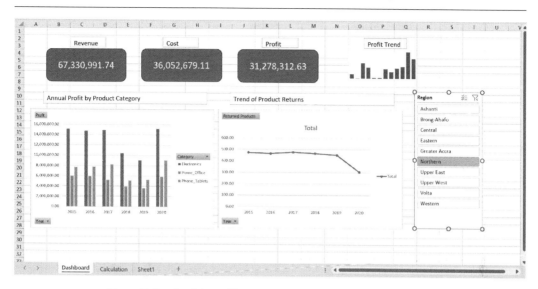

Figure 7.42 – Applying a filter to the dashboard by selecting a slicer

Apart from slicers, we can use other elements such as form controls, data validation, and hyperlinks to help our users interact with or navigate the different components in our dashboard.

Imagine a feature that allows you to display the profit for a selected year from a drop-down list in your dashboard. With a drop-down list, readers can pick a year and the dashboard will update automatically with the corresponding profit.

In Excel, you can insert a drop-down list by going to the **Data Validation** group on the **Data** tab.

Figure 7.43 – Locating the Data Validation feature

When you use drop-down lists in your dashboard, you need to write the required lookup formulas to retrieve the values you want from your calculations or PivotTable summaries.

As an example, let's create the drop-down list to allow the user to select a particular year and see the profit for that year.

To do this, we will need to create a PivotTable that creates a summary of Profit by Year. We can quickly create this by inserting a PivotTable from the Data Model and dragging Profit to **Values** and Year to **Rows**:

	A	B	C	D	E	F	G
1							
2							
3		Row Labels ▾	Profit				
4		2015	28,717,382.06				
5		2016	28,390,179.46				
6		2017	28,365,774.00				
7		2018	19,477,919.43				
8		2019	17,875,261.51				
9		2020	30,037,107.09				
10		Grand Total	19,477,919.43				
11							
12							
13							
14							
15							
16							
17							
18							
19							
20							

Figure 7.44 – Summary PivotTable report showing profit by year

As mentioned, because we want to do a lookup on this table, it will be good to ensure that the PivotTable is on a new sheet without any extra data below.

Our drop-down list of **Data Validation** is going to be placed on the dashboard, so we will select cell R2 and proceed to **Data** > **Data Validation**:

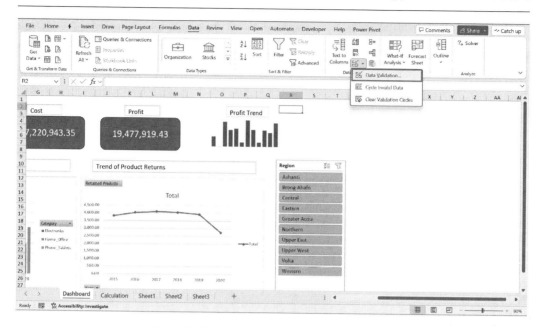

Figure 7.45 – Locating the data validation feature

This brings us to the **Data Validation** dialog box:

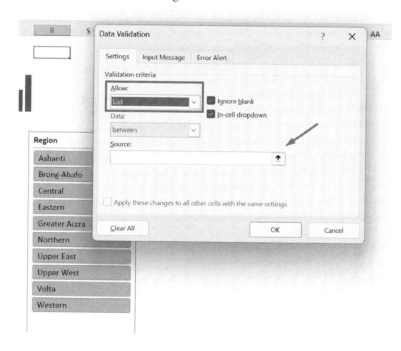

Figure 7.46 – Populating the Data Validation dialog box

We will select **List** and proceed to provide the data source for our list. We can select this from the unique number of years in the summary PivotTable we created or even type the years here separated by commas. You only type them if you do not expect your source list to change; otherwise, the ideal method is to select the range for the source data and the address will be shown in this **field**.

In this example, we will enter the six unique years in our data directly separating each year with a comma.

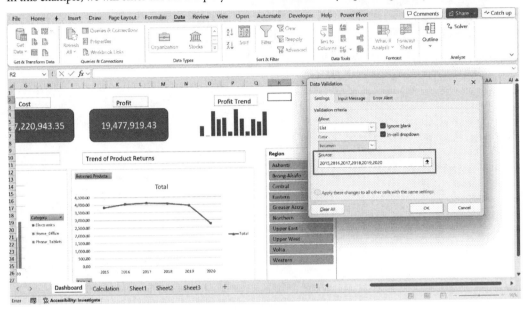

Figure 7.47 – Inputting the values for data in the Data Validation dialog box

This now gives us the unique list of years when we select the cells as follows:

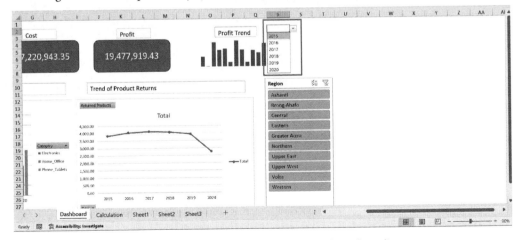

Figure 7.48 – Displaying the values in the drop-down list

We can select 2015 from the list as an example. Moving on to the next cell, we now need to calculate the corresponding profit for the year selected. We can do this using any of these lookup functions in Excel: VLOOKUP, INDEX + MATCH, or XLOOKUP.

While most people are familiar with VLOOKUP, it has a weakness that does not make it ideal for all lookup situations. For the purposes of this book, we will use INDEX + MATCH. XLOOKUP is a new function, and it is not available in all Excel versions.

Starting in cell S2, we will proceed with the INDEX + MATCH formula and calculate the profit for the selected year.

Before we do that, notice that our PivotTable is in Sheet3 and we have to do a cross-sheet reference for our formula. Our formula uses two functions and can be simplified as follow:

```
= INDEX(array, MATCH(lookup value, lookup array, match type))
```

INDEX requires an array, which represents the results we are looking for. In this case, it is the Profit values, which are in column C in Sheet3. When selecting column C in the formula, select the entire column so that if the PivotTable changes, you can still have all the values in the column as a reference. As indicated earlier, make sure there are no other values below the PivotTable.

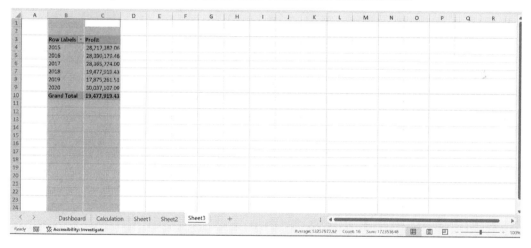

Figure 7.49 – Selecting columns for the INDEX + MATCH formula

MATCH requires a lookup value, which in our case is the year that has been selected. The reference for this is cell R2 in the dashboard. This will be followed by a LOOKUP array. The lookup array is the column that contains the list of years in our source data. This is in column B of Sheet3. We will select it the same way we selected column C earlier, selecting the entire column. Our final input is the match type. We will choose **Exact Match** to finish off the formula. Two brackets will be used to close INDEX + MATCH. Our final formula looks like this:

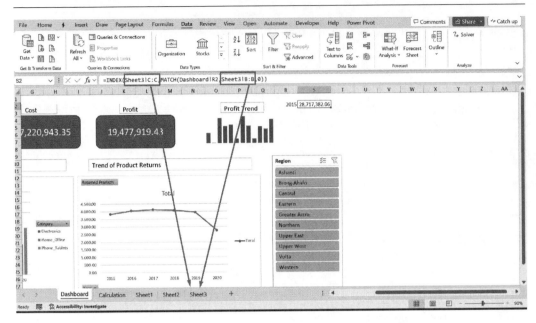

Figure 7.50 – Referencing cells from another sheet for your formula

Now any selection from the drop-down list will show the corresponding profit value. This is one simple example of how you can use a drop-down list or the data validation feature in your dashboard. There are other ways this feature can be used to offer your user more interaction with your dashboard.

Hyperlinks

Hyperlinks are used to link to a location in the same worksheet, a different worksheet, an entirely different Excel file, or even an external website or document.

Hyperlinks can be used in conjunction with shapes, charts, or images to create interactive elements on the dashboard. For example, clicking on a shape could take the user to a related section or report.

Let's try an example by inserting a **Click for details** button on our dashboard.

Insert any shape in the top-right corner of the dashboard. Right-click and insert the link. You can use the shortcut *Ctrl + K*.

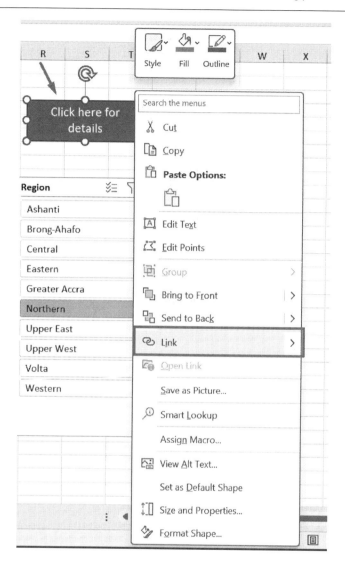

Figure 7.51 – Locating the hyperlink feature

If you're linking to a place in the current workbook, choose **Place in This Document**, then select the desired location.

If you're linking to another file, click **Existing File or Web Page** and browse to the file.

If you're linking to a website, enter the full URL in the **Address** box.

After setting up your link, click **OK** to create the hyperlink.

Your shape is now clickable and will navigate to the desired location when the user clicks on the shape.

Remember, when creating dashboards, it's essential to ensure that the links are intuitive and that the user knows where each link will take them. Using descriptive text or clear button labels can help with this.

As we close out this chapter, remember there are some other final touches you can apply to your dashboard to make it more user-friendly, e.g., taking off gridlines, aligning shapes and elements using mockups or wireframes, and using the appropriate theme.

When you take off gridlines, your dashboard appears cleaner and makes it easier for your users to focus on the important elements. You can take off gridlines by going to **View** > **Gridlines**:

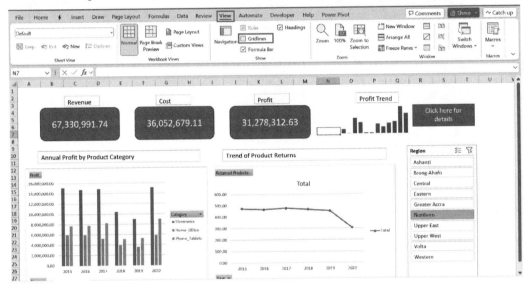

Figure 7.52 – Taking off gridlines from your worksheet

As you take off gridlines, identify all textboxes in your dashboard and turn off the borderlines as well.

One final concept you need to consider when creating dashboards is the use of mockups or wireframes. Using mockups allows you to properly plan and structure the elements in your dashboard. You can use simple borderlines to plan the use of space in your dashboard.

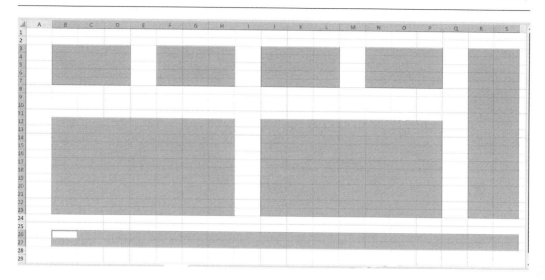

Figure 7.53 – Selecting ranges for mocking up your dashboard

We will begin the next chapter with a deep dive into these concepts.

As you build many dashboards in your career, you can take advantage of these elements to create insightful dashboards. The dummy dashboard we created is nothing close to the final dashboard we will create in the next chapter. We will learn how to format the elements properly, create themes, and use wireframes or mockups to make the dashboard more elegant.

What we have done in this chapter should give us a good foundation to build on in the next chapter.

Summary

In summary, this chapter discussed the use of dashboards in Excel for communicating insights from your Data Model. Dashboards are a powerful tool for visualizing data and presenting insights in an easy-to-understand format. The chapter covered the basics of dashboards, including what they are and how they can be used. It also covered important factors to consider when laying out your dashboard and common dashboard elements.

Finally, it discussed how to make your dashboard interactive to engage your audience. It's important to keep in mind that dashboards are only effective if they are well designed and easy to read and the audience and purpose of the dashboard are taken into account. In the next chapter, we will apply these elements to build the dashboard that will cap our learning in this book.

Visualization Elements for Your Dashboard – Slicers, PivotCharts, Conditional Formatting, and Shapes

In the previous chapter, we learned about the elements of a typical dashboard in Excel. In this chapter, we're rolling up our sleeves and diving into the real stuff. We're going hands-on, step by step, showing you exactly how to create those dashboard elements. And the cool part? We're using some of the calculations we created earlier, so it's like putting the pieces of a puzzle together. We'll walk you through the art of structuring your dashboard using mockups or wireframes. Plus, we'll show you how to add regular shapes that transform into cards – neat little containers to showcase the important numbers on your dashboard.

But we're not stopping there. We'll spice things up with sparklines and conditional formatting. It's like giving your dashboard a splash of color and style, making it more than just numbers and charts. And speaking of charts, get ready for a dash of creativity. We'll show you some tricks to make your charts, such as doughnut and area charts, look amazing with a bit of creative flair.

This chapter is packed with action. Let's dive in and create this amazing dashboard together.

We will cover the following main topics:

- Laying out your dashboard using mockups or wireframes
- Using shapes as cards in your dashboards
- Inserting conditional formatting and sparklines
- Adding and formatting charts
- Inserting slicers for interaction

Laying out your dashboard using mockups or wireframes

A dashboard is more than just a collection of numbers and graphs; it's a visual story waiting to be told. Each element on the canvas plays a vital role in weaving that narrative. A properly orchestrated layout ensures that these elements harmoniously coexist, allowing users to grasp insights swiftly, make informed decisions, and uncover hidden patterns. Imagine entering a well-organized library, where each book resides exactly where you expect it to be. You instinctively know where to find the desired piece of knowledge. In the same vein, the layout of your dashboard holds the key to ease and comprehension. A well-structured layout serves as a guiding path that leads your audience through a sea of information to a clear destination.

Our goal in this chapter is to create the following dashboard from the data we have analyzed in previous chapters. It all starts with properly laying out the elements of the dashboard using wireframes or mockups.

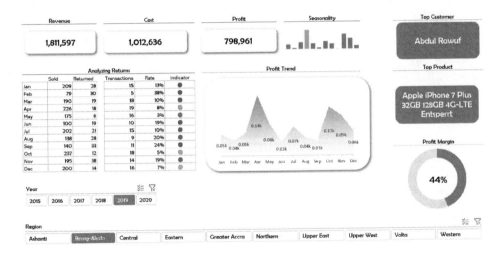

Figure 8.1 – Overview of the final dashboard

Enter mockups and wireframes

Think of mockups and wireframes as your blueprint, your compass in this creative journey. Using mockups provides you with the ability to visualize your dashboard's architecture before diving into the nitty-gritty of data visualization.

Imagine using a pencil to sketch the position of each element in your dashboard on a blank white paper. That is how mockups work, and we can achieve this using simple border lines.

Mockups allow you to tinker with, iterate, and perfect your layout without the constraints of data accuracy or technical intricacies. A mockup, akin to a sketch on an artist's canvas, outlines the grand strokes of your dashboard's design. It sets the stage for what will eventually become an insightful masterpiece.

Wireframes, on the other hand, delve deeper, mapping out the finer details – the placement of graphs, the alignment of labels, the positioning of filters – every element that contributes to the harmonious composition of your dashboard.

Practice your mockup in Excel

To get started, insert a new worksheet in your workbook. If you have practiced up to this stage, this new worksheet will sit in the same workbook as your calculations. In the end, your workbook should be made up of at least one calculation worksheet and another worksheet for your dashboard.

You can lay this out as follows:

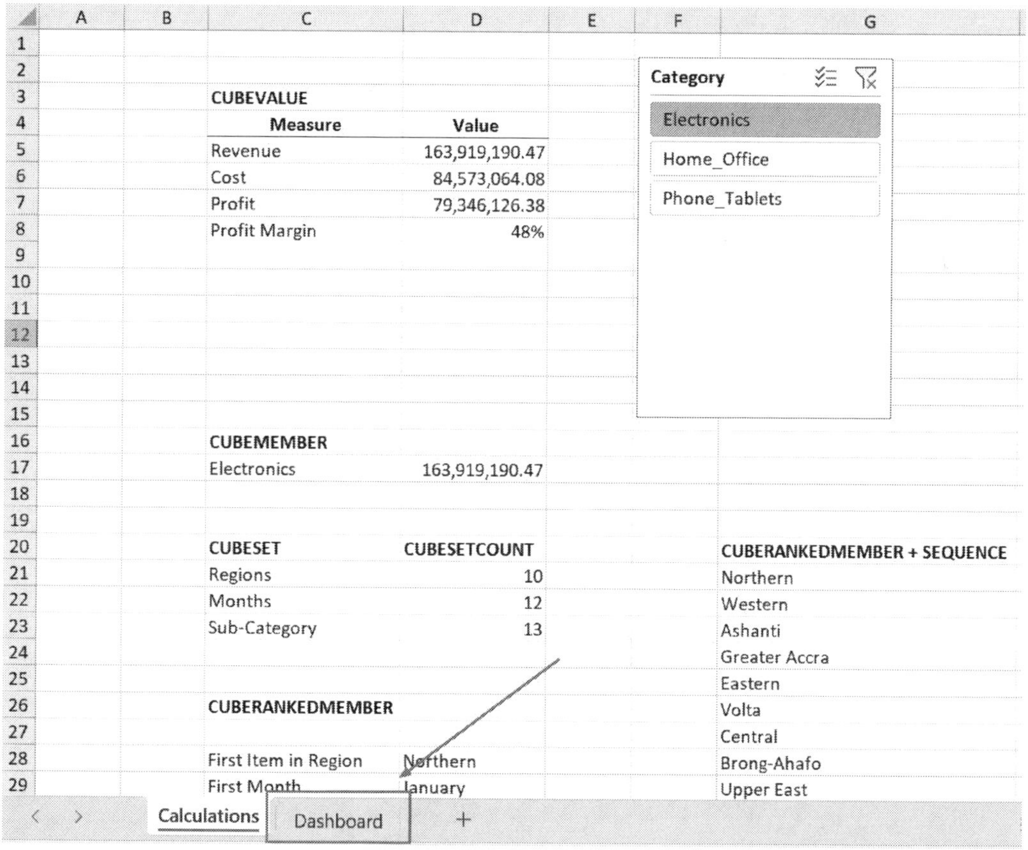

Figure 8.2 – Adding a new Dashboard sheet

You may already have some calculations from the previous chapters in the calculations worksheet. This should not be a problem. We will recalculate all the key indicators on the final dashboard. What is important here is that the workbook you are using contains the data model and transformed data from Power Query.

You can decide to keep your old calculations or delete them to make room for the new ones we will create for the final dashboard. All calculations will reference the data model.

Let's switch to the new **Dashboard** worksheet. This is expected to be blank with the default cell height and width.

One of the important elements of our mockup is to set margins. Setting margins makes it easier for your user to visually separate elements of the dashboard. In the following screenshot, I have highlighted the columns that will be used as margins in our dashboard. This can vary and will normally depend on the kind of design you want to use in your dashboard.

In the following screenshot, I have selected columns A, E, I, M, Q, and U. The width of these columns will be set to 2 to distinguish them from the other columns.

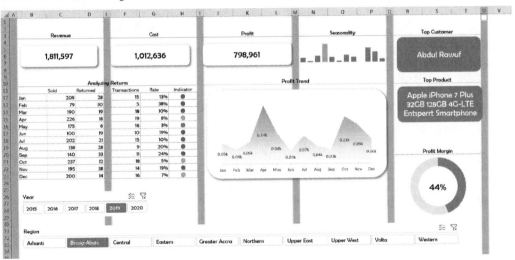

Figure 8.3 – Selecting margins in your dashboard

Let's apply this to our Dashboard workshee:.

1. We begin by selecting cell A1. Hold the *Ctrl* key and select cells A1, E1, I1, M1, O1, and U1. The *Ctrl* key allows you to select non-contiguous cells, that is, cells that are not next to each other. Your worksheet should look like this:

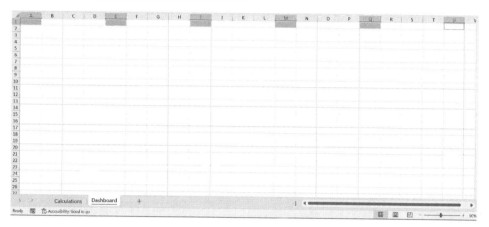

Figure 8.4 – Setting margins in your dashboard

While these cells are selected, we can now reduce the width of the column to 2.

2. You can do this by going to: **Home** > **Format** > **Column Width**. Alternatively, you can use the shortcut *Alt, H, O, W*. You press these keys one after another. You can also right-click to get access to this menu.

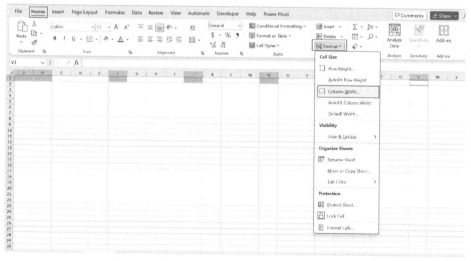

Figure 8.5 – Using column width to set your margins.

When the dialog box for the column width pops up, type 2 in the box and press *Enter*.

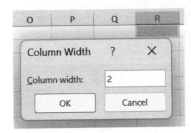

Figure 8.6 – Inserting a number for column width

This should reduce the width of the selected columns to 2.

We will repeat the same procedure for the columns we did not select earlier. However, we will set their width to 10. Select the following columns up to column Y and set the cell width to 10, as shown here:

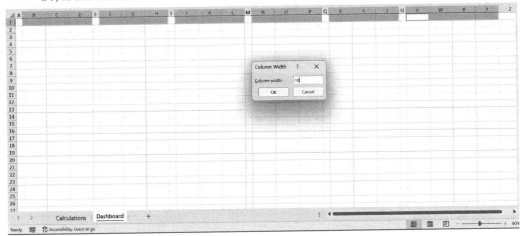

Figure 8.7 – Inserting a number for column width (repeat)

You should now have your columns ready for the mockup of the various sections of our dashboard.

3. We will do this by selecting the range in which we want to place all our indicators and apply outside borders to these selected ranges.

As an example, the first range to select is **B2:D4**.

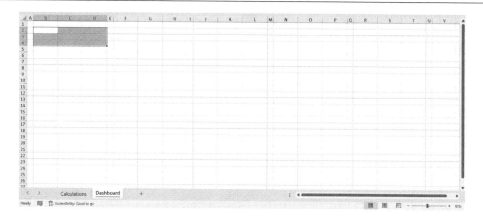

Figure 8.8 – Highlighting a range for drawing your mockup

4. With the selected range, we will proceed and apply an outside border line to the selected range. You can use the shortcut *Alt*, *H*, *B*, *S* (pressed one after another) or directly click with the mouse.

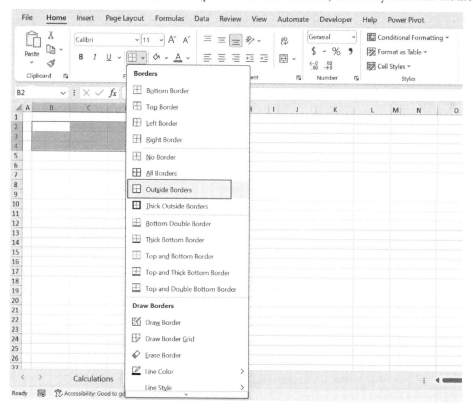

Figure 8.9 – Applying Outside Borders

We will repeat this process for the remaining ranges, as shown in the following screenshot:

Figure 8.10 – Applying Outside Borders to all selected ranges

If the last activity you did before this process was the application of the border line, you can press your *F4* key to repeat the application of the border lines after selecting each range. You can use this shortcut or proceed with the mouse.

As mentioned earlier, the mockup is supposed to be a flexible guide to help you put your dashboard together. It is an iterative process, so you can erase or adjust as you start designing your dashboard.

Using shapes as cards in your dashboards

After setting the stage with our mockup, we will now bring in the first element of our dashboard: a card that displays the calculations for revenue, cost, profit, and profit margin.

Before we proceed with this, let's quickly go over these calculations.

We will switch to the **Calculations** sheet.

The calculations for these metrics can be done using PivotTables or cube functions. Both options have advantages and disadvantages. Let's look at both options.

To use PivotTables, follow this process:

1. Select any cell, preferably cell B3.

2. Go to **Insert** > **PivotTable** > **Data Model**.

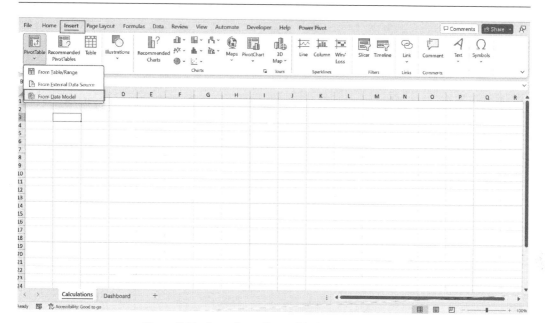

Figure 8.11 – Inserting a PivotTable from a data model

3. Choose **Existing Worksheet** in the dialog box that follows to insert the PivotTable directly in cell B3.

4. Go to the field list of the PivotTable and, under **My Measures**, check the box for **Revenue**, and this will be added to the **Values** section.

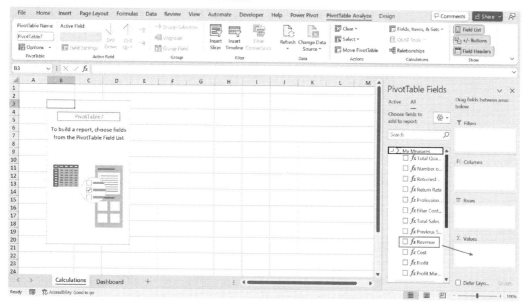

Figure 8.12 – Dragging measures to the Values section

This should give us the value as shown in the following screenshot.

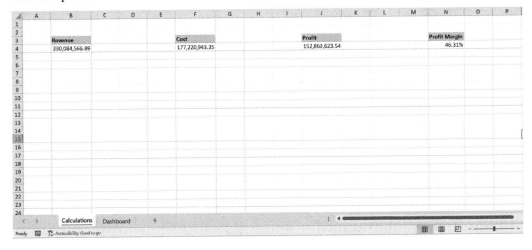

Figure 8.13 – A display of the Revenue measure in a cell

5.   You can then copy and paste the PivotTable to the right of the original version and replace **Revenue** with **Cost**.

When using multiple PivotTables, it is best to have them in different worksheets but if you have to host more than one PivotTable in the same worksheet, place them next to each other and not below. This style is useful if you are not using the **Columns** area of your PivotTable. Allow enough space to separate the PivotTables so that the PivotTable can easily expand if the data source changes.

Your complete set should look like this:

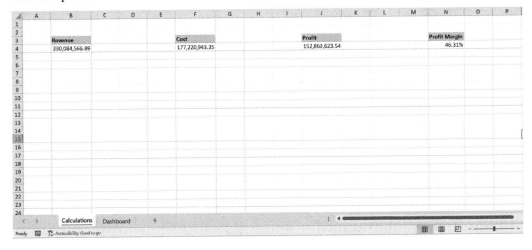

Figure 8.14 – Inserting other measures

We can calculate the same PivotTable values from the data model using cube functions.

Remember we used CUBEVALUE to do this earlier, in *Chapter 6*.

In cell B6, we can enter this formula to return **Revenue**:

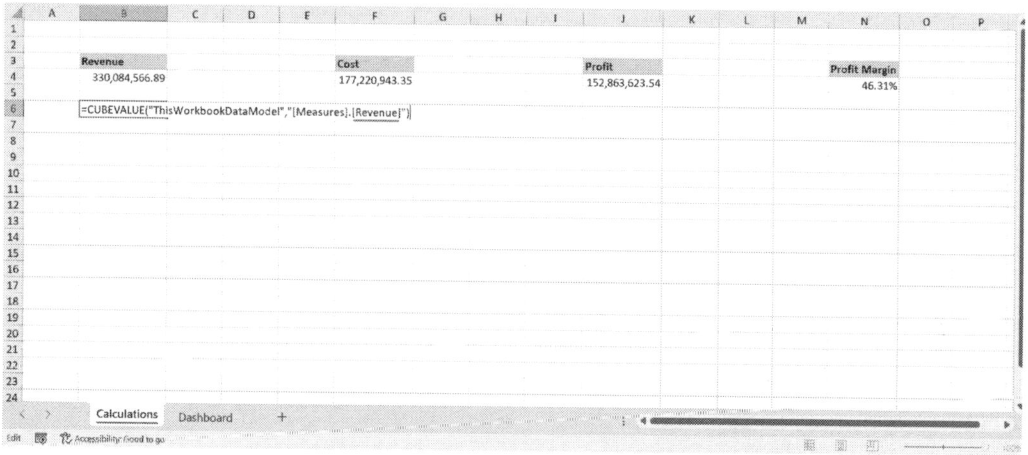

Figure 8.15 – Using the CUBEVALUE function to insert measures

The part of the formula that has been underlined is what will be replaced by Cost and Profit to give us the rest of the indicators. We can use either the PivotTable results or cube formulas for our dashboard input.

The advantage of using PivotTables for these calculations is that it is straightforward and requires you to just drag and drop the required field into the **Values** area of the PivotTable. However, for just a single value output from the PivotTable, it will be easier to use the CUBEVALUE formula than to insert an entire PivotTable.

Cube functions are just like regular functions. In situations where we require just a single value from the PivotTable, it may be easier to calculate it with cube functions. The disadvantage with this approach is that you'd have to remember to include slicer names in your calculations when creating the formulas. For now, we have not created any slicers yet, so these calculations should be fine.

The next thing to do is input these numbers into our dashboard. To do this, we will need to add shapes to the dashboard. We will use the mockup border lines as guides to draw our shapes.

The steps are as follows:

1. Go to the **Dashboard** sheet and click on **Insert** > **Illustrations** > **Shapes** > **Rectangle: Rounded Corners**.

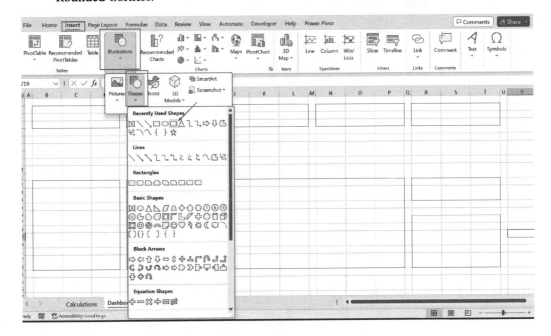

Figure 8.16 – Inserting shapes on your mockup areas

After selecting the shape, draw the rectangle on the range B2:D4. It is a good idea to hold the *Alt* key as you draw this so that it will easily snap to the cells.

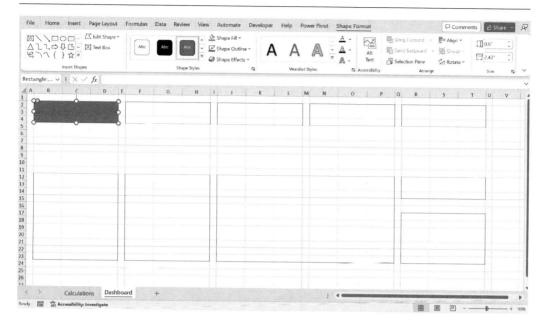

Figure 8.17 – Aligning shapes

2. We will proceed to format the shape as follows:

    I.   Select the shape and select **Shape Format.**

    II.   Fill the shape with **White**.

    III. Select **No Outline** for **Shape Outline**.

    IV.   Under **Shape Effects**, we will add an **Outer** shadow with a **Bottom Right** offset. We will maintain the default settings for the shadow.

    Now you can copy the shape and place it in the next two boxes for the mockups to the right. Do the same for the mockup range J12:P23 as well.

This is shown here:

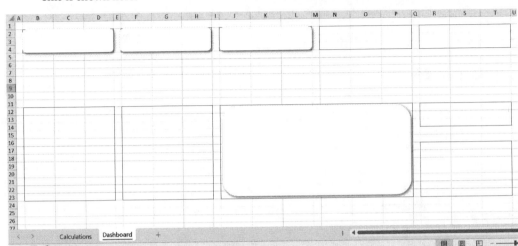

Figure 8.18 – Formatting and duplicating shapes

We will now insert the values we calculated for **Revenue**, **Cost**, and **Profit** in the first three boxes.

3. To insert the values, first select the shape and place an equals sign in the formula bar. You can select the values from the calculation sheet.

    If you are using the PivotTable values, you may encounter an error if GETPIVOTDATA is active for the PivotTable.

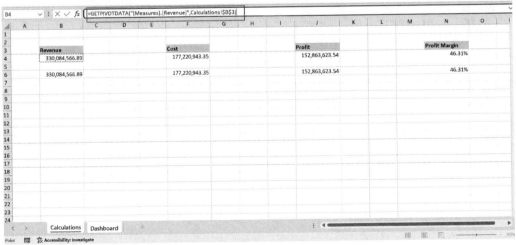

Figure 8.19 – Working with GETPIVOTDATA function

You may have to turn this off in the PivotTable settings before selecting the value.

4.   To do this, select the PivotTable and uncheck **Generate GetPivotData**.

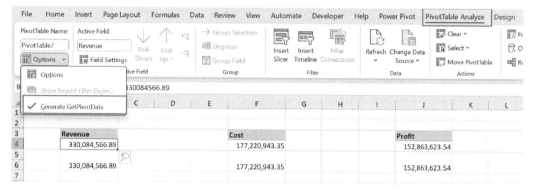

Figure 8.20   Unchecking the GETPIVOTDATA function

You can now select the first shape, which is for **Revenue**, and reference the revenue calculation in the calculations sheet. Do the same for the next two shapes for **Cost** and **Profit** by referencing their respective values in the calculation sheet. Center and middle align the value in the shape.

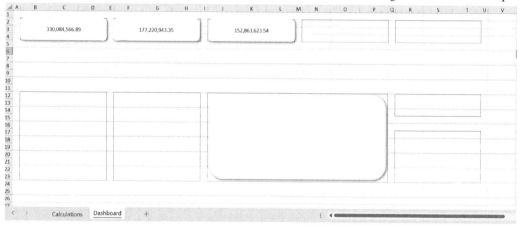

Figure 8.21 – Inserting measures in your shapes

The completed process should look like the preceding image.

Inserting conditional formatting and sparklines

In this section, we will learn how to add sparklines and conditional formatting to our dashboard.

Sparklines

In the previous chapter, we learned that sparklines are mini charts placed in single cells, each representing a row of data in your selection.

In our dashboard, we want to use a sparkline to determine the seasonality or pattern of revenue for our branches during the twelve months of the year. Instead of using a bulky chart, the sparkline will allow us to fit a mini 12-column chart in a selected cell.

To do this, we have to create the PivotTable that will provide the data.

We will insert a new PivotTable in the calculation sheet that will break down revenue by the months of the year using the following steps:

1. Select cell B10 of the Calculation sheet.

2. Go to **Insert** > **PivotTable** > **From Data Model** > **Existing Worksheet**.

3. Drag the **Revenue** measure to the **Values** section.

4. On the **Calendar** Table, go to **Data Hierarchy**, and drag **Month** to the **Rows** section.

You should get the following results from the PivotTable:

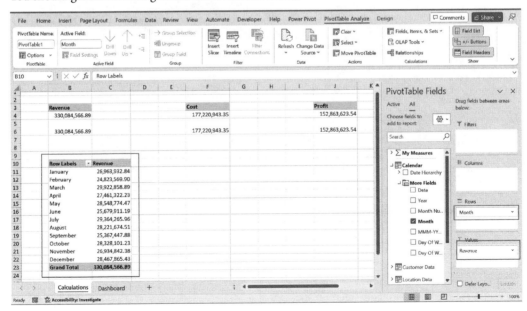

Figure 8.22 – Creating a summary PivotTable report on monthly revenue

From this PivotTable, we can create a sparkline. As of the time of writing this book, it is not possible to insert sparklines directly from PivotTable data. The workaround is to mirror the output in the PivotTable in a range of cells.

We can do this by referencing the entire data in the PivotTable into a range of cells.

To do this, follow these steps:

1. Select the range E11:F22.

2. Place an equals sign in E11 and then select the data from January to the last value for December in the PivotTable (B11:C22).

3. Press *Ctrl + Enter* to populate range E11:F22 with the PivotTable data.

The results should be as follows:

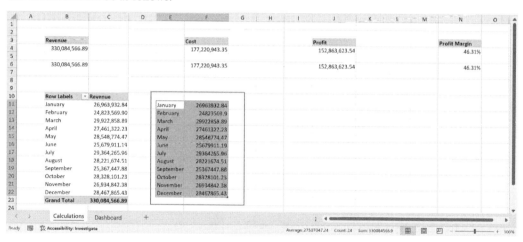

Figure 8.23 – Creating a mirror of formulas from the PivotTable report

The sparkline that will be inserted on this PivotTable will respond to slicers. To display all 12 months every time, go to **PivotTable** > **Display** and check the option to **Show items with no data on rows**, as shown here:

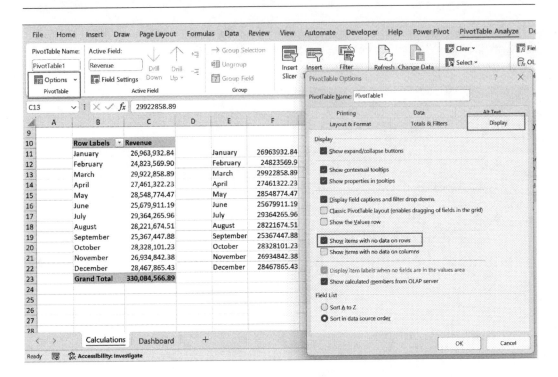

Figure 8.24 – Setting the display of the PivotTable to show all 12 months

If your version does not show this under **Display**, you can right-click on any of the month names in the **Pivot Table** > **Field Settings** > **Layout and Print** and you will find this setting there.

We will now insert our sparklines on this range using the following steps:

1. Go to the **Dashboard** sheet.

2. Click on cell N2.

3. Go to **Insert** > **Sparklines** > **Column.**

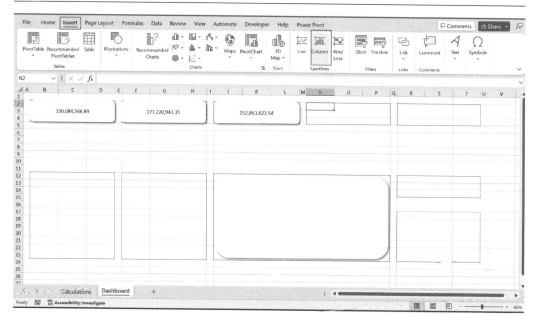

Figure 8.25 – Inserting sparklines

In the dialog box that pops up, select the values range for the mirrored data from the PivotTable in the Calculations sheet:

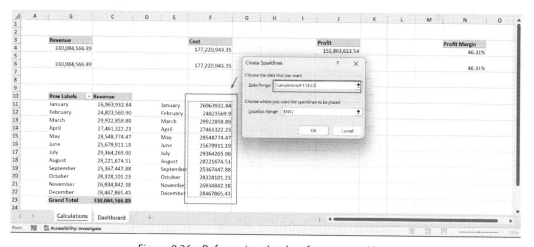

Figure 8.26 – Referencing the data for your sparklines

This should give you the sparkline in cell N2. Now, to make it show in the entire range we dedicated for the sparkline in the mockup, we have to merge the cells N2:P4.

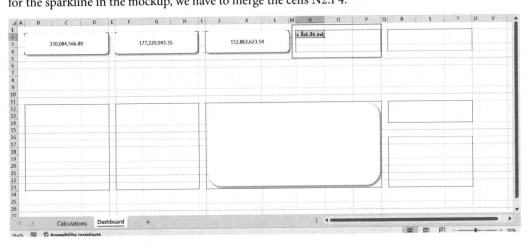

Figure 8.27 – Inserting your sparkline from your data

Select the range N2:P4 and merge them to make the bars appear bigger in that range. Your final sparkline should look like this:

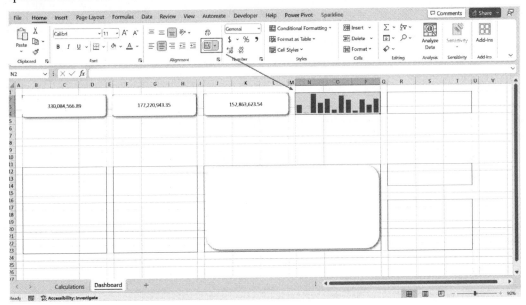

Figure 8.28 – Resizing your sparkline

In the next chapter, we will come back and format the sparkline to match the selected theme in our dashboard. Well done on coming this far!

Conditional formatting

We will now proceed and add our next visual to the dashboard, a conditional format that will help the user track return rate for selected shops and years. By now, you should know the pattern. All visuals that are displayed in the dashboard are driven by calculations from either the PivotTable or cube functions.

We will now create the PivotTable for this from the Calculations sheet. As indicated earlier, when you have to host multiple PivotTables in the same worksheet, it is advisable to place them next to each other so that the PivotTables can always expand vertically if the data source changes. This is when you are not using the **Columns** section of the PivotTable. The exception to the rule is when PivotTables return a single value. We really do not expect these PivotTables to expand vertically.

We will place this new PivotTable in cell J10 and go through the following steps:

1. Insert a PivotTable from the data model.

2. Place **Months** in the **Rows** section.

3. Drag the following measures to **Values** section: **Total Quantity**, **Returned Products**, **Number of Transactions**, and **Return Rate**. We calculated all these in the previous chapters, so they should be available in the list of measures.

Your completed PivotTable should look like this:

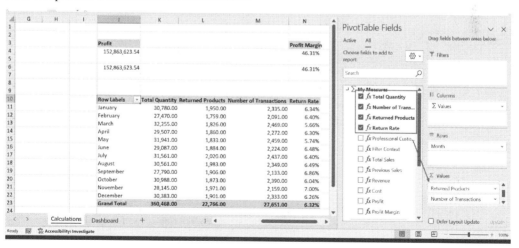

Figure 8.29 – Creating a PivotTable report on Monthly quantity sold and returns

You will notice that the values are displayed in comma-separated, two decimal-place format. We can always change this in the PivotTable. To format a number in a PivotTable, you can select a single cell in a particular field, right-click on the cell, and use **Number Format** to apply the right format. This approach ensures that the format stays in the field when the PivotTable is updated.

We can now use the numbers in the PivotTable to populate the dashboard using the following steps:

1. In cell B12, we will reference the list of month names with an equals sign and select the cell containing January in the PivotTable from the Calculations sheet. You can now drag this down to complete the list for the 12 months for that range.

2. The next cell, which is C12, will be populated with Total Quantity and Returned Products. Because these columns are next to each other, we can drag the month column we just populated in the dashboard to the right to fill up the cells in columns C and D.

3. We will skip the margin in column E and select F12. This cell will be filled with the Number of Transactions field from the PivotTable. You will copy this down for the cells below it as well.

4. Then, in G12, we will populate the cell with the return rate field. The numbers may appear as decimals. You can highlight the range of numbers and format as a percentage.

5. In H12, we will reference the values in G12. We are creating this duplicate to help us create our conditional format in column H.

Your completed work should look like this:

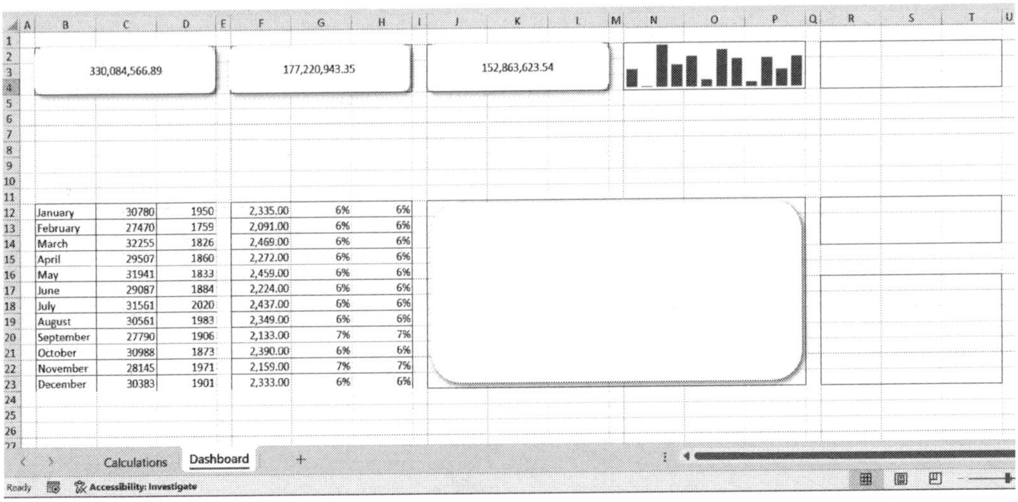

Figure 8.30 – Referencing your PivotTable in your dashboard

We will now add conditional formatting to show different indicators for the rate of return for the different months.

We will use the 3-traffic light icon sets with the following rules:

- A return rate of more than 10% should be displayed in red

- Less than 10% but more than 5% should be yellow, and less than 5% should be green

We can do this using the following steps:

1. Go to **Home** > **Conditional Formatting** > **New Rule**:

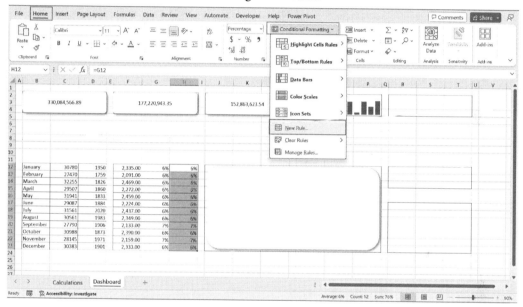

Figure 8.31 – Adding Conditional Formatting icon.

2. In the new rule dialog box, go through the following steps:

   I.   Select **Format all cells based on their values**.

   II. **Reverse icon order** to swap the arrangement of the icons. This will ensure that the first rule starts with the red circle.

   III. Select **Show Icon only** to only display the icons in the cells and not the values.

3. Then for our rule, input the following thresholds:

   - Red when the value is >=0.1

   - Yellow when the value is < 0.1 and >=0.05

   - Green when the value is < 0.05

4.   Select **Number** as **Type** for all the rules at each level.

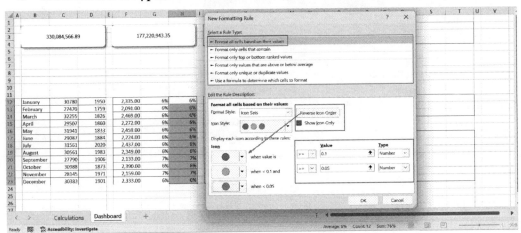

Figure 8.33 – Editing conditional formatting rules

After clicking **OK**, you will see the icons appear in the selected range in our dashboard. All the cells are yellow because no slicers have been introduced yet. These will be introduced in the next chapter, and the final dashboard will have different icon colors based on the inputs selected from the slicer.

We will format all these visual outputs in the next chapter. For now, the focus is on learning how to create and add these elements to your dashboard.

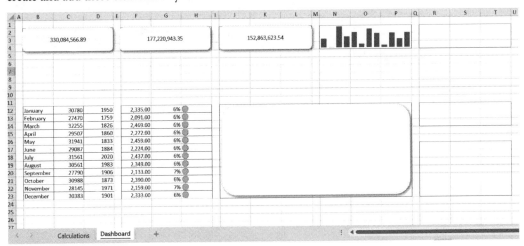

Figure 8.34 – Displaying conditional formatting icons

Adding and formatting charts

Next up are charts. In this dashboard, we are going to insert two popular charts. We will add some formats to enhance how they appear in our dashboard.

The first chart is the area chart. This chart falls into the group of charts that are useful for visualizing trends. We are going to use this chart to show the trend of profits for the period that we select.

We will go through these steps:

1. Create a PivotTable in the Calculations sheet in cell Q10.
2. Put **Months** in the **Row** section and the **Profit** measure in the **Values** section.

This should give us the following PivotTable:

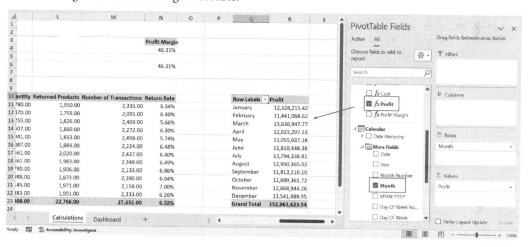

Figure 8.35 – Creating a PivotTable report on monthly profit

From here, we will select any cell in the PivotTable we just created and insert a PivotChart. In the chart options, we will select the **Area** chart:

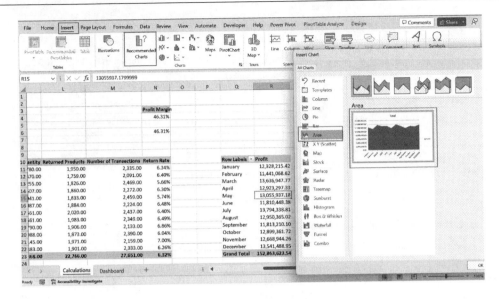

Figure 8.36 – Inserting an area chart

We will reduce the clutter on the PivotChart by removing the chart title and the legend, and hide the field buttons. These are the gray buttons on the chart that can be used to filter the chart's data. You can do this by selecting the **Field Buttons** icon and selecting **Hide All**. Your goal is to help your user focus on the key elements of the charts and remove distractions.

We will also delete the Y axis labels from the left side of the chart. We will add these labels to the chart later when we format it.

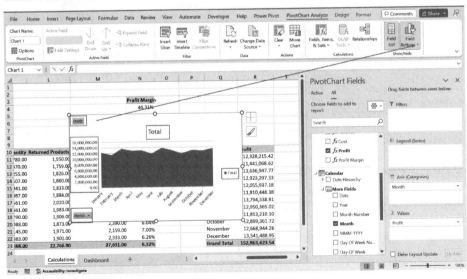

Figure 8.37 – Turning off field buttons in your PivotChart

You can now cut the chart and place it in the mock area in the range J12: P23 on the dashboard. You can use the shape in that range as a placeholder to help you resize the chart.

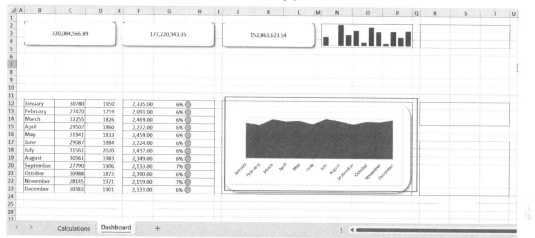

Figure 8.38 – Aligning your area chart

The next chart we will insert in our dashboard is a doughnut chart. We will use this chart to display the profit margin. We will begin with the calculations. The doughnut chart will display the part that represents the profit margin percentage we have selected and show a different color for the remainder.

For example, if the profit margin percentage is 20%, the remainder will be automatically calculated as 80%. We will use these two inputs to create the chart. The calculations will be done just by the profit margin cell in the calculations sheet.

In cell P4, type the label Actual, and in P5, type Remainder:

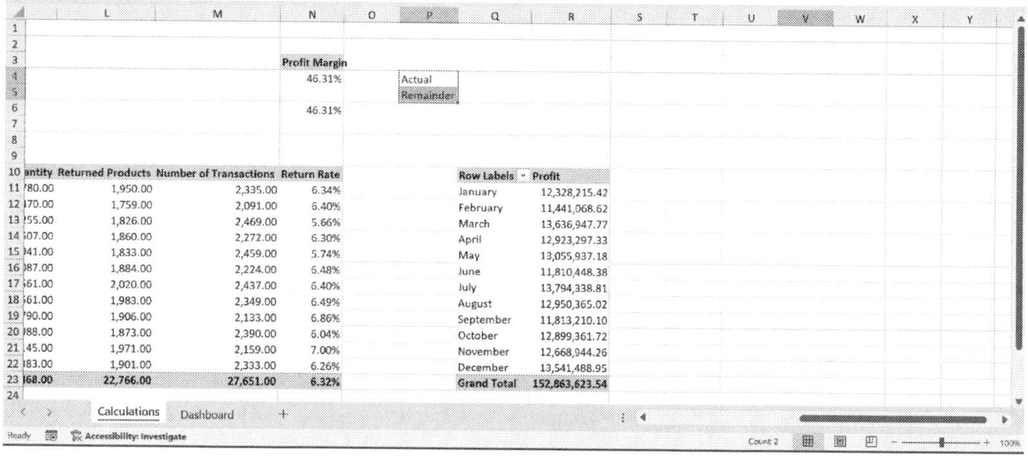

Figure 8.39 – Creating labels for your doughnut chart calculations

We will now calculate these two values:

- The calculation for **Actual** will be = `MIN(1,N3)`. This formula ensures that the chart will display a full blue ring for values above 100%.

- The calculation for **Remainder** is = `1 - Q4`. This is the difference between Actual and the maximum value of 100%.

The final values are shown in the following screenshot:

	L	M	N	O	P	Q	R
1							
2							
3			Profit Margin				
4			46.31%		Actual	46.31%	
5					Remainder	53.69%	
6			46.31%				
7							
8							
9							

Figure 8.40 – Calculations for your doughnut chart

We can now insert the chart on it by using the following steps:

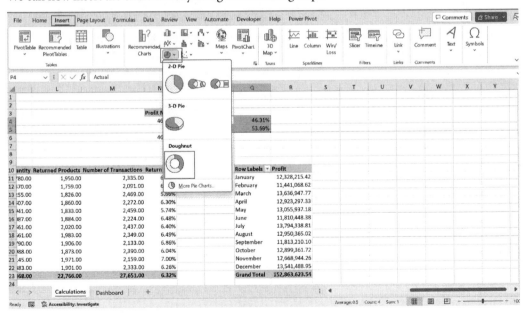

Figure 8.41 – Inserting your doughnut chart

1. At this point, you can remove the chart title and legend and place it on the dashboard:

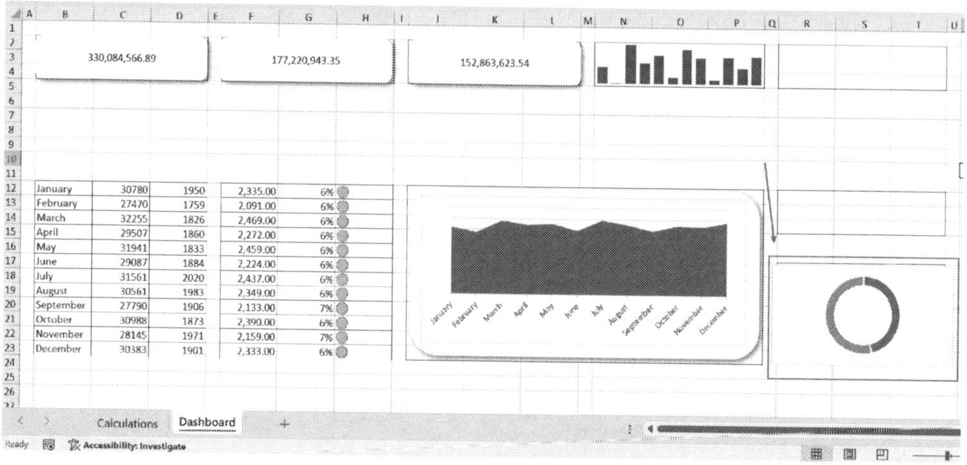

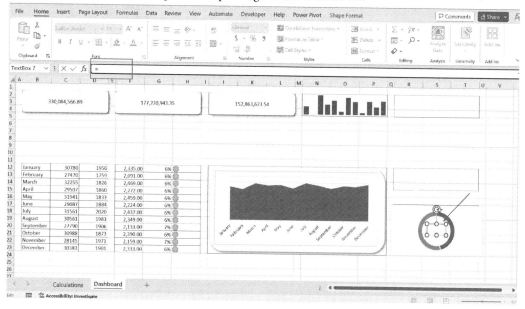

Figure 8.42 – Aligning your doughnut chart

2. We will now insert the data label for the chart inside the ring. We can do this by inserting a text box in the chart.

    Go to **Insert** > **Textbox** and then gently draw the text box in the middle of the doughnut chart. Select the text box and place an equals sign in the formula bar.

Figure 8.43 – Inserting a textbox in your doughnut chart

3. Select the cell that has the original PivotTable calculation for Profit Margin from the Calculations sheet. That will be in cell N4. Press *Enter*. This should bring the value inside the text box in the chart.

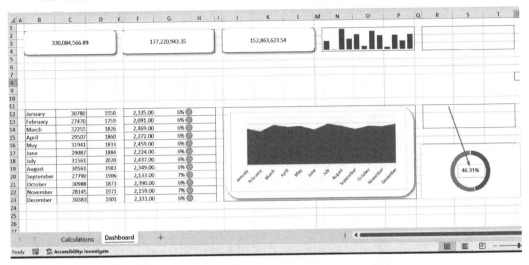

Figure 8.44 – Aligning textbox in your doughnut chart

Our dashboard is now taking shape. There are two more visuals we need to add for top customer and top product by revenue. This will always show the top-ranking customer and product based on the selected branch or period.

We will begin by inserting a PivotTable for these two visuals.

Having selected cell T10 in your calculation sheet, insert a PivotTable from the data model and drag the **Revenue** measure to the **Values** section.

We want to break down the revenue with customer names from our Customers table. If you take a look at the Customers table, you will observe that we do not have a column that has the full names of customers. The names are split into first name and last name. We can go back to Power Query and create this new column, and this will be reflected in our PivotTable.

To go back to Power Query, go to **Data** > **Queries & Connections** and double-click on **Customer Data**.

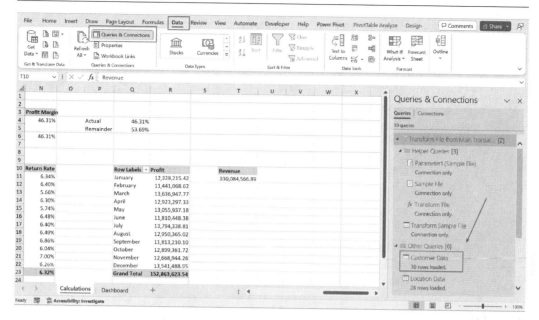

Figure 8.45 – Accessing the Power Query editor

This will open the Power Query editor. The key learning here is that you can always go back to Power Query to make transformations to your data after loading the original query.

To create the new column with the first and last name of the customers, we will go to the **Add Column** tab and click on **Merge Columns**.

Select the two columns in the order you want to see in the merged column, **First Name** and then **Last Name**, and then click on **Merge Columns** in the ribbon:

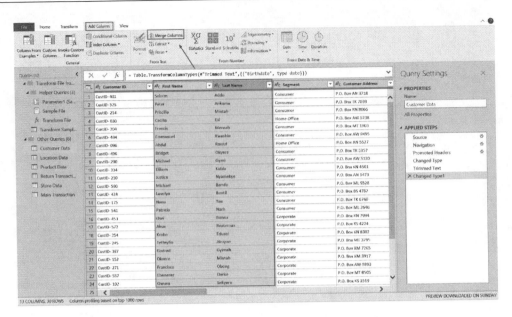

Figure 8.46 – Merging columns in the Power Query editor

This brings up the following dialog box:

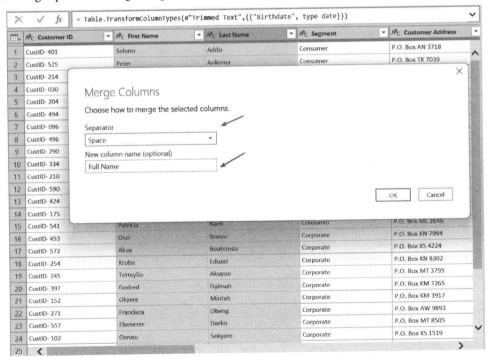

Figure 8.47 – Dialog box for merging columns in the Power Query editor

Select **Space** as a separator and add `Full Name` as the name of the new column. When you click **OK**, this should add a new column to the extreme right of the table named **Full Name**.

We can now go to **Home** > **Close and Load**.

Our PivotTable is now updated with the Full Name column. We can now drag it to the **Rows** section of the PivotTable we are working on.

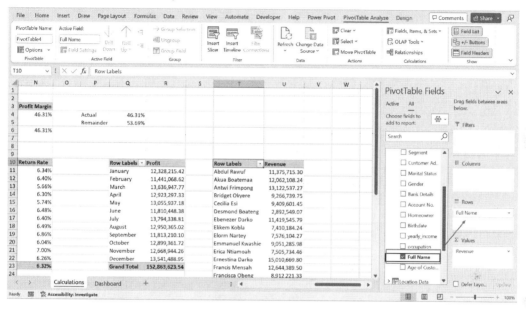

Figure 8.48 – Dragging the new column to the Rows section

This gives us the names of all our customers. However, we want to just have the top customer by revenue. In a PivotTable, you can filter names based on ranking.

Right-click on any of the names in the customer list, then click on **Filter** > **Top 10**.

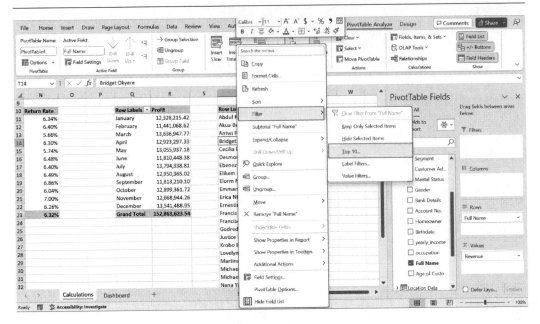

Figure 8.49 – Filtering the report to the top customer

In the dialog box that pops up, change **10** to **1** to reduce the PivotTable to the customer with the highest revenue.

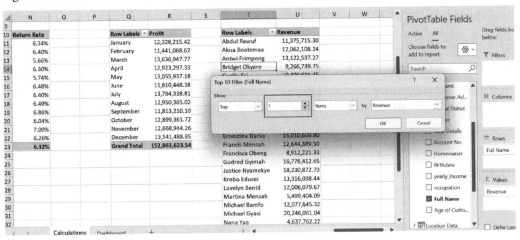

Figure 8.50 – Dialog box for filtering in PivotTables

This will now give us Osei Bonsu:

	T	U	V	W
	Row Labels ▼	Revenue		
	Osei Bonsu	20,823,181.35		
	Grand Total	20,823,181.35		

Figure 8.51 – Displaying the top customer in a PivotTable

We can now repeat the same process for the top Product Name by inserting a new PivotTable in cell X10.

See if you can go through the process of displaying the top Product Name. Product Name is available in the Product Data table. Your completed PivotTable should look like this:

	X	Y	Z
	Row Labels ▼	Revenue	
	UltraHD Smart TV	28,704,081.90	
	Grand Total	28,704,081.90	

Figure 8.52 – Display of top product in a PivotTable.

After this, we can reference the top customer name and product name in our dashboard. We will do this with a shape. This is like what we did earlier with Revenue, Cost, and Profit.

Back in the dashboard, we will insert a shape over the mockup range R2:T4. Place an equals sign in the formula bar and reference Osei Bonsu from the PivotTable on the Calculations sheet.

Your final result should be like this:

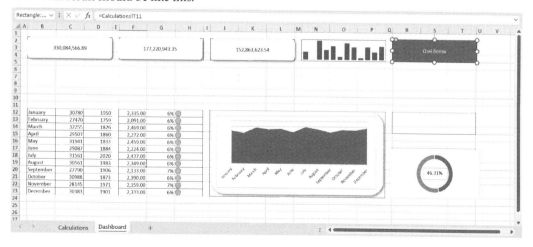

Figure 8.53 – Inserting top customer name in a shape

Repeat the same process for Product Name and place it in the range R12:T15. That should give you the completed shape with text:

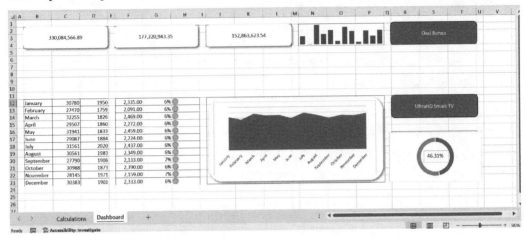

Figure 8.54 – Inserting the top product name in a shape

Inserting slicers for interaction

We have now created all the primary components of our dashboard. At this point, the visuals are not formatted, and they are only flat displays without any interaction.

To bring in some interaction, we will insert slicers to help users dice and slice to bring out some insights from these charts.

We can insert the slicers directly from the data model. To do that, go to **Insert** > **Slicer** > **Data Model**.

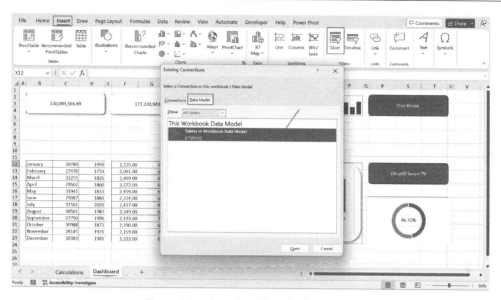

Figure 8.55 – Inserting slicers for interaction

This should bring up all the tables in our data model.

For this dashboard, we want users to slice using **Year** from the **Calendar** table and **Region** from the **Location** table.

This should bring up the two slicers:

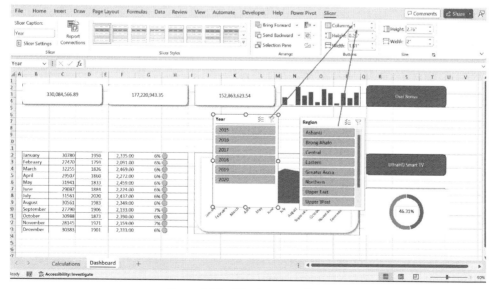

Figure 8.56 – Aligning your slicers

We can split the buttons into columns representing the number of items we have in each slicer. So, we set 6 columns for the **Year** slicer and 10 for the **Region** slicer. You can always come back and make changes to these.

Resize the slicers and place them below the dashboard in such a way that they are still in view for the user to see all the elements at a glance.

Congratulations on coming this far. You have taken an important step toward creating your final dashboard. In the next chapter, we will learn how to format and choose an appropriate theme that will bring this dashboard to life.

Look at the following screenshot to see how all the elements should be placed in the dashboard:

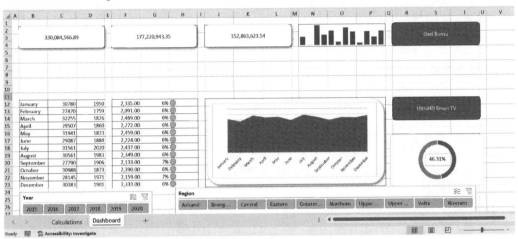

Figure 8.57 – Dashboard in its final state

Summary

In this chapter, we have applied some of the elements you can use to create your dashboard. You are now familiar with how to use mockups and layouts to set the stage for your dashboard. You learned how to use shapes and cards to project the key indicators in your dashboard. Apart from shapes, we covered how you can create sparklines, which are in-cell charts that can be used when you have limited space to present your visual.

The chapter also discussed the use of conditional formatting to apply icons to your values. We also covered some creative ways to enhance regular charts such as doughnut and area charts and how you can add slicers to add some interaction to your dashboard.

These concepts will give you a good foundation to build more complex dashboards. In the next chapter, we will add some color to what we have built so far.

9

Choosing the Right Design Themes – Less Is More with Colors

In *Chapter 8*, we delved into the mechanics of visualization elements such as slicers, pivot charts, conditional formatting, and shapes. These tools are foundational in creating an interactive dashboard. However, the aesthetic design, particularly the color theme, plays a crucial role in ensuring our dashboards are not just functional but also visually appealing and easy to interpret. In this chapter, we'll explore the significance of color choice, how it impacts user perception, and best practices to ensure your dashboard's design enhances its utility.

To view the images in this chapter in color, please refer to the free ebook.

We will cover the following main topics:

- Understanding your users
- How to reduce noise in your presentation
- Using colors to tell a story

Understanding your users

Before diving into the intricacies of color selection, it's vital to understand your users. A dashboard's purpose is to provide valuable insights, and its design should cater to its audience.

Know your audience's preferences

Different audiences have different preferences. A financial analyst might prefer a more data-dense dashboard, while a marketing executive might opt for something more graphical. Consider the final dashboard's end users and tailor the design to their preferences.

Accessibility is key

Ensure that your color choices are distinguishable for all users, including those with color blindness. Tools such as the Color Blindness Simulator can help you check how your dashboard looks to those with various forms of color vision deficiencies.

Consistency is crucial

The design theme should be consistent throughout the dashboard. For instance, if you've used a specific color for a product category in one chart, use the same color for that category in all other visualizations.

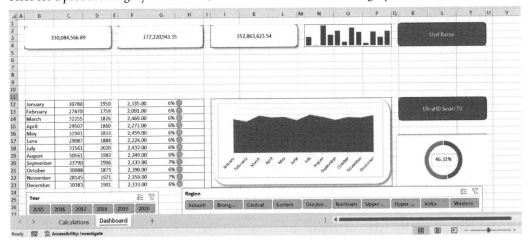

Figure 9.1 – Dashboard from the previous chapter (WIP)

Skill 1 practice

Open the dashboard and list who your potential users might be. Based on this list, decide on a primary and secondary color that you believe would appeal to this audience. Remember, the goal is to answer the key questions your users might have.

Let's now proceed and set the theme for our dashboard based on the above.

In Excel, a theme refers to a collection of coordinated design elements that provide a consistent and visually appealing look for your workbook, including fonts, colors, effects, and background styles. Themes are designed to simplify the process of creating professional-looking spreadsheets by ensuring that all the design elements across different sheets and workbooks are consistent and harmonious.

When you apply a theme to an Excel workbook, it affects various design aspects, such as the following:

- **Colors**: Themes define a set of colors for text, backgrounds, headings, and other elements within your spreadsheet. These colors are chosen to complement each other and maintain a consistent visual style.

- **Fonts**: Themes include specific font styles for headings and body text. These fonts are selected to provide readability and visual appeal.

- **Effects**: Themes might also include visual effects such as shadows, reflections, and gradients that can be applied to shapes, charts, and other graphical elements.

- **Cell Styles**: Themes can define specific cell styles that include combinations of font colors, fill colors, and border styles for various types of data.

By using themes in Excel, you can easily change the overall appearance of your workbook without manually adjusting each element's formatting. If you decide to change the theme later, all the design elements that use that theme will automatically update to the new styles. This is particularly useful when you're creating multiple sheets or workbooks that need to maintain a consistent look and feel.

Let's now create a theme for our dashboard.

We will create a theme by modifying the existing colors, fonts, and effects in our current workbook.

Go to **Page Layout**:

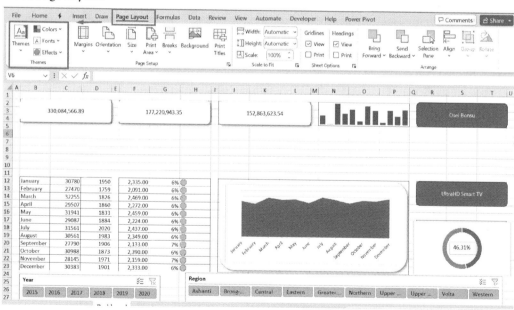

Figure 9.2 – Accessing Themes from the ribbon

On the left, you will find a tab called **Themes**. Close to the tab are options to modify the colors, fonts, and effects of the current theme. We will create our custom theme by modifying these.

Begin by selecting **Colors** > **Customize Colors…**.

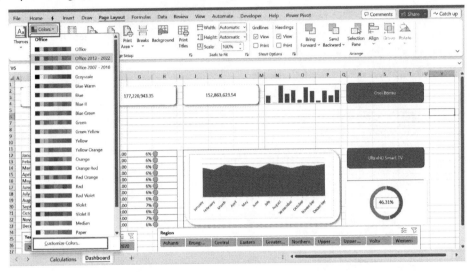

Figure 9.3 – Customizing colors in your theme

This brings up the dialogue box to select our theme colors. Our dashboard will be dominated by teal green. We will input the hex code or RGB code for this color for **Accent 1** as shown:

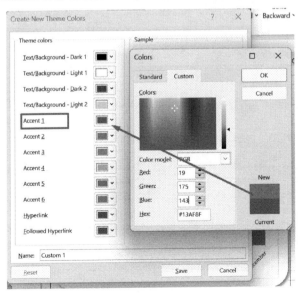

Figure 9.4 – Modifying colors in your theme

We will make **Accent 2** white. These are the two dominant colors in our final dashboard. We will leave the rest at default and proceed to rename the theme. Here, you can give it any custom name.

For consistency, it will be good if you use the same name for fonts and effects later. I have named mine `Finex` as shown in the following screenshot:

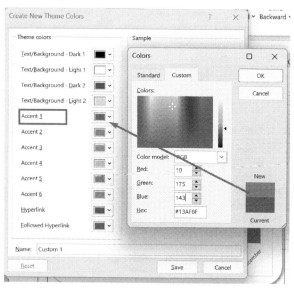

Figure 9.5 – Renaming your theme colors

You will notice that the colors for the shapes, charts, and slicers change instantly after saving. Using **Themes** saves you time and makes it easy for you to generate a consistent color for the elements of your dashboard.

We will now proceed with the font type. For dashboard designs, popular font types are Segoe UI, Poppins, Montserrat, and Red Hat.

You can use any of these or set the font style to your favorite. For this case study, I will set both **Heading font** and **Body font** in the font dialogue box to **Segoe UI**. We will save this with the name `Finex` as well. The dialogue box is shown in the following figure:

Figure 9.6 – Modifying your theme fonts

After saving, all the values in cells, change to the new font style. You will notice that the values in the textboxes do not change. We can select the textboxes and then apply our new font to these directly. The advantage here is that our selected font will always appear on top for selection, and we do not have to search through the list.

How to reduce noise in your presentation

A well-designed dashboard should direct the user's attention to the most critical data without overwhelming them with too much information.

Here are some ideas to help in this objective:

- **Limit the number of colors**: Too many colors can make a dashboard look chaotic. Limit your primary colors and use shades of these colors to maintain consistency while distinguishing data points.

- **Use neutral backgrounds**: A neutral background allows your data to stand out. Avoid using bright colors that can distract from the data.

- **Consistent fonts**: Just as with colors, limit the number of fonts you use. Stick to one or two fonts to maintain a clean look.

- **Whitespace is your friend**: Allow some space between visual elements. This gives your dashboard a clean look and helps users focus on the data.

- **Skill 2 practice**: Identify any areas where there might be too many "noisy" or redundant elements and adjust these elements to reduce visual noise. Examples of noisy elements include gridlines, chart titles, field buttons, legends, and so on. Sometimes these elements are already part of your dashboard setup. It is therefore important to remove them so that the user can focus on the key elements of the chart.

By applying these tips to our dashboard, we can make our dashboard cleaner by removing the gridlines. You can do this by going to **View** and unchecking the **Gridlines** box, as shown in the following screenshot:

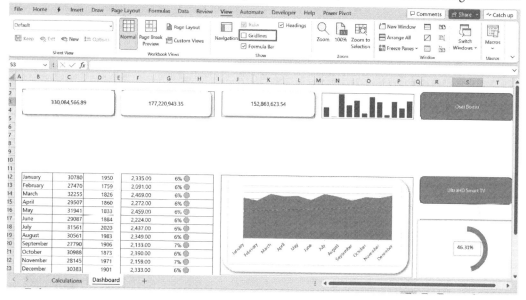

Figure 9.7 – Removing gridlines

Removing gridlines when designing dashboards in Excel can offer several advantages:

- **Improved aesthetics**: Gridlines can make a dashboard appear cluttered and less visually appealing. By removing them, you can create a cleaner and more professional-looking design.

- **Enhanced focus**: Without gridlines, the data and visual elements on the dashboard stand out more prominently. This can help users focus on the information presented rather than getting distracted by the gridlines.

- **Simpler interpretation**: Gridlines can sometimes make it harder to distinguish between data points, especially if the colors used in the gridlines are similar to the data colors. Removing gridlines can make it easier to interpret the data and identify trends.

- **Consistency**: Gridlines might not align perfectly with the data points, especially when using certain chart types or positioning elements precisely. Removing gridlines can help maintain the consistent and accurate alignment of data and visual elements.

- **Ease of printing and exporting**: Dashboards designed without gridlines tend to look better when printed or exported to other formats, such as PDF. Gridlines may not always render well in these formats, leading to inconsistent appearances.

However, it's important to consider your audience's preferences and needs. Some users might find gridlines helpful for reading data precisely, especially when working with numerical values. Therefore, you could provide an option to toggle gridlines on or off based on user preference or context. Ultimately, the decision to remove gridlines should be made based on the overall design goals and the user experience you want to provide.

After removing gridlines, another concept that will enhance our dashboard is the use of white space. You will notice that columns A, E, I, M, and Q are already serving as white spaces to separate the major elements in our dashboard.

For consistency, we can reduce the number of rows between row 5 and row 11 by cutting some rows and inserting them at the top. Taking into account the headers for the charts, let's select rows 6 – 8, cut these rows, and insert them in row 1, as shown in the following screenshot:

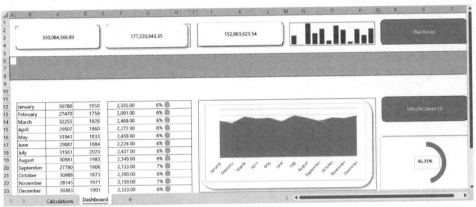

Figure 9.8 – Inserting extra rows in your dashboard for consistency

After inserting the cut rows in row 1, your dashboard should look like the following screenshot:

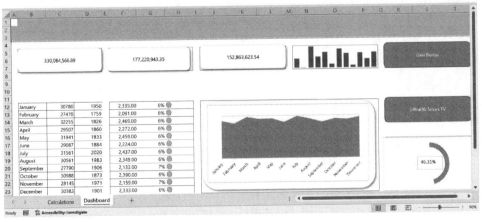

Figure 9.9 – Inserting extra rows at the top of your dashboard for consistency

After we put in our headers and other labels, we will end up with consistent white space between our rows and columns.

Now that we are done with reducing the noise and distracting elements in our dashboard, it is time to add some extra colors to the elements in our dashboard.

Using colors to tell a story

Colors can be powerful storytellers. They, highlight important data points and guide the user's eyes to where you want them to focus.

Associative colors

Colors often have associations. For example, red might indicate a decline or danger, while green might indicate growth or safety. Use these associations to your advantage, but also be aware of cultural differences in color interpretation. In North America and Europe, red is often associated with passion, love, anger, danger, energy, and youth.

In Central and South America, red is also associated with passion and emotion, and it's frequently used in religious practices, often in combination with white, symbolizing the blood of Christ and the crucifixion.

In Asian cultures, particularly China, red symbolizes honor, success, prosperity, good luck, and a long life, and is often worn by brides as it's believed to bring happiness and good luck to their marriage. You can read more here: `https://tinyurl.com/cculture57d`.

Red, yellow, and green are common colors. These three colors have come to be associated with performance indicators. You should always consider how they blend with the colors in your theme and apply them effectively.

This is the same concept that has been used to format our conditional formatting icons in our dashboard – red for high return rates, yellow for medium return rates, and green for low return rates.

Using gradient colors for scales

For data that is on a scale (e.g., low to high), use gradient colors. This provides a visual cue to users about the data's progression.

Apart from this, gradient colors can be used to vary the appearance of the elements of your charts. Let's look at our area chart. The green fill color makes it appear "flat."

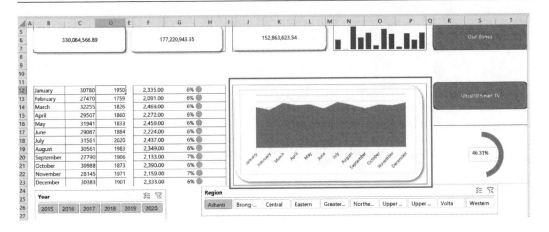

Figure 9.10 – Applying a gradient fill to a chart

We can vary the green fill color with a gradient fill to make it more elegant. As always, less is more when you are adding elements to your charts.

To add the gradient fill, let's go through the following steps:

1. Right-click on the filled area and select **Format Data Series**.

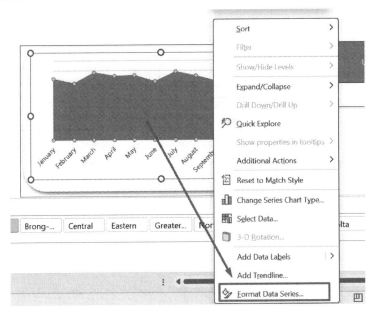

Figure 9.11 – Accessing the gradient fill dialog box

2. Under the **Fill** and **Line** icons, select **Gradient fill** and enter the settings shown in the following dialog box.

Figure 9.12 – Changing the gradient settings

The gradient type we chose here is **Linear** and for **Direction**, we chose **Linear Down** with **Angle** at 90 degrees. When you are creating gradients, you can add stops to give you different shades or colors of your gradient. In this case, we chose two stops. On the left side is a green shade from our theme with hex code #13AF8F, and on the right is a white color.

While we are working on this chart, let's remove the gridlines to make it cleaner. Usually, if you do not have any axis labels to the left of your chart, you can consider taking off the gridlines of your chart to give it a cleaner look.

Another way we can improve the appearance of this chart is to abbreviate the month names. Remember, the column used in this chart is the month name column in the calendar table. We created the calendar table in the data model using Power Pivot.

We need to go back to Power Pivot and make the changes from there. To access the data model, we will go to **Data** and click on the **Go to Power Pivot** icon from the **Data Tools** group. Alternatively, you can access the same icon from the **Power Pivot** tab.

Figure 9.13 – Accessing the Power Pivot window

When the Power Pivot window opens, go to the calendar Table, select the column that has the month names, and make changes to the formula by removing one **M** from the format. This should now render the month names in an abbreviated form.

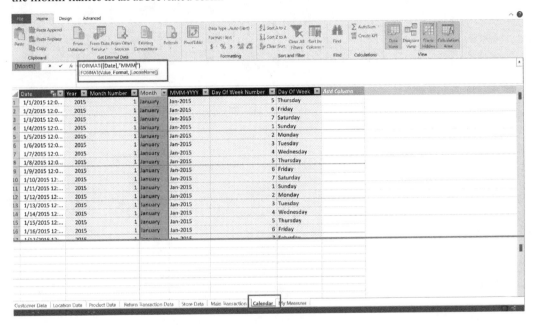

Figure 9.14 – Modifying the format for months

After this, we need to sort the columns again by month number so that they are displayed in chronological order in our PivotTable.

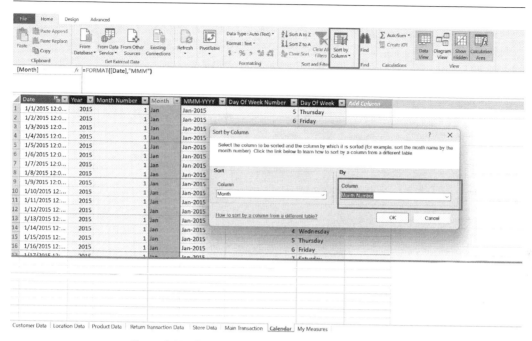

Figure 9.15 – Sorting the month names by month values

We should see the effect of these changes after we click **OK** and go back to the worksheet in Excel. Our chart now shows an abbreviated form of the month names.

Our final chart looks like this:

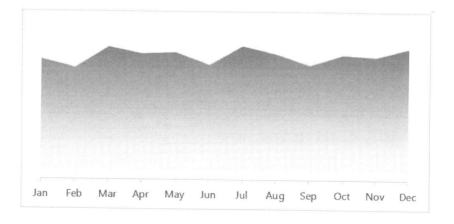

Figure 9.16 – Effect of sorting the month names by month values

We can now add the data labels by clicking on the plus icon on the chart and selecting the **Data Labels** checkbox.

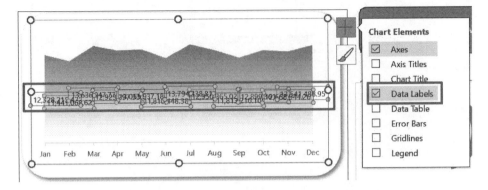

Figure 9.17 – Adding data labels to the area chart

This poses an obvious challenge. The numbers appear cluttered. But we can always format this nicely by applying a custom format.

While the numbers are selected, press *Ctrl + 1* or right-click and access the dialog box to format the numbers.

Figure 9.18 – Customizing the data labels of your area chart

Switch to **Custom**, enter the `0.0,,"M"` script, and click **Add**.

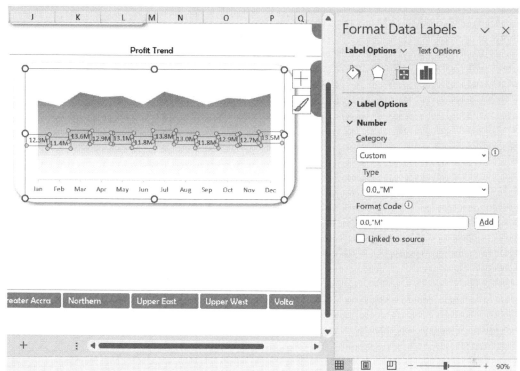

Figure 9.19 – Applying Format Code to values in your chart

The custom format `0.0,,` with the added text `"M"` is used in Excel to format numerical values in a specific way. Let's break down what each component of this format means:

- **0.0**: This part of the format specifies how the numerical value should be displayed in terms of decimal places. The 0 signifies a digit placeholder, and the 0 after the dot indicates that the number will be displayed with exactly one decimal place.

- **,,**: Usually, commas are used in large numbers in a way that separates every three digits for better readability. When we place a comma after 0.0 in a custom script, we are truncating the original value by removing three digits, which represents a thousand; if it's two commas, that will be six digits, representing a million, and so on. In this case, we will apply a double comma ",," to truncate the number by removing the million part.

- **"M"**: This is a text string that you want to add to the formatted number. In this case, "M" stands for "million," so it's often used to indicate that the number has been scaled down by a factor of one million.

You can find out more about custom formatting here: `https://tinyurl.com/nformats`.

Our chart now looks like this:

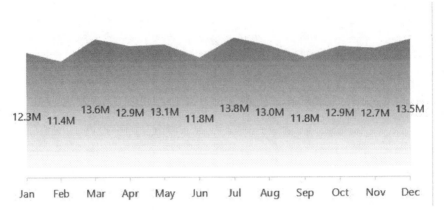

Figure 9.20 – Effect of applying Format Code to values in your chart

Let's finish it off with some final touches. We will remove the outer border line of the chart.

It would be nice to have the numbers placed at the top of the filled area of the chart. Unfortunately, as of the time of writing this book, there is no direct way to make this change in an area chart in Excel. You can, however, drag these values directly to the top.

Let's now apply the same concepts to format our doughnut chart, sparkline, and our textboxes.

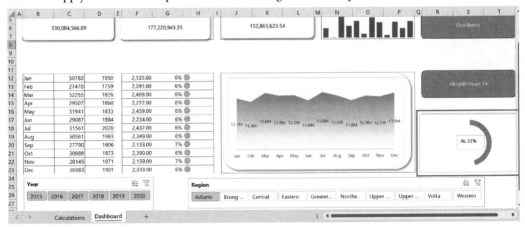

Figure 9.21 – Dashboard after formatting area chart

This is currently the state of our dashboard.

Now, think of some creative ways to make this dashboard even better. Still looking at colors, we will maintain the green portion of the ring, which shows the portion of the profit margin, and select a light shade of gray for the remainder of the ring. You can do this by directly selecting the left side of the ring, pressing *Ctrl + 1*, or by right-clicking for the fill and line settings and applying the gray color with the hex code #F2F2F2.

This highlights the other portion of the ring but in a more subdued way. We want the user to focus on the green part. You can take off the border line of the textbox, so it sits in the middle of the chart without the box frame. To do this, you can select the textbox and go to **Shape Format** > **Shape Outline** > **No Outline**. Ensure that the edges of the textbox are nicely tucked inside the ring of the doughnut chart.

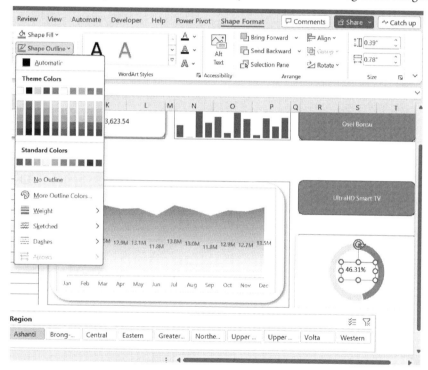

Figure 9.22 – Removing border lines from your textbox

Your complete chart should look like the following screenshot:

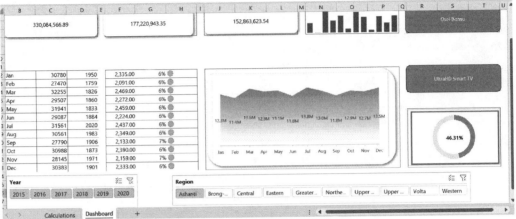

Figure 9.23 – Effect of removing border lines from your textbox

We'll move on to format our sparklines using the same color concept.

Select the **Sparkline** tab. This should bring up the contextual tab to format the sparkline in the ribbon. Apply a green color (hex code: #13AF8F) to the bars in the sparkline.

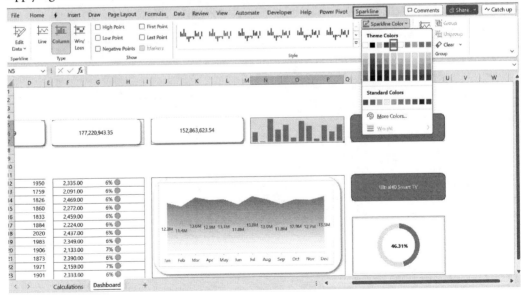

Figure 9.24 – Formatting your sparkline

We will then change the color of **High Point** under **Marker Color** to gray (hex code: #D9D9D9) to make this bar stand out from the other green bars.

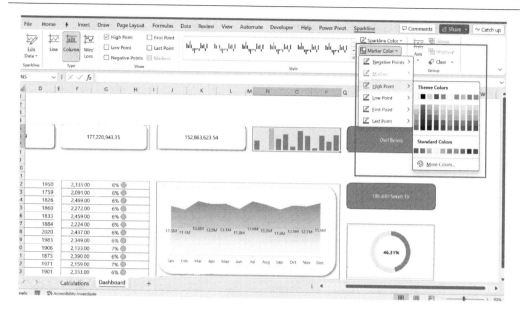

Figure 9.25 – Accessing color formatting options for your sparkline

Highlighting key data

Use bolder fonts to highlight key data points or sections of your dashboard that you want users to focus on.

Skill 3 practice

Examine the dashboard. Identify areas where bolder fonts could be used to emphasize a particular story or data point. We will put in captions and labels after this exercise.

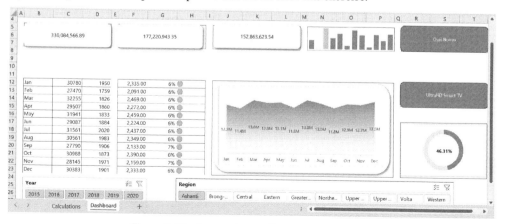

Figure 9.26 – Formatting outliers in your sparkline

We can increase the font size in the textboxes to make it easier for our users to pick the key numbers. While doing this, we can change the font type as well, so it syncs with the theme fonts in the cells.

You can select all the textboxes together by holding the *Ctrl* key and selecting one after the other. Then increase the font size to **18** and change the font type to **Segoe UI (Headings)** as shown in the following screenshot:

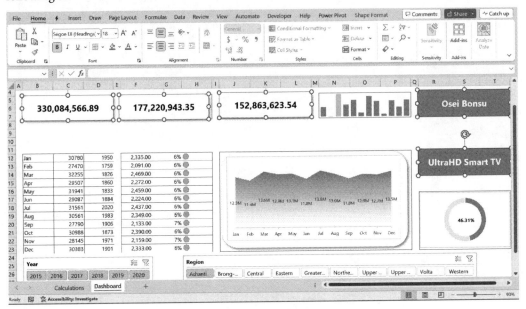

Figure 9.27 – Formatting shapes and content

After this step, we can reduce the decimal places in the first three textboxes to reduce the length of the values. You may also want to format the values using the custom million format we used earlier for the area chart. The formatting of the numbers can be done directly in the cells that contain the values in the **Calculations** sheet.

We are almost there. The next step in the design stage is to remove border lines. This will include the ones we used for the mockup, the borderline for the green textboxes, and those around the area chart as well.

To remove the borderlines, highlight the range of cells that have border lines and apply no border lines to the range. Repeat for the other sections of the dashboard apart from the summary table at the bottom left part of the dashboard.

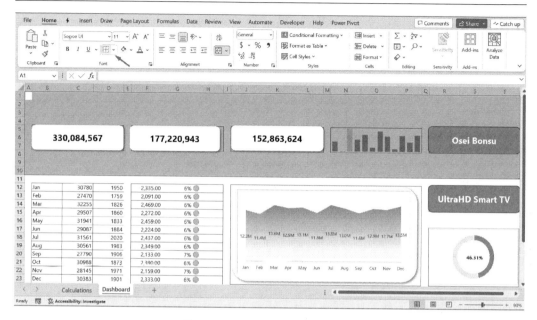

Figure 9.28 – Removing borderlines

This will give the dashboard a clean look, as shown in the following screenshot.

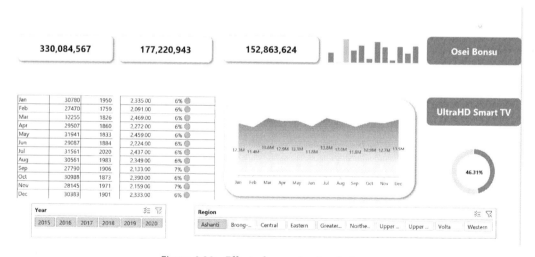

Figure 9.29 – Effect of removing borderlines

We now have to apply our captions or labels to each element of our dashboard. We made some room for this when we were creating our white spaces.

We apply them using a consistent format that will align the headings nicely with the chart or textbox.

Let's start with the first label, for **Revenue**. We will place this label in cell B3, as shown:

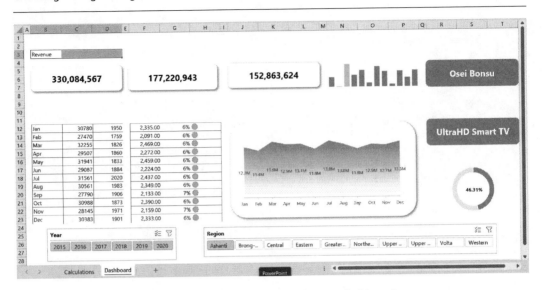

Figure 9.30 – Creating captions for your dashboard

After typing the label, select the range B3:D3 and press *Ctrl + 1* or right-click to access the format cells dialog box. Ensure that your cursor is not in edit mode. To be sure, you can press the *Esc* key before pressing *Ctrl + 1*. In the dialog box, we want to center the text over the selected range:

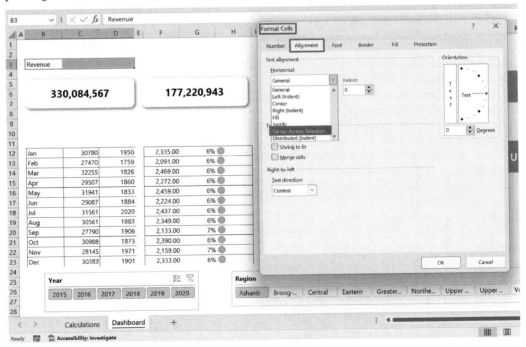

Figure 9.31 – Accessing the Center Across Selection menu

Go to **Alignment** and then choose **Center Across Selection**. This approach is better than merging the cells because it maintains the respective columns while centering the text over the range.

While the range is selected, apply a border line to the label. Your complete label should look like the following screenshot:

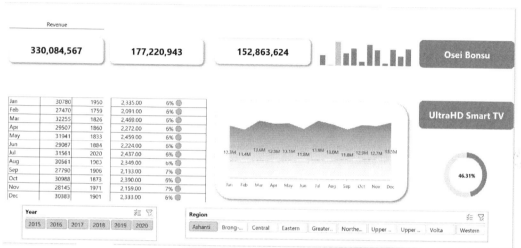

Figure 9.31 – Applying captions to the rest of the dashboard components

Now repeat the process for the rest of the elements in the dashboard by copying and pasting into the respective cells indicated in the following screenshot. This should bring our dashboard to the following stage. The cells marked in red should be the first cells you select to paste the copied label. This will ensure consistency.

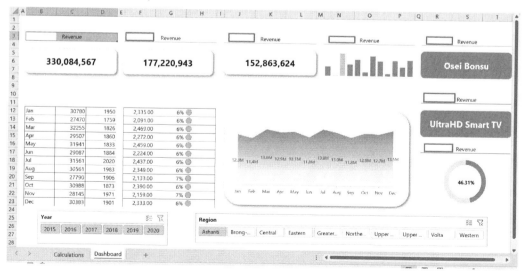

Figure 9.32 – Determining active cells to paste the copied label

We can repeat the process for the summary table, starting with cell B10. Before we do that, let's type the captions for the month name and the headers of the table, as shown:

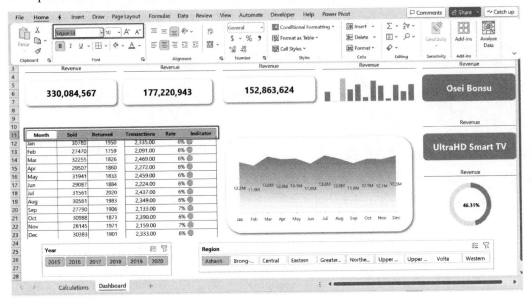

Figure 9.33 – Modifying the font size of your captions

We will set the font size of these labels to 9 to differentiate it from that of the main headers. After this, we can apply the main caption on top of these sub-labels.

We will apply the same concept we used to create the **revenue** label earlier by selecting the range B10:H10. The title we will use here is Analyzing Returns, as shown in the following figure. After typing this, press *Ctrl + 1* and select **Center Across Selection**.

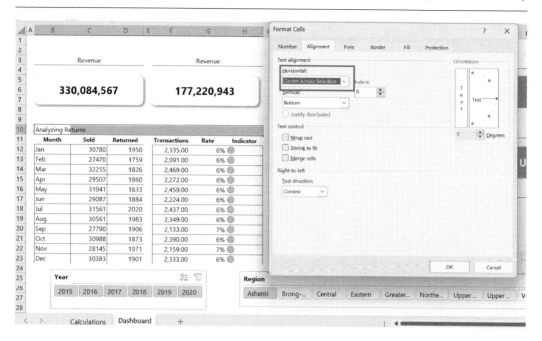

Figure 9.34 – Applying Center Across Selection to your caption

Apply borderlines to this. Copy and paste this in cell J10 for the caption of the area chart.

You can now change the names of the various captions as shown:

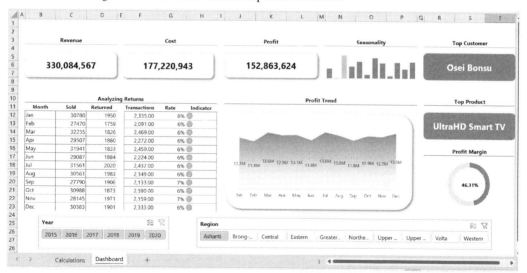

Figure 9.35 – Modifying your captions

Remember that even though the values appear to be sitting in the middle of the range, the active cell that has the caption is the first cell in the range. You should select the first cell and type your text in each case. You can make it bold afterward.

This should bring our dashboard to this stage:

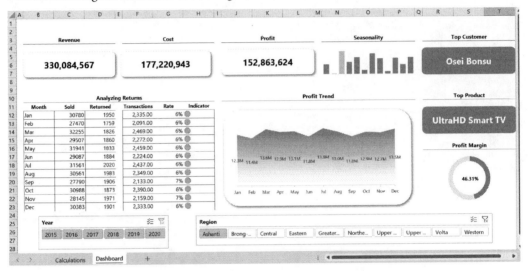

Figure 9.36 – Dashboard after applying captions

The last design activity will be to connect and format our slicers.

Slicers are a powerful tool for filtering data, but sometimes, you want them to match your workbook's unique style or branding. Fortunately, Excel allows you to create your own slicer styles and modify them to suit your needs. Let's explore this process step by step.

Duplicating an existing slicer style

Before we can start customizing our slicer style, we need to duplicate an existing style as a starting point. This ensures we don't mess up the default styles that Excel provides.

Here's how to do it.

Select any of the slicers by clicking on it. This will activate the **Slicer** tools contextual tab in the Excel ribbon.

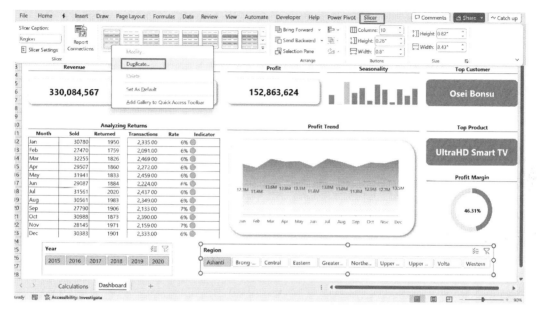

Figure 9.37 – Duplicating slicers

Right-click on the first slicer and click **Duplicate**.

In the dialog box that pops up, we have the option to rename the slicer. I have changed mine to Finex, as shown:

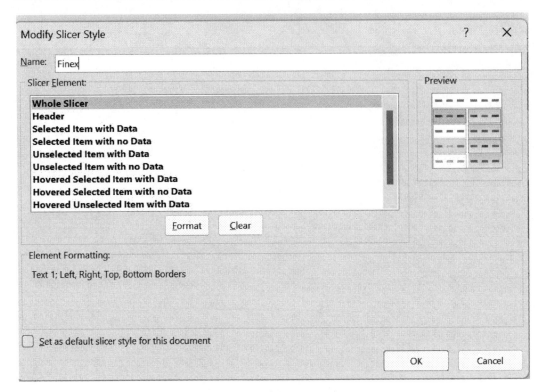

Figure 9.38 – Renaming your slicers

Following are all the various components of the slicer. Depending on the style you want for the slicer, you can edit **Font**, **Border**, and **Fill** for each element by clicking on the **Format** button.

The dialog box shows you a preview of the effect of your changes on the right. In most cases, editing the first six elements should be enough to give you the style you want.

Let's quickly go through what each of these six styles represents:

- **Whole Slicer**: This refers to the entire slicer control, including all its components, such as the header, selected items, and unselected items. Modifying the **Whole Slicer** element allows you to make broad changes to the overall appearance of the slicer.

- **Header**: The header is the top part of the slicer, which usually contains the title or label of the slicer. You can modify the font, color, background, and borders of the header to make it stand out or match your workbook's style.

- **Selected Item with Data**: This is the style applied to items in the slicer that are selected and have associated data. For example, if you have a list of countries in your slicer, this style would be applied to the country names that you've selected.

- **Selected Item with no Data**: Similar to **Selected Item with Data**, this style applies to selected items, but specifically to those without associated data. For instance, if you select a category in the slicer that has no data in your worksheet, it will use this style.

- **Unselected Item with Data**: This style is for items in the slicer that are not selected but have associated data. It allows you to control how these items look when they are not chosen.

- **Unselected Item with no Data**: Like the **Unselected Item with Data**, this style applies to items that are not selected and don't have associated data. It helps you distinguish these items from the selected ones.

By customizing these individual slicer elements, you can create a slicer that not only matches your workbook's design but also makes it easier for users to interact with and understand your data.

Let's now make changes to the first three of these elements, starting with **Whole Slicer**:

- Whole Slicer:

  - **Font**: Segoe UI (Headings), Color is Black,

  - **Border**: No Border

  - **Fill**: No Fill

- Header:

  - **Font**: Segoe UI (Body), Color is Black,

  - **Border**: Bottom Border Line, Color: Green (Hex code: #13AF8F)

  - **Fill**: No Fill

- Selected Item with Data:

  - **Font**: Segoe UI, Size is 12, Color is White,

  - **Border**: Top, Bottom, Left, Right Border Line, Color: Gray (Hex code: #999999)

  - **Fill**: Green (Hex code: #13AF8F)

We can leave the rest of the elements as the defaults because they reflect the green and white theme we set earlier.

You can now click **OK** and exit the dialog box. To apply the new style to the slicers, select each slicer, go to **Slicer styles**, and select the new **Finex** slicer style, as shown:

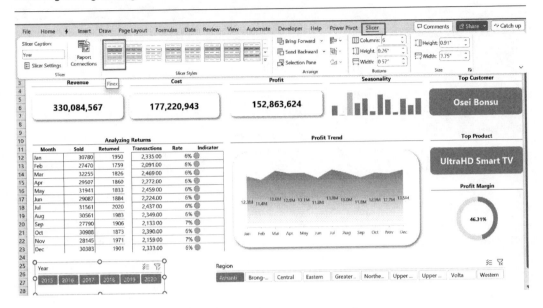

Figure 9.39 – Applying your custom slicer

We can now align our slicers at the bottom of our page. The final thing we need to do is to connect our slicers to the PivotTables that drive the charts and calculations in our dashboard.

To do that, right-click on **Slicer** and select **Report Connections**:

Figure 9.40 – Connecting your slicers using Report Connections

This brings up all the PivotTables we used in our calculations. Ideally, you should name the PivotTables to help you know which specific PivotTable you are connecting to. Sometimes, it may not be helpful to connect some slicers to PivotTables that have the same attributes.

In our case, we are using **Year** and **Region**, which can be used to slice all the calculations we have in our dashboard. We will therefore connect to all the PivotTables listed in the dialog box as shown in the following screenshot:

Figure 9.41 – Connecting your slicers to PivotTables

Repeat the process for the **Region** slicer.

You'll notice that the slicers are now filtering all the visuals in this dashboard as expected. This makes your dashboard interactive and helps you drill down to specific values.

We are done apart from some final touches to the border lines on our **Sales Returns Summary** table. Reapply the border lines to the range and center the icons. Our final dashboard now looks like this:

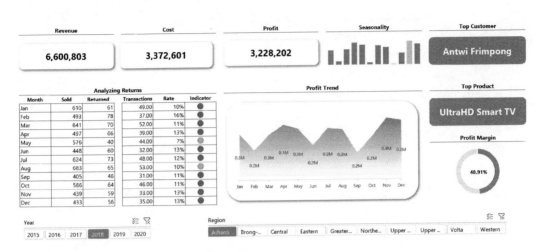

Figure 9.42 – Final dashboard

Congratulations! Well done practicing. Now you can apply some of these concepts to create your own dashboards in Excel.

Summary

In this chapter, we have applied some design concepts to complete our final dashboard. Design plays a pivotal role in the effectiveness of a dashboard. The colors and themes you choose can greatly influence user interpretation and engagement. By understanding your users, reducing visual noise, and using colors to tell a story, you can create a dashboard that is not only functional but also compelling.

As we wrap up this chapter, reflect on the skills you've gained and consider how they'll aid in finalizing the design of your dashboard. Remember, less truly is more when it comes to color.

Publication and Deployment – Sharing with Report Users

The dashboard we created in the previous chapter must now be shared with users. Creating an Excel dashboard is just the beginning. Sharing it securely and effectively with others is an important part of the process. This chapter will help you navigate through securing your data, making it easy for others to collaborate, and choosing the right ways to share it online. Our aim is to help you keep your dashboard flexible for updates while ensuring the data remains accurate.

We will cover the following main topics:

- Protecting your workbook
- Collaboration
- Publishing online via OneDrive/SharePoint
- Exporting your data model to Power BI

Protecting your workbook

Keeping your data safe is key when sharing your workbook. Excel has a bunch of tools to help you do this. Excel lets you protect different parts of your workbook, including individual cells, sheets, or the entire workbook. This way, you can control who sees or edits what. The **Protect Sheet** and **Protect Workbook** features are simple yet effective ways to keep your workbook safe. They provide you with the option to add passwords to further secure the data and formulas in your workbook.

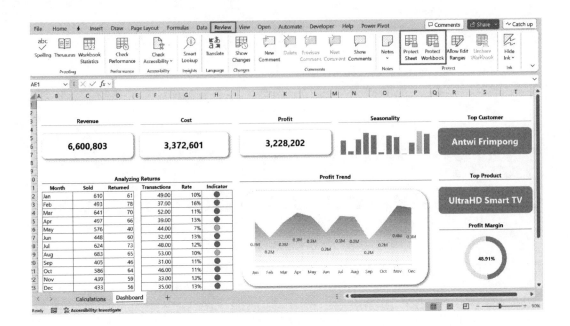

Figure 10.1 – The Protect Sheet and Protect Workbook features

The **Protect Workbook** feature in Excel prevents others from making big changes such as adding or deleting sheets. This is handy when sharing with many people who may not know their way around your workbook.

Protecting certain cells or sheets with the **Protect Sheet** feature in your Excel dashboard is a good idea when you have sensitive information or formulas. This keeps important data from being changed or deleted by mistake.

Now let's look at some practical ways to achieve this.

Skill one – restricting access to sensitive parts of your workbook

Our final dashboard contains a mix of shapes, charts, values in cells, slicers, sparklines, and conditional formatting. In Excel, we can broadly classify the elements we can protect in a workbook into three main areas.

Objects

In Excel, objects refer to items such as charts, text boxes, images, or shapes that you can insert into your spreadsheet. These objects normally sit on top of your cells. Protecting objects prevents others from modifying or deleting these items, which helps in maintaining the integrity of the graphical or visual elements in your workbook.

Structure

The structure of a workbook refers to the organization of sheets within it. This includes the addition, deletion, hiding, unhiding, renaming, or reordering of sheets. Protecting the structure prevents others from making changes to the overall organization of the workbook, which can be crucial for maintaining the desired layout and function of the workbook.

Cells

Cells are the individual units in a spreadsheet where data is entered. Each cell can contain text, numbers, or formulas. Protecting cells prevents others from modifying the content of these cells. This is particularly important when you have formulas or data that should not be altered to ensure the accuracy and functionality of the spreadsheet.

These protection features help in managing access and editing rights, ensuring that the critical or sensitive parts of the workbook remain unchanged.

Here are some further notes to consider when applying these features:

1. All these features are locked by default. You enforce this locking feature by activating the **Protect Sheet** icon under the **Review** tab.

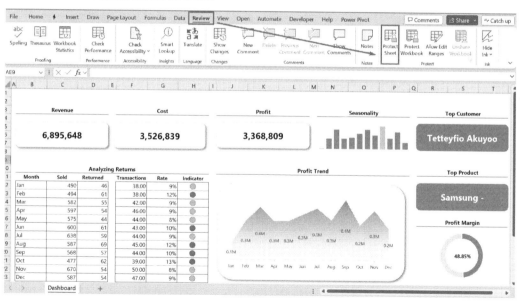

Figure 10.2 – Accessing the Protect Sheet feature

2. After applying the **Protect Sheet** feature, the user is now limited to only selecting locked and unlocked cells by default. However, you can allow the user to perform certain actions by checking these from this list:

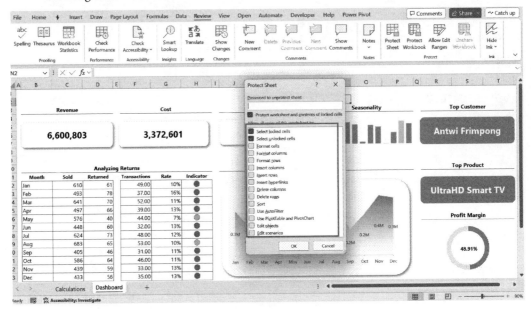

Figure 10.3 – List of allowed actions under the Protect Sheet feature

3. If you do not want to lock any of these elements in your dashboard, you must change the locked feature by accessing the property of that element. For cells and ranges, you can select the cell or range, right-click, and select **Format Cells**....

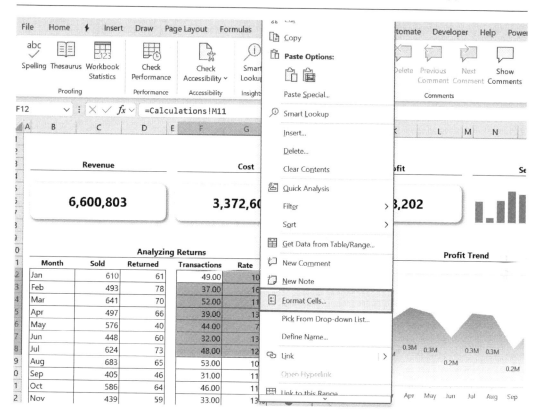

Figure 10.4 – Accessing the Format Cells dialog box

Go to the **Protection** tab when the **Format Cells** dialog box pops up.

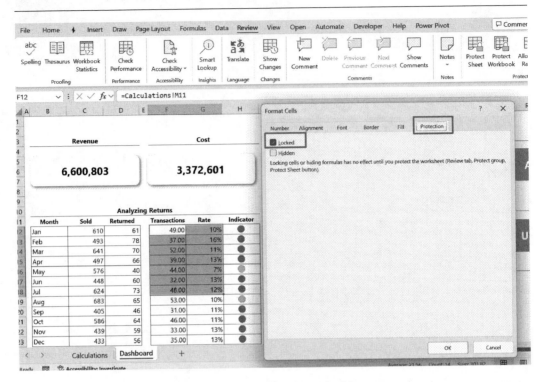

Figure 10.5 – Unchecking the Locked feature

Here, you can uncheck the **Locked** feature to make that cell or range unlocked.

You will notice that there is also a **Hidden** box. The **Hidden** feature in the **Format Cells** dialog box in Excel serves to obscure the content or formulas in cells from being visible in the formula bar to others while at the same time protecting those cells from being modified. This feature is particularly useful when you have formulas or data that you don't want to be easily seen or altered by others.

Let us apply these concepts discussed to our dashboard. First, we need to determine which aspects of our dashboard we need to unlock. Approaching it in this way makes it easier for you. Remember, if we just applied the **Protect Sheet** feature, all the elements would be locked, and our user may not be able to use slicers and other features to interact with our dashboard.

To unlock our slicers, select the slicer, right-click, and select **Size and Properties…**.

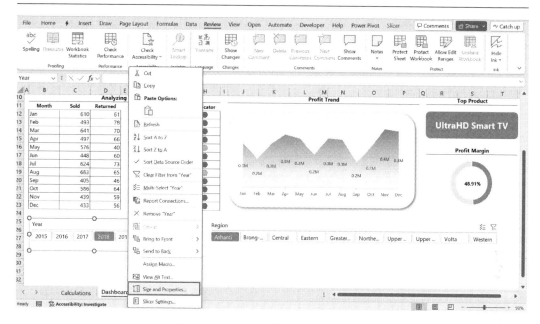

Figure 10.6 – Accessing the Size and Properties feature

In the **Format Slicer** pane that pops up, click to uncheck the **Locked** feature to make sure the slicer remains unlocked when we apply the **Protect Sheet** feature.

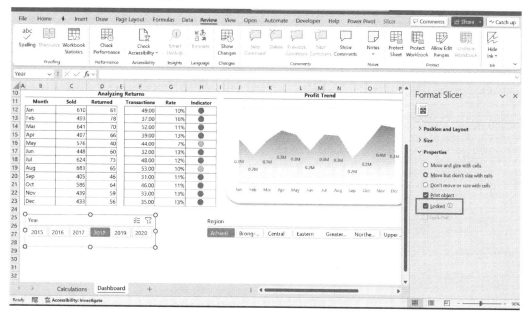

Figure 10.7 – Unchecking the Locked feature in the pane

After doing this, we also have the option to restrict users from changing the position of the slicer. This ensures that the structure of our dashboard remains intact.

To do this, we can move to the **Position and Layout** option in the same pane, expand it, and check **Disable resizing and moving**.

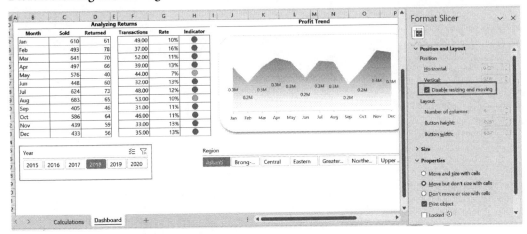

Figure 10.8 – Disabling the resizing and moving option

These two options—unlocking the object and disabling resizing and moving—ensure that the user can access the slicer and will not be able to modify the structure when we apply protection to our sheet. If we had other interactive elements such as **Form Controls** in our dashboard, we would use the same approach before applying protection to our sheet.

Please go ahead and apply the same settings to the second slicer. After this, we can now apply the **Protect Sheet** feature by going to **Review** and selecting **Protect Sheet**:

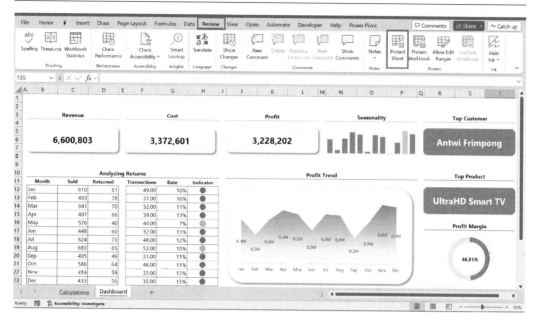

Figure 10.9 – Applying the Protect Sheet feature

In the list of actions we want the user to do, we will leave it at the default setting by allowing users to select both locked and unlocked cells. You can put in your password. Remember to keep it safe and do not forget it. Excel will prompt you to re-enter your password if you choose to enter your password.

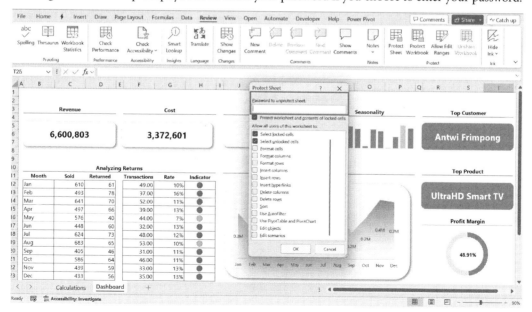

Figure 10.10 – Option to put in a password

After applying the **Protect Sheet** feature, you will now notice that any attempt to delete or modify the content of your sheet will give you the following warning:

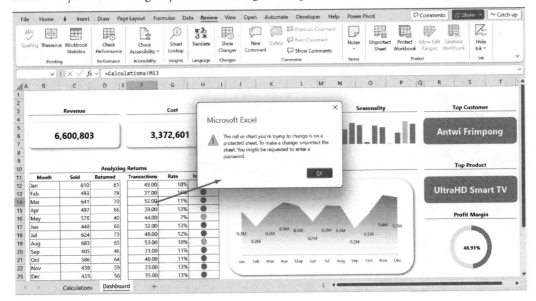

Figure 10.11 – Testing the locked feature

However, the user can use the slicer to filter the charts and other calculations without the ability to move them. We now turn our attention to the other worksheets in our workbook. These will usually be our calculations sheet or data sheet. Normally, we may want to only make the dashboard visible while we make these other sheets inaccessible to our users by hiding them. It will be more effective to hide these and protect the workbook structure so that the user is unable to access them without a password.

This is where we use the **Protect Workbook** feature. First, we right-click on the sheet we want to hide and select **Hide**:

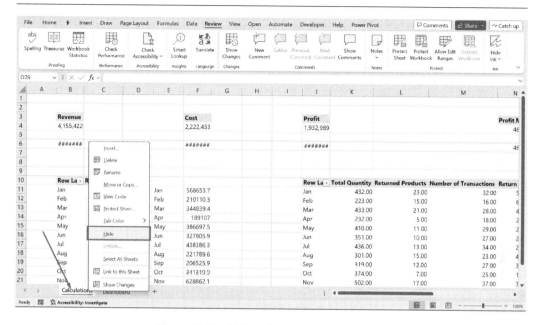

Figure 10.12 – Hiding sheets in your dashboard

After hiding the sheet, we can now apply the **Protect Workbook** feature to ensure that the user cannot unhide the sheet or add extra sheets to the original workbook.

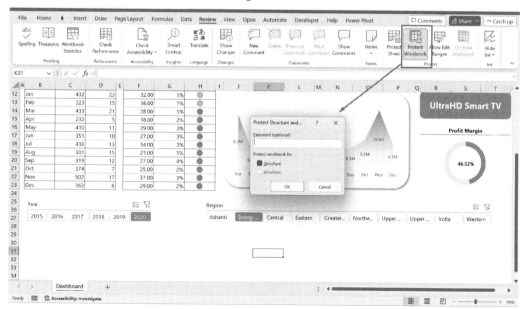

Figure 10.13 – Adding a password to the Protect Workbook feature

After doing this, you will notice that both the **Hide** and **Unhide** options in the right-click menu are now grayed out:

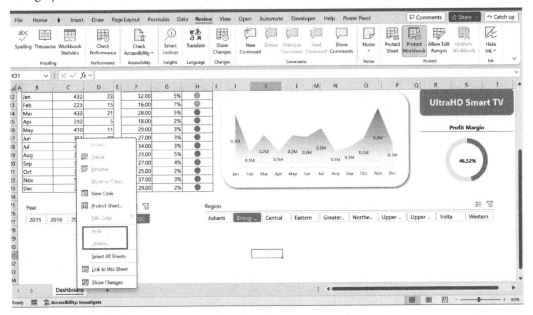

Figure 10.14 – Grayed out Hide and Unhide features

While applying these features is not foolproof, it ensures that the structure and content of your dashboard remain intact. In extreme cases, passwords can be removed by third-party tools or custom VBA scripts.

It is still advisable to apply these protections to ensure that you can share your work without worrying about any major changes to your structure and content.

If you work in an organization that requires other team members to collaborate with you, it may be important to apply these features before sharing your work with others. Let's now look at ways you can share your work or collaborate with others on your dashboard.

Collaboration

Working together in Excel can make your projects better. It's easy for everyone to chip in with their ideas when they can work on the dashboard at the same time. When you use platforms such as OneDrive or SharePoint with Excel, many people can work on the same workbook all at once. This helps get things done faster and makes sure the data is accurate. The **Share** feature in Excel lets you invite others to view or edit your workbook. This is great for big projects with many people involved.

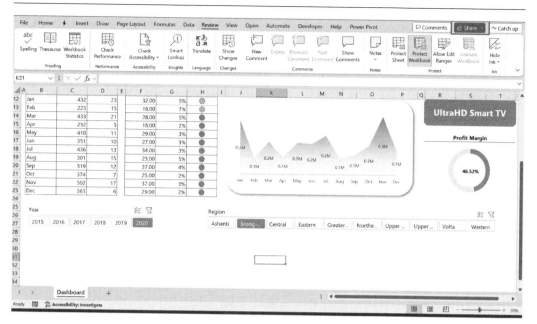

Figure 10.15 – Accessing the Share option

You can set different permission levels, such as **Can view** or **Can edit**. This way, you control who can change your workbook.

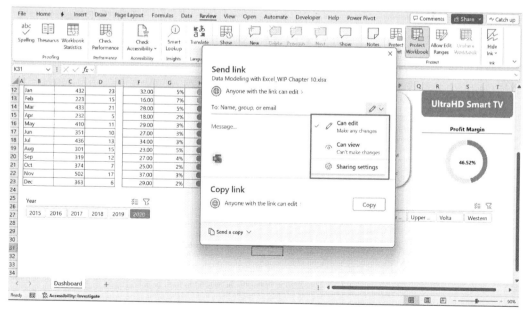

Figure 10.16 – Setting permission levels

Before allowing others to collaborate with you on your workbook or dashboard, let's look at a few considerations:

- **Determine access levels**: Decide who needs edit access versus who only needs view access. It's important to control who can make changes to prevent accidental or unauthorized modifications.

- **Protection and permissions**: Set up protection for cells, worksheets, and workbooks to prevent unwanted changes. We covered this in an earlier section. Please note that some of the protection features may not work well when files are opened online. Excel's online version has seen a lot of improvements over the last few years, and hopefully these features will be fixed soon to sync the offline and online protection features.

- **Use a cloud platform**: Save your workbook on a cloud platform such as OneDrive or SharePoint to enable real-time collaboration. Ensure all collaborators have the necessary accounts and access to the cloud platform.

- **Invite collaborators**: Use the **Share** feature in Excel to invite collaborators. Provide collaborators with clear instructions on how to access and edit the workbook. You can add this in the form of a message in the invitation dialog box:

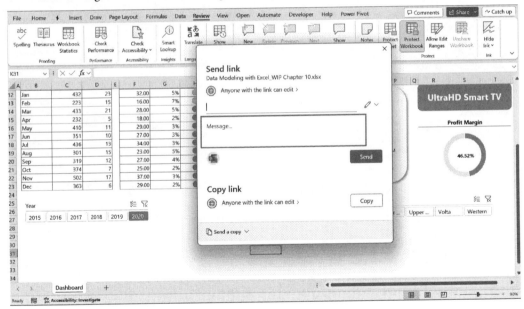

Figure 10.17 – Option to include instructions

- **Communication**: Establish clear communication channels for collaborators to discuss changes, ask questions, and provide feedback. Consider using a collaboration tool such as Microsoft Teams alongside Excel for more efficient communication.

- **Version control**: Make use of version history to track changes over time and to revert to previous versions if necessary.

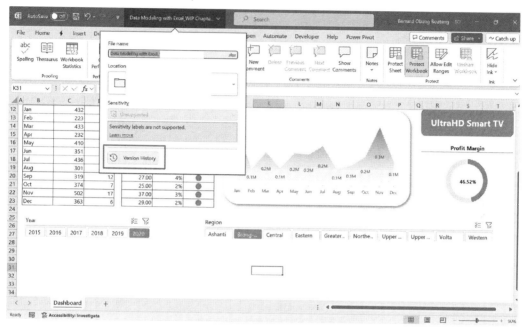

Figure 10.18 – Accessing the version history

- **Education and training**: Ensure that all collaborators are familiar with Excel and its collaboration features. Provide training or resources as necessary to help collaborators use this effectively.

- **Regular reviews**: Schedule regular reviews to check the data for accuracy and completeness. Evaluate the collaboration process and make adjustments as necessary to improve efficiency.

- **Backup**: Regularly back up the workbook to protect against data loss.

- **Documentation**: Document the process, settings, and any special instructions for future reference.

These steps and considerations aim at creating a secure and efficient collaborative environment. We will now apply these concepts to our dashboard by using the **Share** feature to invite a colleague to collaborate.

Skill two – inviting people to collaborate

We first need to ensure that our workbook is saved to OneDrive or SharePoint.

We will find the option to share in the top-right corner of the workbook. Click on it:

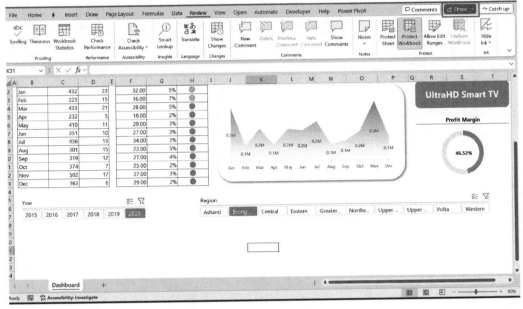

Figure 10.19 – Accessing the Share feature

Type in the email addresses of the people you want to share with:

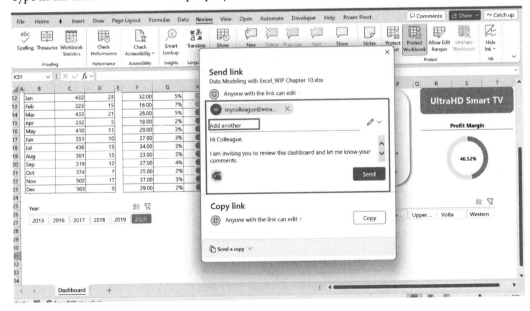

Figure 10.20 – Including email addresses

You have the option to add another email address just below the original email address.

Choose the permissions (**Can view or Can edit**) and click **Send**:

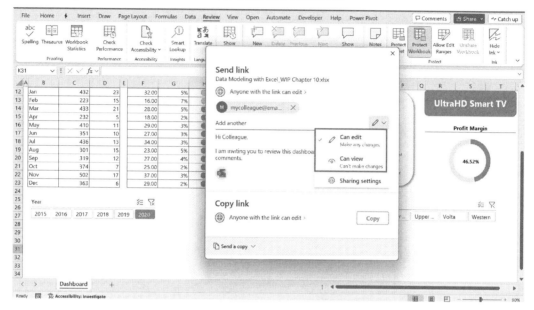

Figure 10.21 – Managing permissions

Your colleague should now receive an email to access the workbook. If viewed offline, it maintains all the protection features we used earlier. However, for online viewing, some of the protected elements may still be accessible.

If you really want to share your final dashboard for online viewing, a better way to do this is to publish a **View Only** version of the dashboard. This restricts users to just the dashboard and generates an embedded code you can share with a broader audience.

Let's look at how this works in the next section.

Publishing a view-only online version via OneDrive/ SharePoint

When we invite people to collaborate on shared workbooks in Excel, the changes they make in the workbook can impact the original workbook depending on the permissions we set for them. Creating an interactive view-only dashboard in Excel can enhance collaboration and ensure that the people we share our dashboard with can access and view the same dashboard without impacting each other's changes.

To do this, we can generate a custom URL linked to our dashboard and share this link with others. Sharing it this way means people can see your workbook anytime, anywhere.

Skill three – using OneDrive/SharePoint as a means to share your final work

There are a few things we need to consider first. We will go through them step by step:

1. **Saving on OneDrive/SharePoint**: The process begins by ensuring that our dashboard is saved on OneDrive or SharePoint. We then need to adjust the settings and configurations of the workbook to allow for interactivity but not editing. This includes locking cells and protecting sheets as necessary. It will be useful if the only visible worksheet in your workbook is the dashboard sheet. Ensure all other worksheets are hidden. We have already covered this in an earlier section, so our dashboard should be fine.

2. We will now proceed and access our dashboard online in OneDrive or SharePoint. You can do this by selecting the file in the folder, right-clicking on the file, and choosing **View online**:

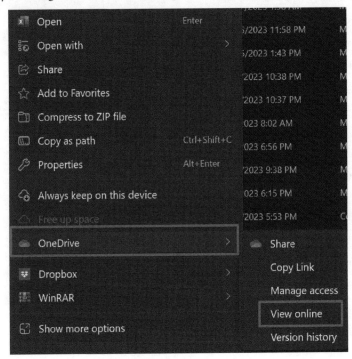

Figure 10.22 – Opening a file in OneDrive

This should open the file in OneDrive or SharePoint Online:

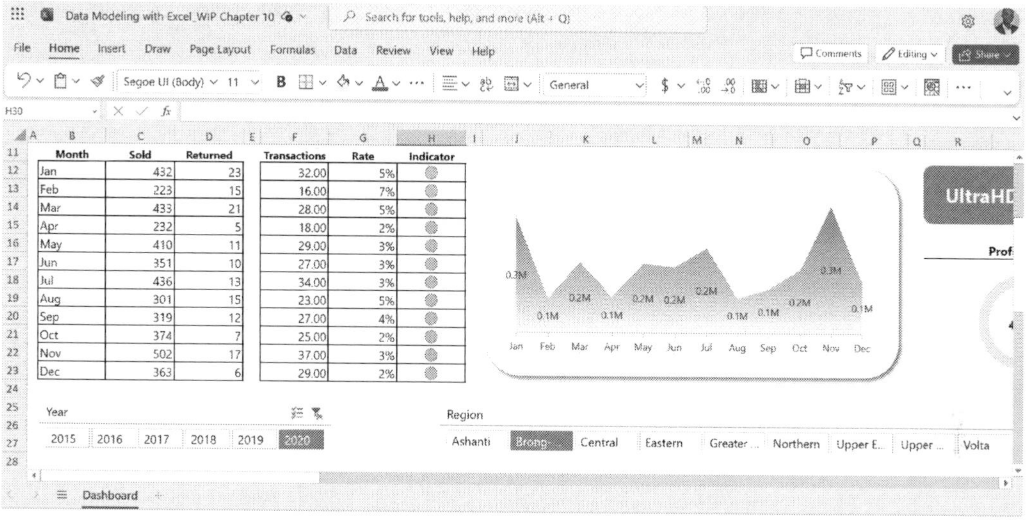

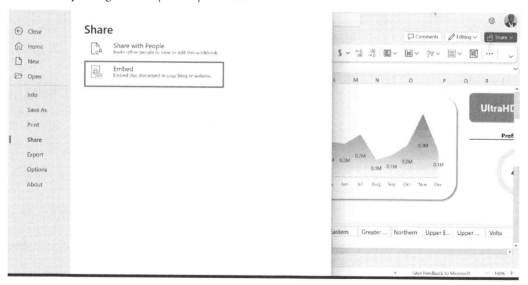

Figure 10.23 – A OneDrive view of your dashboard

Alternatively, we can open the file directly in our OneDrive folder.

The next step is to go to **File | Share | Embed**:

Figure 10.24 – Accessing the Embed feature

This will open up a dialog box for us to generate our embed code. Click on **Generate** and you will see the following screen, which displays some settings we can use to make it easier for our users to access and navigate the dashboard:

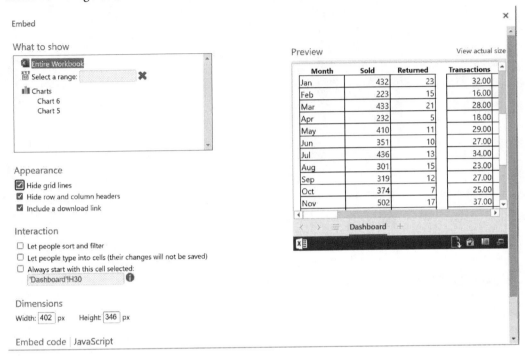

Figure 10.25 – Managing Embed settings

There are a few options we can play with to alter the appearance of the dashboard.

There are three main sections:

- **What to show**

- **Appearance**

- **Interaction**

Under **What to show**, we can select the entire workbook. This option is useful when the dashboard is the only sheet in your workbook. We can also select a range in the displayed dashboard for a more custom view. If you already have a named range in your original dashboard, you can put the name in here. There are also options to display some specific charts in the dashboard as well. We will leave our selection at the default view to display the entire workbook.

Under **Appearance**, we can toggle between showing the grid lines and hiding rows and column headers, and we can also decide whether to include a download link or not. Apart from these, there is an option to manage the interaction settings by allowing people to sort and filter, type into cells, or choose the default start cell when our dashboard is displayed. You can choose whether to allow a download link for users who may want to view the dashboard offline. This is not advisable if you have some sensitive company data you want to restrict access to. In our case, we will select all the options and change the start cell to A1 by directly selecting the cell:

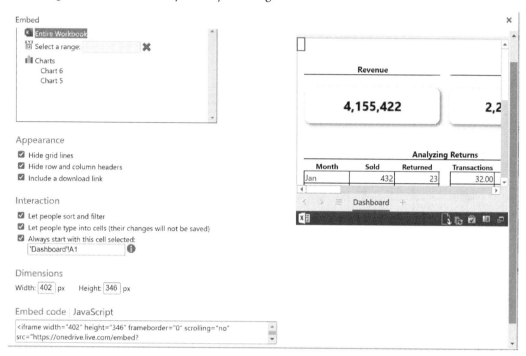

Figure 10.26 – Generating final embed code

We can now see that the embed code has been generated below the screen based on the settings we chose. You can now copy the embed code:

Figure 10.27 – Copying the embed code

This embed code is designed to fit into a blog or website using an iframe dimension. The text beginning with <iframe up to the double quote before https can now be removed. To do this, you can paste it into Notepad and make the necessary changes to the URL:

```
<iframe width="402" height="346" frameborder="0" scrolling="no" src="https://onedrive.live.com/embed?resid=
8243AA7D1A3C60C5%2156848&authkey=%21ANB0YNh8TFzpdQg&em=2&AllowTyping=True&ActiveCell='Dashboard'!A1
&wdHideGridlines=True&wdHideHeaders=True&wdDownloadButton=True&wdInConfigurator=True&wdInConfigurator=True"></iframe>
```

Figure 10.28 – Modifying the embed code

We will also remove the suffix that begins with a double quotation mark after the last True value, as shown in *Figure 10.28*.

Our final link should now look like this:

```
https://onedrive.live.com/embed?resid=8243AA7D1A3C60C5%2156848&authkey=%21ANB0YNh8TFzpdQg&em=2
&AllowTyping=True&ActiveCell='Dashboard'!A1
&wdHideGridlines=True&wdHideHeaders=True&wdDownloadButton=True&wdInConfigurator=True&wdInConfigurator=True
```

Figure 10.29 – Modified embed code

You can always modify the true or false values that are generated based on your settings. This link can now be pasted in any web browser, and it will display our dashboard online.

Ideally, our slicers should be responsive when we click on the buttons. However, it is possible you may encounter the following error if you choose to apply the slicers:

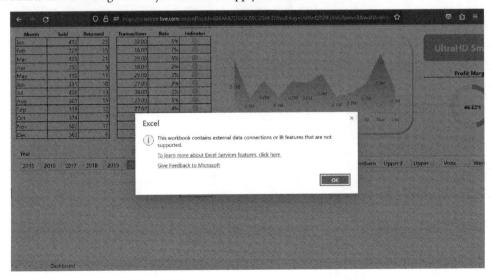

Figure 10.30 – External data connection warning

This happens because, by default, a guest link URL that is provided by OneDrive or SharePoint doesn't include the required parameters for guests to use workbooks that contain data connections to data models or BI.

We can fix this by adding the `&action=embedview&wdbipreview=true` suffix to the end of the original code we copied. Your sample code now looks like this:

```
https://onedrive.live.com/embed?resid=8243AA7D1A3C60C5%2156848&authkey=%21ANB0YNh8TFzpdQg&em=2
&AllowTyping=True&ActiveCell='Dashboard'!A1
&wdHideGridlines=True&wdHideHeaders=True&wdDownloadButton=True&wdInConfigurator=True&wdInConfigurator=True
&action=embedview&wdbipreview=true
```

Figure 10.31 – Modifying embed code to allow for slicing

This will now allow our slicer to be responsive.

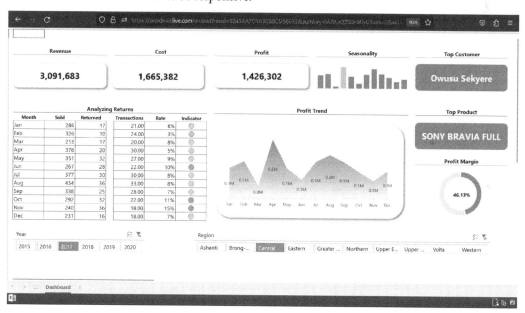

Figure 10.32 – Final interactive dashboard

The good thing about sharing a **view-only** interactive web link is that all changes to the dashboard online do not impact your original file. Your file stays intact while making your dashboard available to a broader audience.

So far, we have explored options to share our final work in Excel. However, beyond sharing our dashboard in Excel, we can also export the data model, our transformed dataset in Power Query, and all our measures in Excel to Power BI to further analyze or create more stunning visualizations.

Although this is beyond the scope of the book, the next section will introduce us to how we can export our data model from Excel to Power BI for further analysis and visualization.

Exporting your data model to Power BI

Exporting a data model from Excel to Power BI, including all measures and Power Query transformations, is a seamless process that involves importing the Excel workbook into Power BI Desktop. The two programs work together smoothly, so you can move your data over without a hitch.

Power BI can handle big, complex datasets. This is great when you have a lot of information to work with.

Let's go through the steps:

1. We begin by opening Power BI Desktop. This is free and you will not require an account to use this. However, a licensed version gives you more advantages when you bring in the data model from Excel.

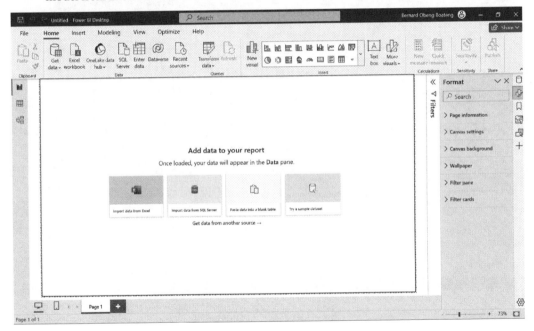

Figure 10.33 – Power BI Desktop

2. After opening Power BI Desktop, you can now go to **File** | **Import** and choose the **Power Query, Power Pivot, Power View** option:

Figure 10.34 – Accessing the Import option

Ensure that your Excel file containing the dashboard, the data model, measures, and Power Query transformations you want to export to Power BI is closed before proceeding.

3. Follow the path to the saved Excel workbook and open it. You will see a dialog box that summarizes the process. Click on **Start**:

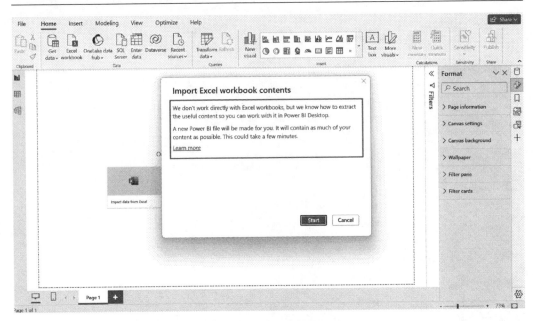

Figure 10.35 – Import Excel workbook contents warning

After you click **Start**, you now will see all the content that has been extracted in a list, as shown:

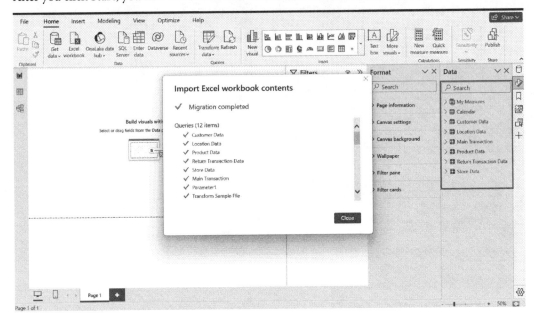

Figure 10.36 – List of migrated content

This includes all the measures, the transformed queries, and the data model we worked on in Excel. You can proceed with further analysis and visualization in Power BI. Your datasets are still linked to the original data source we used in our Excel dashboard workbook.

There are lots of features in Power BI. We will probably explore these features in a sequel to this book.

Summary

Beyond creating your dashboard in Excel, you have now learned about various ways you can share, collaborate on, and publish your final work. Now you know how to keep your workbook safe with the **Protect Sheet** and workbook features and share it online. Using OneDrive, SharePoint, and Power BI, you can reach a wider audience and make your data work harder. The skills you've learned in this chapter will help you share your Excel dashboard effectively, keeping it flexible for updates while making sure the data stays accurate.

As we wrap up this book, reflect on the skills you've gained and consider how they'll aid you in creating an effective data model in Excel and building an interactive dashboard that will provide your users with key insights for decision-making.

Index

`Packtpub.com`

Subscribe to our online digital library for full access to over 7,000 books and videos, as well as industry leading tools to help you plan your personal development and advance your career. For more information, please visit our website.

Why subscribe?

- Spend less time learning and more time coding with practical eBooks and Videos from over 4,000 industry professionals

- Improve your learning with Skill Plans built especially for you

- Get a free eBook or video every month

- Fully searchable for easy access to vital information

- Copy and paste, print, and bookmark content

Did you know that Packt offers eBook versions of every book published, with PDF and ePub files available? You can upgrade to the eBook version at `packtpub.com` and as a print book customer, you are entitled to a discount on the eBook copy. Get in touch with us at `customercare@packtpub.com` for more details.

At `www.packtpub.com`, you can also read a collection of free technical articles, sign up for a range of free newsletters, and receive exclusive discounts and offers on Packt books and eBooks.

Other Books You May Enjoy

If you enjoyed this book, you may be interested in these other books by Packt:

Data Modeling with Tableau

Kirk Munroe

ISBN: 9781803248028

- Showcase Tableau published data sources and embedded connections
- Apply Ask Data in data cataloging and natural language query
- Understand the features of Tableau Prep Builder with the help of hands-on exercises
- Model data with Tableau Desktop using examples
- Formulate a governed data strategy using Tableau Server and Tableau Cloud
- Optimize data models for Ask and Explain Data

Data Modeling with Snowflake

Serge Gershkovich

ISBN: 9781837634453

- Discover the time-saving benefits and applications of data modeling
- Learn about Snowflake's cloud-native architecture and its features
- Understand and apply modeling techniques using Snowflake objects
- Universal modeling concepts and language through Snowflake objects
- Get comfortable reading and transforming semistructured data
- Learn directly with pre-built recipes and examples
- Learn to apply modeling frameworks from Star to Data Vault

Packt is searching for authors like you

If you're interested in becoming an author for Packt, please visit `authors.packtpub.com` and apply today. We have worked with thousands of developers and tech professionals, just like you, to help them share their insight with the global tech community. You can make a general application, apply for a specific hot topic that we are recruiting an author for, or submit your own idea.

Share Your Thoughts

Now you've finished *Data Modeling with Microsoft Excel*, we'd love to hear your thoughts! Scan the QR code below to go straight to the Amazon review page for this book and share your feedback or leave a review on the site that you purchased it from.

`https://packt.link/r/1-803-24028-8`

Your review is important to us and the tech community and will help us make sure we're delivering excellent quality content.

Download a free PDF copy of this book

Thanks for purchasing this book!

Do you like to read on the go but are unable to carry your print books everywhere? Is your eBook purchase not compatible with the device of your choice?

Don't worry, now with every Packt book you get a DRM-free PDF version of that book at no cost.

Read anywhere, any place, on any device. Search, copy, and paste code from your favorite technical books directly into your application.

The perks don't stop there, you can get exclusive access to discounts, newsletters, and great free content in your inbox daily

Follow these simple steps to get the benefits:

1. Scan the QR code or visit the link below

https://packt.link/free-ebook/9781803240282

2. Submit your proof of purchase
3. That's it! We'll send your free PDF and other benefits to your email directly

Made in the USA
Middletown, DE
28 March 2024

52242526R00177